Victorian Literary Cultures

Victorian Literary Cultures

Studies in Textual Subversion

Edited by Kenneth Womack and James M. Decker

FAIRLEIGH DICKINSON UNIVERSITY PRESS
Madison • Teaneck

Published by Fairleigh Dickinson University Press
Copublished by The Rowman & Littlefield Publishing Group, Inc.
4501 Forbes Boulevard, Suite 200, Lanham, Maryland 20706
www.rowman.com

Unit A, Whitacre Mews, 26-34 Stannary Street, London SE11 4AB

British Library Cataloguing in Publication Information Available

Library of Congress Cataloging-in-Publication Data

Library of Congress Cataloging-in-Publication Data Available

ISBN 978-1-61147-664-4 (cloth: alk. paper)
ISBN 978-1-61147-665-1 (electronic)

Printed in the United States of America

For William Baker,
Bibliographer, Teacher, Critic

Contents

Acknowledgments

Special thanks are due to the many friends and colleagues who made this volume possible. The editors are particularly grateful to the supportive and highly professional team at Fairleigh Dickinson University Press, especially the esteemed Harry Keyishian, the Director of the press and Professor Emeritus of English. At Monmouth University, we would like to thank Lynne Clay, Nancy Mezey, Judy Ramos, and Michael Thomas. We would like to thank Penn State Altoona's Lori J. Bechtel-Wherry, Brian Black, Michele Kennedy, Peter Moran, and Nancy Vogel. Finally, we are indebted to our Illinois Central College colleagues, including Susan Hillabold and Stuart Boyd. Ken would like to thank his wife Jeanine for her steadfast love and support. James would like to thank Stephanie Guedet for her unflagging love and keen critical eye, as well as his children, Siobhan, Anastazia, and Evan, for their inspiration.

Introduction: Subversive Literary Cultures

Kenneth Womack and James M. Decker

In a recent study, Astrid Peterle considers a central paradox of subversion: its simultaneous ability to critique dominant ideology by "shifting hegemonic meanings and codes" and its "mainstream" tendency to reinforce prevailing social mores. Judith Butler implicitly concurs in her observation that "subversive performances always run the risk of becoming deadening clichés . . . through their repetition within commodity culture where 'subversion' carries market value" (xxii). Such a variance in meaning calls to mind Terry Eagleton's comment on overly broad definitions of ideology that it "threatens to expand to vanishing point." By being both ideologically "dangerous" and utterly normative, the concept of subversion risks losing critical potency or, at the very least, forfeiting its ability to "enable the possibility of action" (Lui 56). Nevertheless, as Peterle somewhat grudgingly acknowledges, "artistic practice has the potential to open up alternative ways of perception by making visible, switching, affirming (and so on) hegemonic meanings." *Victorian Literary Cultures: Studies in Textual Subversion* explores such artistic practice—from writers both socially committed and otherwise—and provides readers with close textual analyses regarding how subversion either critiques or reinforces the so-called mainstream. By drawing clear cultural contexts for the writers under review—including such canonical figures as George Eliot, Charlotte Brontë, and Sir Arthur Conan Doyle, as well as new readings of lesser-known works by Carlton Dawe and Helen Dickens—the critics in this anthology offer diverse example of subversion—both "intentional" and unintentional—as an enduring literary phenomenon.

A notoriously unstable term, *subversion* can refer to multiple practices and concepts. At the center of the controversy lie the entangled relationships among writer, text, and reader. For some theorists, such as Leo Strauss, the writer initiates the subversive act, concealing "obtrusively enigmatic features" (36) in plain sight so as to pass along potentially radical ideas to a select group of readers who can see "between the lines" (24). In this way, as José Manuel Losada Goya and Marta Guirao Ochoa would have it, "subversion is carried out with an end in mind" (3). The effectiveness of this overt action, however, is called into question by theorists such as Louis Althusser, who argues that such subversion merely "contributes to the maintenance and nourishment" (157) of the dominant ideological state apparatuses, a position echoed by Stephen Greenblatt (via Foucault's views on power in works such as *Discipline and Punish*): "power defines itself in relation to such [subversive] threats" (50). For Greenblatt, authority can quickly and seamlessly "contain" such "alien forces" (52–53). In other words, the active subversion proposed by Strauss may ultimately reinforce, rather than destroy, the dominant ideology, for it is merely co-extensive with it.

Others, such as M. M. Bakhtin and Judith Butler, take a more sanguine view and submit that in certain circumstances "intentional" subversion can succeed in challenging the hegemony. Bakhtin's concept of carnival, with its mockery and "grotesque realism" suggest, contra Greenblatt, that subversion could break through its sanctioned (contained) space and demonstrate that the dominant ideology could indeed be questioned in narrative (19). Butler, although aware that power relations such as those discussed by Althusser could negate or "postpone the . . . task of rethinking subversive possibilities for sexuality and identity" (42), nevertheless argues that intentionally subversive performances could expose the "phantasmatic structure" (42) of normative identity because "the very multiplicity of their construction holds out the possibility of a disruption of their univocal posturing" (44). For both Butler and Bakhtin, the presence of multiple voices casts doubt on the naturalized state of the dominant ideology and implies that an intentional author—or series of intentional authors—can effect lasting change.

Roland Barthes and Tony Bennett, however, minimize the role of the writer and highlight the subversive nature of the text itself, particularly when engaged by an active reader. In *S/Z*, Barthes outlines his concept of a "plural" text in which a "galaxy of signifiers" (5) resist a singular meaning and "subvert the opposition between true and false" (44). The infinitely connotative possibilities of such narratives are by their nature subversive in that no officially sanctioned interpretation can negate the possibility of heterodox ones. Tony Bennett, thus, can claim that the task of a subversive reader (Marxist for Bennett, but the principle applies beyond a single ideology) "is not that of reflecting or bringing to light the politics which is already there as a latent presence [but of] producing a new position for it within the field of cultural relations and, thereby, new forms of use and effectively within the broader social process" (136). In other words, as Keith M. Booker writes, "the role of the critic [is] activating the subversive potential of a text" (10).

The critics in this volume stake a position that attempts to balance the roles of the writer, text, and reader as subversive agent. For a variety of nineteenth- and early twentieth-century British novelists, subversion existed as a central aspect of their writerly existence. Although—or perhaps because—a great number of Victorian authors composed their works for a general and mixed audience, many writers employed strategies designed to subvert genteel expectations. In addition to using coded and oblique subject matter, such figures also hid their transgressive material "in plain sight" á la Strauss. Although some writers sought to critique, and even destabilize, their society, others juxtaposed subversive themes and aesthetics negatively with communal norms in hopes of quashing progressive agendas. Others, however, do not appear to advance a clearly subversive agenda, and it is here that Booker's idea of critic-as-activist comes into play and with it the desire to transform the text into a socially meaningful tool.

This overarching concept receives considerable attention in the present anthology's first subsection, which explores works by and about "Subversive Women." In "The Mysterious Identity of Helen Dickens, Victorian Novelist," Troy J. Bassett investigates the inherently subversive life and work of Helen Dickens, possibly a pseudonym or, even more intriguingly, potentially the sister-in-law of the renowned novelist. The author of six novels and a short story collection between 1872 and 1905, Helen Dickens fervently sought to make her name by appropriating intentionally sentimental and sensational modes throughout her work and across a career in which the well-known Dickens family neither claimed nor disclaimed the author as a relation. For Bassett, this only marks the beginning of this unresolved Victorian literary mystery.

In "Moonrise and the Ascent of Eve, the Woman Titan: Charlotte Brontë's Epiphanies of the Fourfold Elemental Feminine," Martin Bidney addresses the subversive structural patterns of literary epiphanies in Brontë's novels *Shirley*, *Villette*, and *Jane Eyre*. Drawing on the insights of philosopher-critic Gaston Bachelard, Bidney asserts that Brontë offers epiphanies representing conceptions of idealized womanhood and that the novelist's epiphanic paradigm depicts the feminine sublime as maternal. Nancy Henry's "Condoning Adultery: Problems of Marriage and Divorce in George Eliot's Life and Writing" explores subversive issues at the heart of Eliot's biographical life. Namely, Henry interrogates the biographical commonplace that George Henry Lewes could not divorce his wife Agnes and marry Eliot because of Agnes's adultery, thus making Lewes and Eliot victims of a rigid and unforgiving legal system and Agnes's unrepentant ways. As Henry points out, such biographical maneuvers shift the emphasis away from Eliot and Lewes's own adulterous relationship. "Biographers and critics have failed to question this reduction of a complex legal problem to an act of good will," Henry writes, "and instead have repeated the claim so often that its truth seems beyond doubt." By questioning the facticity of these oft-repeated claims, Henry succeeds in subverting a century of biographical assertions.

The anthology's second subsection investigates the subversive ideologies inherent in a wide range of prevailing ethical, philosophical, and literary practices. In "Unraveling Orientalism: Dawe's 'Yellow and

White,'" James M. Decker draws on Edward Said's conceptions of simultaneous repulsion and attraction in an original reading of a short story by Dawe, the Australian expatriate author of more than seventy works. For Decker, Dawe's "Yellow and White" affords readers with a quintessential example of an Orientalist representation of China, while also offering a demonstration of the binary that underpins Said's explanation of the Orientalist fascination with the Eastern Other. Joseph Lennon's "'A Familiar Kinde of Chastisement': Fasting in the Nineteenth-Century" identifies images of hunger and fasting in a variety of late nineteenth-century Irish texts. For Lennon, fasting can be interpreted as a transitive action in which, "fasting on, against, or for something, we see its nascent potential." Through readings of texts such as William Maunsell Hennessy's translation of *Aislinge Meic Conglinne*, Whitely Stokes's edition of *The Tripartite Life of St. Patrick*, and the Rev. Evelyn Baring-Gould's address on Celtic Saints, Lennon examines the seemingly contradictory aspects of fasting in these narratives, while highlighting the strikingly similar ways in which they distance themselves from fasting as an ancient practice.

In "The Effect of Emerging New Media on Book Publishing: Lessons from the Origins of Cross Media Storytelling in the Early Twentieth Century for Contemporary Transmedia Researchers," Alexis Weedon reminds us of the many ways in which the history of the book can shed light on present-day publishing practices. In particular, Weedon reveals key parallels between the early days of the cross over between film, radio, and publishing at the onset of the twentieth century, when subversive new practices were emerging in comparison with specific examples of current trends in the digital book and reading. In so doing, Weedon provides a new framework for understanding the complexity of contemporary trends in media publishing. In "'And this also has been one of the dark places of the earth': Reading Levinasian Ethics and Literary Impressionism in Conrad's *Heart of Darkness*," Kenneth Womack also looks to the dawn of a new century as Conrad posited deeply fraught images of colonialism in arguably his most renowned work. Drawing on Emmanuel Levinas's philosophical conceptions of alterity, Womack interprets *Heart of Darkness* as a subversive text that challenges readers to reconsider their ethical positions about Empire and the cultural yen for colonization. With *Heart of Darkness*, Womack writes, "Conrad merges the over-arching Victorian desire for storytelling—for engaging in the act of storytelling or, perhaps more pointedly, for serving as the audience for other storytellers—with the penchant for irony that characterizes modernism's necessarily complex and uncommitted attitude toward social critique."

The final subsection in this anthology considers the generic properties of textual subversion in works by Bram Stoker, Sir Arthur Conan Doyle, and Henry James, among others. Ira B. Nadel's "'Count Me In': Comedy in *Dracula*" discusses stage and filmic adaptations of Stoker's classic work. In so doing, Nadel demonstrates the ways in which these often campy presentation of Dracula's environs "masks the horrific, while emphasizing the Gothic." For Nadel, the visually comedic images in these texts serve as antidotes Stoker's "world of dark and dreadful things." In Nadel's reading, then, *Dracula* emerges less as a novel about horror and more as a study in "comic, if not melodramatic, extremes." In "'The Seasoned Spirit of the Cunning Reader': The Textual Subversions of *The Turn of the Screw*," Ruth Robbins addresses the notion of genre itself, arguing that genre "at its simplest is the set of clues which direct (or misdirect) readers how to read." In her interpretation of James's novella, Robbins sees genre as both a guide and a red herring. For Robbins, "James's text subverts and mixes the genres to which it apparently belongs," while also acting as a means for establishing intentionally misleading conclusions in the mind of the reader.

In "'Fallen' Clergymen: The Wages of Sin in Hawthorne's *The Scarlet Letter*, Charles Reade's *The Cloister and the Hearth*, and Henry Arthur Jones's *Michael and His Lost Angel*," Jeanette Shumaker demonstrates the ways in which Reade, Hawthorne, and Jones examine the dilemmas of adulterous priests and ministers who emulate Christ, thereby subverting the genre of the traditional Romance. For Shumaker, these figures can be interpreted as moving "from the feminized angle of resistance to temptation rather than from mere masculine self-mastery." In this way, Shumaker highlights the ways in which Hawthorne, Reade, and Jones expose their own crises of identity by ultimately adopting a feminized notion of virtue. Finally, Joseph Wiesenfarth's "Sherlock Holmes: The Criminal in the Detective" reads Conan Doyle's efforts to liberate himself from his most famous character as a "case of premeditated murder." Understanding that the author had grown tired, professionally, of having to breathe life into Holmes in one adventure after another, Wiesenfarth identifies the ways in which Holmes had become inseparable from his creator. As Wiesenfarth concludes, Conan Doyle's attempt to destabilize—even destroy—his most famous incarnation underscores the larger aims of Victorian-era textual subversion: the careful sublimation of love and sex through brute reason and machine-like logic. In Wiesenfarth's reading, Conan Doyle's world represents an era in which intelligence invariably wins the day. As Wiesenfarth sagely concludes, "That is one myth, surely, that it would be a pleasure to recover for contemporary life—even for contemporary fiction—in any way we can."

The editors and authors of *Victorian Literary Cultures: Studies in Textual Subversion* proudly dedicate their efforts in producing this anthology to William Baker, renowned literary critic and bibliographer. Emeritus Professor of English and University Libraries at Northern Illinois University, Baker has impacted the professional lives of our contributors in indelible ways. Indeed, he has enjoyed a prolific career as an expositor and bibliographer of such literary luminaries as George Eliot, George Henry Lewes, Harold Pinter, and Tom Stoppard, among a host of others. Having earned his doctorate at the University of London in 1974, Baker has authored or edited more than forty volumes, while also serving as editor and founder of *George Eliot-George Henry Lewes Studies* and as co-editor of the *Year's Work in English Studies*. At Northern Illinois University, he was honored as a Board of Trustees Professor and earned a Distinguished Research Professorship. His work has been supported by a number of revered agencies, including the National Endowment for the Humanities and the Andrew Mellon Fellowships, among others. As with the writers under consideration in this volume, Professor Baker has long championed the importance of textual subversion, of working to uphold the highest standards of scholarship, without compromise to—and often despite—the vicissitudes of critical fashion. As a bibliographer and textual critic working in the self-perpetuating age of the theoretical project, Baker has proven himself, and our profession at large, as enduringly subversive forces indeed.

WORKS CITED

Althusser, Louis. *Lenin and Philosophy*. Translated by Ben Brewster. Monthly Review Press, 1971.

Bakhtin, Mikhail. *Rabelais and His World*. Translated by Hélène Iswolsky. Indiana UP, 1984.

Barthes, Roland. *S/Z*. Translated by Richard Miller. Hill and Wang, 1974.

Bennett, Tony. *Formalism and Marxism*. Routledge, 2003.

Booker, Keith M. *Techniques of Subversion in Modern Literature: Transgression, Abjection, and the Carnivalesque*. U of Florida P, 1991.

Butler, Judith. *Gender Trouble: Feminism and the Subversion of Identity*. Routledge, 2006.

Eagleton, Terry. *Ideology: An Introduction*. Verso, 1998.

Greenblatt, Stephen. "Invisible Bullets: Renaissance Authority and Its Subversion." *Glyph*, vol. 8, 1981, pp. 40–61.

Losada Goya, José Manuel, and Guirao Ochoa, Marta. *Myth and Subversion in the Contemporary Novel*. Cambridge Scholars, 2012.

Lui, Alan. "Wordsworth and Subversion, 1793–1804: Trying Cultural Criticism." *Yale Journal of Criticism*, vol. 2, no. 2, 1989, pp. 55–100.

Peterle, Astrid. "Thinking through Subversion in the Time of Its Impossibility." *Institute for Human Sciences*. Junior Visiting Fellows Conferences XXIII. 2009, http://www. iwm.at/publications/5-junior-visiting-fellows-conferences/vol-xxiii/astrid-peterle/. Accessed 14 August 2016.

Strauss, Leo. *Persecution and the Art of Writing*. U of Chicago P, 1988.

Part I

Subversive Women

ONE

The Mysterious Identity of Helen Dickens, Victorian Novelist

Troy J. Bassett

In November 1895, the anonymous M. H. wrote a query letter to the editor of *The Literary World* asking, "Is Helen Dickens, author of *Married at Last, The Mill Wheel, Wild Wood*, etc., any relative of Charles Dickens?" This question referred to a handful of undistinguished three-volume novels published between 1872 and 1881 in England under the name "Helen Dickens." But as the weeks slipped by, no one answered his question in the columns of the periodical, and the question, much like its original subject, was quickly forgotten. This essay attempts to answer the correspondent's question through an examination of the works of novelist Helen Dickens (fl. 1872–1905) and the extended family of Charles Dickens. Though as yet no definitive evidence has been found, I will show that a sister-in-law of the famous novelist could very well be the author of these novels.

1. HELEN DICKENS: THE NOVELIST

Helen Dickens the novelist wrote six novels, one collection of short stories, and four additional short stories between 1872 and 1905. Her fiction shows the influence of the popular novels of the time, especially the sentimental and the sensational, and exhibits a familiarity with the works of Mary Elizabeth Braddon, Charlotte Brontë, and Ellen Wood (to name a few). All of her works were produced by publishers of the lowest rank: Thomas Cautley Newby, Charles Joseph Skeet, and Henry J. Drane.[1] In contrast to her model authors, Dickens's novels left little mark with her contemporaries, rating only middling reviews whenever reviewers deigned to notice them at all.

Newby, a notorious publisher in his day, brought out Dickens's first two novels *Wild Wood* (three volumes, 1872) and *The Mill Wheel* (three volumes, 1874). Both novels are highly sensationalistic, involving inheritance plots, murders, and family secrets. *Wild Wood* follows the lives of the eight Drever children, the eldest of whom, Durill Drever, manages their father's estate and struggles with one dissolute alcoholic brother Gilbert and another debt-ridden one Crispin. The plot hinges on the dead father's missing will, the attempted murder of Durill by Gilbert, and forged promissory notes by Crispin.[2] The novel received polite reviews from the *Morning Post* and *The Spectator*; the former sees within it "the germ of a future career in this sphere of literature," whereas the latter rates it "fairly open to ridicule" but "not without some cleverness and much good feeling." The plot of *The Mill Wheel* draws somewhat on Braddon's *Lady Audley's Secret* (1862). The novel follows the career of the orphaned Renie Rudkin as she struggles to become a professional painter, suffers unrequited love for Rufus, another painter, and discovers the fate of her aunt (who years before ran away with gypsies). The plot depends on her uncle's surprise marriage to a penniless woman, his mysterious death, and his estate passing to his despicable relation Gunstan after the drowning of his heir. The end of the novel reveals Gunstan responsible for both deaths. The third volume of the novel also contains the short story "Lost: A Tale." Set in Lancashire, the story recounts the doomed love between a poor girl and a lord. *The Mill Wheel* received a scathing review from the *Athenaeum* that castigated its "vulgarity" of language, lack of wit, and improbable story.

Newby had an infamous reputation for sharp practice (Arbuckle). In the 1840s, he published the Brontë sisters Anne and Emily implying in advertisements their novels were by their sister Charlotte (newly famous as the author of *Jane Eyre*), and he published Anthony Trollope's first novel implying in advertisements it was by his more famous mother, Fanny. In 1865, Newby published a novel call *It May Be True* by Mrs. Wood, which forced Ellen Wood (better known as "Mrs. Henry Wood") to write to the *Athenaeum* disclaiming the work and demanding an apology. Newby feigned surprise at the confusion and he clarified the identity of the author as Mrs. Harcourt Wood ("Our Weekly Gossip"). Eight years later, in the same year *Wild Wood* by Helen Dickens appeared, Newby also published another novel by Frank Trollope. The latter author was no relation to the family of Anthony Trollope; but the names of Dickens and Trollope on Newby's fiction list suggest a least some intention to mislead readers by filling his lists with recognizable names. Nowhere does Newby claim or disclaim the author as a relation to Charles Dickens; likewise, nowhere does the Dickens family claim or disclaim the author as a relation. Certainly the name "Helen Dickens" could be a pseudonym, but because (as we shall see) at least one Helen Dickens existed there also was no attempt to clarify the authorial identity. The handful of reviewers who noticed Dickens's novels also did not explicitly connect the author with the family of Charles Dickens; in the reviews, she is described as "Miss Dickens," a widely used convention for female authors of unknown marital status. One excerpt from a *Daily Guardian* review used in a Newby advertisement in the *Athenaeum* says, "The literary fame of the Dickens family will never decline so long as Miss Helen Dickens produces such interesting and talented novels as 'The Mill Wheel'" —a rather coy attempt by Newby to suggest a family connection. Away from London, *The Australian Journal* (August 1874) announced *The Mill Wheel* "has been written by Miss Helen Dickens, daughter of Charles Dickens, and is highly praised," a clear mistake because Dickens did not have a daughter named Helen.

Shortly after the publication of *The Mill Wheel*, Newby retired from publishing and the publisher Charles Joseph (C. J.) Skeet brought out Dickens's next three novels: *Married at Last* (two volumes, 1877), *The Home of Faith* (three volumes, 1880), and *A Woman's Requital* (three volumes, 1881).[3] Skeet (1812–1892) began as a bookseller in King William's Street and branched out into publishing (usually on commission) in the 1850s—in thirty years, he published more than eighty novels. Skeet never made much mark as a publisher; as his fellow publisher William Tinsley remarked, Skeet was "more a seller of old books than a publisher of new ones" (qtd. in Newbolt 82). *Married at Last* follows the narrator Penny, who because of her poverty, accepts a governess position with a wealthy relation. Jocky, another poor relation from Yorkshire, visits and falls in love with the eldest son, Yorke. The unsolved murder of Yorke's friend casts a shadow of guilt over the man and soon after Jocky runs away. Years later, Jocky reveals her fugitive brother as the killer and she and Yorke wed. The second volume of the novel contains two additional short stories: the first is called "Harvest Queen" about four siblings sent to England from Demerara. When their parents die abroad, they must make their own ways in the world: one son immigrates to Canada where he dies; the youngest daughter dies of fever; and another daughter becomes an actress. The second short story called "Fairy" centers on Frances, the youngest daughter of the Rector of Boscobel in Sussex. A tomboy, she is dubbed "Fairy" by her cousin Alexander Stewart who is dispatched with his army unit to Bombay. A few years later he returns still smitten by his cousin and they wed. When the novel appeared, the reviewer for the *Standard* recognized a "certain crude cleverness in the book"; the *Athenaeum* said it "cannot be asserted that Miss Dickens has greatly improved her style since she wrote her first novel"; and the *Academy* dismissed the novel altogether.

Dickens followed *Married at Last* with two novels that both draw heavily on Brontë's *Jane Eyre* (1848). In *The Home of Faith*, the governess

Faith Lurgan waits years for her lover to return from India, only to have him drown on his voyage home. Meantime, the daughter of her employer Meggie meets Colonel Dundas but her father refuses the match. He marries another wealthy woman and inherits a title. Meggie, now poor, works as a governess for Dundas's son and discovers his wife is now an odious alcoholic. Dundas fakes his wife's death and marries Meggie, but she leaves him after his ruse is revealed. Reviewers, especially the *Athenaeum* and *The Literary World*, unfavorably noted the novel's resemblance to Brontë's *Jane Eyre*, especially the governess characters, bigamy plot, and the mad wife. The bigamy plot device gets used again in *A Woman's Requital*. Grace Sharland, the daughter of nobleman's son and a singer, supports herself as a music teacher after the death of her parents. She falls in love with William Lovering, her proud and taciturn landlord, and the two secretly wed. When Grace discovers William has a living wife who deserted him, she flees to London. Later, she inherits a fortune and learns the wife has died. On her return to William, she finds he has gone mad from grief. In an affecting scene, Grace visits William in his Yorkshire asylum. Only the *Spectator* reviewed the novel, saying "this is a very dreary story" (967).

Shortly after the last novel was published, Skeet retired from publishing. Dickens's three novels published by Skeet did not make any mark with reviewers or readers nor did they call for cheaper reprint editions.[4] With the seeming failure of her five novels thus far and the end of her publishers, Helen Dickens stopped writing for the next twenty years. Then, in 1901, she published the collection of short stories *Puffs of Wind* with publisher Henry J. Drane (1859–1932). Drane, like Newby and Skeet, was a minor Victorian publisher, beginning his business in the late 1880s and lasting until the 1920s. The collection of ten stories advertised "by Helen Dickens author of *Married at Last, The House of Faith* [sic], etc. etc." ran the gamut from ghost stories to romantic vignettes to mysteries.[5] The story "Between the Lights" concerns a naturalist and his family who take a Norfolk cottage during Christmas time. Seeing a ghost renews the man's belief in the supernatural. Two of the stories involve bigamy plots: "A Thousand Pound" concerns a dissolute clergyman's attempt to marry a rich woman despite having a living wife, and "For Ever and a Day" tells of a singer's decline and death after accidentally meeting her lover's wife. The last story in the collection, and arguably the best, "Gate Ahoy!" is narrated by an East End doctor who moves to a village in Yorkshire. There, he recounts the murder of a gatekeeper and a love triangle between the gatekeeper's son, a woman, and her male cousin. The title of the story refers to the ghostly sound the narrator hears near the site of the murder. The collection garnered better reviews than her previous books, including the *Athenaeum* reviewer's praise that "several of the stories are well fancied, and the writer has a gift for narrative."

Four years later, Dickens published her last work of fiction, *The Door on the Latch* (1905), with Drane. Inexplicably, the novel appeared under the pseudonym "Appleton Ellis," the "author of *Puffs of Wind*, etc." and the back pages include a full-page advertisement for Dickens's previous collection of stories (identified as "by the author of *The Door on the Latch*"). Why the author took such a transparent pseudonym remains a mystery. The novel itself concerns the lives of the Hardcastle family consisting of a widowed mother and her nine children. The eldest daughter Marjoriedel, a pious and level-headed spinster, narrates the story of her siblings, including the accident murder of a patient by her alcoholic brother and the unhappy marriage of her sister with a solicitor. The novel received one brief notice: the *Manchester Courier* found the novel "nicely written and full of interest."

What information, if any, can be gleaned about the life of Helen Dickens the author from her works? She was active from 1872 until 1905, suggesting she was born before 1854 and died after 1905. Two of the novels have dedications. Dickens dedicates *The Home of Faith* (1880) to Mrs. H. B. Garling "as a token that sympathy is appreciated and kindness never forgotten." The dedicatee was Marian (d. 1903), the youngest daughter of publisher Thomas Cautley Newby and wife of Henry Bayly Garling (1822–1909). According to his obituary in the *Times*, Garling was an architect who married Marian Newby in 1871 and retired to Folkestone in 1879. His father-in-law Newby spent his retirement years living with them until his death in 1882. The connection between Helen and Marian is suggestive—did she introduce the budding author to her publisher father, or did the friendship develop after the publication of her first novel? Dickens dedicates *A Woman's Requital* (1881) to "my dear and only sister" but the sister is not named. None of her works contain any other biographical information such as prefaces or introductions. Besides her knowledge of popular fiction, the author of these novels exhibits some familiarity with poetry: she liberally quotes Longfellow, Shelley, and the poets in the collection *Translations from the German Poets* (1879) often.

The settings and characters of Dickens's fiction present less reliable information about their author—though authors tend to write about what they know. London and southeast England serve as the setting most often: the estate in *The Mill Wheel* is on the coast of Sussex; the family resides in Surrey in *Married at Last*; the central character flees to London in *A Woman's Requital*; and the characters all live in London in *The Door on the Latch*. Northern England figures in many of Dickens's works: the narrator of "Lost: A Tale" lives in Lancashire; the character Jocky lives near Ripon, Yorkshire, in *Married at Last*; the Yelverton family in *The Home of Faith* resides in Mosston near the "largest northern seaport town" (1) (in all likelihood Newcastle-upon-Tyne or Kingston-upon-Hull); Lovering is sent to a Yorkshire asylum near Skipton in *A Woman's*

Requital; and the doctor's village in "Gate Ahoy!" is Kirkston, Yorkshire. The only other notable setting occurs in *A Woman's Requital* where the narrator's village is near a textile mill outside Manchester. Oddly, only Dickens's first novel *Wild Wood* does not have a specific setting: the estate lies near Maldon, a nondescript village, in the south of England. Few locations outside of England figure in her fiction; some male characters go off to the colonies (Australia, Canada, India, and South Africa) and the family in "The Harvest Queen" come from Demerara (though colonial life is not depicted in any of these works). The men characters have occupations including art, business, engineering, law, medicine, music, and religion. The women characters tend to be governesses and teachers, such as Penny in *Married at Last*, Faith and Meggie in *The Home of Faith*, Grace in *A Woman's Requital*, and several characters in the short stories. Notably, women actors and musicians frequently appear: Jocky takes to the stage in *Married at Last*; the eldest sister becomes a famous actress in the story "The Harvest Queen"; Grace Sharland participates in amateur theatricals and later supports herself as a musician in *A Woman's Requital*; and the central character in the story "For Ever and a Day" trains as a professional singer. Renie in *The Mill Wheel* becomes a professional artist and the narrator of *The Door on the Latch* confesses to being an author.

All in all, the works of Helen Dickens fail to rise above the most pedestrian fiction of her day, though she does show herself competent at constructing a sensational plot. Her penchant for doomed love seems to be the prevailing keynote in her stories, one that probably stood her in good stead with her readers.

2. HELEN DOBSON DICKENS: THE SISTER-IN-LAW OF CHARLES DICKENS

Supposing "Helen Dickens" is not a pseudonym, who could she have been? According to the 1871 and 1881 British Censuses,[6] a handful of women named Helen Dickens lived in England. Of the group, the only woman old enough to have authored a novel in 1872 is a forty-seven-year-old Yorkshire-born widow with four children. This Helen Dickens, living in London in 1871 and 1881, was the sister-in-law of Charles Dickens.

Charles's younger brother Alfred Lamert Dickens was born on 11 March 1822 in Chatham, the seventh child and fourth son of John and Elizabeth Dickens (Slater 12). Through the assistance of his eldest brother Charles, Alfred studied civil engineering in Tamworth, Staffordshire, as a young man and by 1844 worked as a civil engineer for John Cass Birkinshaw of York who oversaw the building of new railroad lines in the East Riding of Yorkshire (Pilgrim 4:98; Cooper 15). In 1846, with the passing of the Malton and Driffield Junction Railway Act, Alfred moved to Malton,

Yorkshire, to supervise the building of the new line (Cooper 17). It was during this time he met Helen Dobson (born in 1826), the daughter of Robert and Ann Dobson. Helen's father was the stationmaster at Strensall, outside York, on the York-Scarsborough line—presumably, Alfred passed through the station frequently in the course of his duties and become acquainted with the stationmaster's daughter. On 16 May 1846, Alfred and Helen married at St. Andrew, Holborn, London, in the presence of Charles and other members of the Dickens family and Charles hosted the wedding breakfast. The young couple—he was twenty-four and she was not yet twenty-one years old—lived in York before moving to Derwent Cottage, Norton, near Malton where Alfred had his office. Alfred and Helen had four children while living at Norton: Alfred Charles (born 1847),[7] Edmund Henry (born 1849), Florence Helen (born 1850), and Katherine Louise (born 1854). In 1848, the Public Health Act created the General Board of Health and the government named Alfred an inspector. Eventually, in 1854, Alfred rose to Superintendent Inspector (Pilgrim 7.410). One of his colleagues at the Board of Health was Henry Austin (d. 1861), the husband of his older sister Letitia Mary Dickens (1816–1893). As part of his duties, Alfred traveled often, visiting urban areas and writing reports about the conditions, one of which was published as *Sewerage, Drainage and Supply of Water and the Sanitary Condition of the Inhabitants of West Ham* (1855). Sometime in 1854 Alfred and Helen's family moved south to Hampstead where their last child Augusta Maud was born in 1855. Over the years of their married life, Alfred frequently met Charles and other members of the Dickens family as Charles's letters show, including visits by Charles to Yorkshire and trips by Alfred to London, Brighton, and once Paris to see his brother. Helen, often, did not accompany her husband on these trips. On one trip north, in 1848, Charles bought Helen "a little bracelet" (Pilgrim 5:221); in 1852 he arranged for tickets to a performance in Manchester for the couple (Pilgrim 6:751); and later he sent copies of his books to the couple. Alfred, ten years Charles's junior, shared his brother's love of the stage and acted in *The Frozen Deep* (first performed 5 January 1857) and other of Charles's amateur productions (Slater 413).[8] In addition, according to Charles's daughter Kate, Alfred was "a talented amateur water-colour artist" (Storey 79; Hawkley 65). He was also an active Freemason of the Universal Lodge in London ("Mr. Joseph Charles Parkinson" 11). His later obituary noted, though not an author himself, "his tastes were eminently literary; and he [was] . . . a brilliant conversationalist and humourist" ("Latest Intelligence").

In 1860, Alfred's position as sanitary inspector took him to Manchester where he fell seriously ill with pleurisy in late June. His wife and children rushed to his side, where Helen nursed her husband through his deteriorating condition. He never recovered and died on July 27 at the Moseley Arms Hotel, Manchester. Notified by telegraph of his brother's condition, Charles unfortunately arrived three hours too late to attend his death. As he observed to a friend after the death, Alfred "had been habitually out very late at night for two or three years. I had seen him at his own house in the morning, a very few weeks before, and had come home here greatly shocked and impressed by his shattered condition before he was wound up for the day" (Pilgrim 9:289). Charles brought the grieving widow and "five little witnesses" (ages thirteen, eleven, ten, six, and five years old) back to London (Pilgrim 9:280). He installed them in a farmhouse near his new home Gad's Hill in Kent while he worked to settle them permanently. According to Charles's letters, Alfred left Helen with £90 in debts: Charles paid them and supported the family for the next ten years, including £280 in the first two years (Pilgrim 9:280).[9] He wrote of the pressures to Mrs. Frances Dickinson: "I have been involved in great anxiety and worry by the unexpected death of my poor brother Alfred. He had no opportunity of providing for his family—died worth nothing—and has left a widow and five children—you may suppose to whom. Day after day I have schemed myself into broken rest and low spirits" (Pilgrim 9:287). In particular, Charles wrote to the Earl of Carlisle asking for aid in helping his two nephews and he arranged for his friend J. C. Parkinson to assist in his sister-in-law's affairs (Pilgrim 9:279–80, 283).

By mid-August the proximity of Helen and her young children proved to be too distracting for Charles—the children, in particular, interrupted his work: "Even while I have been writing this [letter], I have had black figures, little and big, coming in and wistfully questioning me about what is to be done in this wise or that" (Pilgrim 9:289). He struck upon the idea to use his sister-in-law as the caretaker for his ailing mother; for some time, Elizabeth Dickens had been suffering from senility and needed full-time care. Charles rented 4 Grafton Terrace, Camden, and bundled off his dependents to London with furniture left over from the old Tavistock House residence that he had recently sold. Over the next three years, Helen cared for her mother-in-law all the while complaining to Charles about her money problems, her difficulties with caring for Elizabeth, the future of her children, and the poor drains at Grafton Terrace—complaints Charles relegated to his other sister-in-law and helpmeet Georgina Hogarth (Pilgrim 10:22, 10:185). The only extant letters written by Helen Dickens come from this period: a letter from 23 May 1861 addressed to her brother-in-law Frederick Dickens during a "fortnight leave of absence from head-quarters" to visit her family in York and another letter from 9 October 1861 to Frederick announcing the death of their brother-in-law Henry Austin (Free Library of Philadelphia).[10] (The death of Austin added another dependent to Charles's growing rolls, joining the widowed Helen and the abandoned Harriet, wife of his brother Augustus Dickens.) The two letters show Helen to be a thoroughly competent writer who maintained close contacts with her husband's extended family, especially Charles's estranged brother Frederick and widowed sister Letitia, who Helen assisted in finding lodgings (Pilgrim 9:533).

Her mother-in-law, Elizabeth Dickens, died suddenly on 13 September 1863. Charles immediately arranged to let the Grafton Terrace house by the end of the year and encouraged Helen to move back to Yorkshire (Pilgrim 10:290, 296). She refused and remained in the London area, though the exact address is unknown. Charles continued to support Helen and her family: he paid the tuition for the daughters to attend the North London Collegiate girls' school in Camden (Nayder 207); he once again enlisted his friend Parkinson to assist one of the daughters Augusta in getting a place in a charity school (Pilgrim 10:440)[11] ; and he continued to give the family money through at least 1867 (Pilgrim 11:190, 11:314). But clearly Charles grew weary of dealing with his sister-in-law. In April 1866, he served as a reference for a new "London-suburban house" at £37 per annum that she later complained was "alive with bugs" (Pilgrim 11:179, 11:190). A few months later in August 1866, Charles wrote to Georgina,

> I never will go to her house, and that it is my fixed purpose (without any abatement of kindness otherwise), to hold as little personal communication with her as I possibly can. You may add—as you like—either that you do, or that you do not, know the reason for this. . . . About the house, I can give no opinion. She must decide the question out of her own daily experience of it and domestic knowledge of it. If she has any question to ask me of her boy, she can either write it to me or to you. . . . It is pretty clear to me that she very well knows what is amiss, and *has been put up by somebody to trying to get hold of me*. (Pilgrim 11:228; emphasis added)

The letter hints at more trouble than just the house or finances: the "somebody" may very well be either of Charles's estranged brothers, Frederick or Augustus. Years before, in November 1859, Helen had written a letter to Charles interceding on Augustus's behalf, who was living in Chicago with a second woman after abandoning his blind wife Harriett. At that time, Charles gently explained in his reply his desire to have nothing to do with his estranged brother (Pilgrim 9:158–60). And, as we have seen, Helen also maintained a friendly correspondence with Frederick, who, by 1866, lived a dissolute life in London after abandoning his own wife. Charles's letter to Georgina suggests either Augustus or Frederick may have used Helen to contact Charles. A year later, Charles's annoyance toward Helen had not abated; he wrote Georgina "Enclosed is that disagreeable woman's cheque" for £25 (Pilgrim 11.314). The last reference to Helen and her family in Charles's extant correspondence came in 1868 when he presented Edmund £25 for his eighteenth birthday (Pilgrim 12.88).

When Charles Dickens died on 9 June 1870, he left nothing in his will to Helen or to any of her children. Alfred and Helen's twenty-two-year-old son Edmund attended the funeral of Charles as the representative of their family. Though no records of this period exist for the family, presumably the family suffered with the sudden loss of Charles's financial support. In 1871, less than a year later, Helen, Edmund, Florence, and Augusta lived at 39 Queen's Crescent, Camden, according to the census. Edmund worked as the secretary to the Telegraph Construction and Maintenance Co., Augusta was in school, and the two others had no listed occupations in the census. The middle daughter Katherine (age seventeen) was visiting the ship owner Thomas D. Woodhead and his young family in Kingston-upon-Hull, Yorkshire.[12] Alfred no longer lived with the family; he had joined the 16th Queen's Lancers by this time, eventually rising to the rank of sergeant. He died on 20 August 1878 and was buried in Aldershot Military Cemetery, Hampshire.[13] In 1881, according to the census, Helen lived at 14 Richmond Gardens, Hammersmith, with her daughters Florence and Augusta and her elder sister Emma Dobson (age sixty-nine). Edmund (age thirty-two) was visiting the celebrated steamship captain Robert Charles Halpin in Kent (probably as a work-related trip); Katherine (age twenty-seven) was visiting her widowed aunts Letitia Austin (widow of Henry Austin) and Harriett Dickens (widow of Augustus) in Paddington (in perhaps an attempt to economize).

At least one member of the family turned to literature. In 1873, Florence wrote and illustrated a children's book with the unfortunate title *The Ten Little Niggers*. The demy quarto book published anonymously by Frederick Warne as volume five in their Juvenile Drolleries series featured lavish color illustrations accompanying the words and music of the story. The success of the book called for a sequel, *Nine Niggers More*, the following year also published anonymously by Warne in his Juvenile Drolleries series. The publishing agreement for the latter book, dated 1 July 1874, records that Warne paid Florence Dickens £40 for the copyright and that her mother Helen witnessed the contract.[14] Warne republished the two works (with new illustrations) a few years later in a collection of children's songs. Besides these two children's books, no other books authored by Florence have been traced.

In 1886, Edmund married Frances Eleanor, the widow of retired army captain Edward Thornton, and the couple had two sons. In 1891, Helen still resided in Hammersmith with her daughter Augusta. Edmund and his wife lived in Berkshire, with sister Florence (age forty-one) visiting.[15] By the turn of the century, Helen had moved to a house at 53 Culmington Road, Ealing, where she lived with her daughters Florence (age fifty-one) and Augusta (age forty-six). Daughter Katherine lived in Kent with Elizabeth Pentland as a "companion," suggesting the continual need to earn an income or economize. In 1908, Augusta (age fifty-three) married the artist Harry Colls (age fifty-two) in London and the couple moved to Surrey. Colls regularly exhibited his sea- and landscapes at the Royal Academy and he came from a large artistic family centered in Barnes; his father Lebbeus Colls owned a London art gallery and his brother Walter L. Colls was an engraver.[16] In May 1910, Edmund died after a long illness leaving a widow and two sons; an obituary in *The Dickensian* lauded Edmund as "a well-known and acknowledged authority on all things connected with his famous uncle's life and works" (189).

His mother Helen continued living in Ealing with Florence and Katherine until her death in April 1915 at age eighty-nine. At her death, she left a modest estate of £965 to her eldest daughter. Despite her familial connection to Charles Dickens as his sister-in-law, no newspaper noted her passing. Shortly after her death, the three surviving daughters and one husband joined households and shared a house at 10 Byfeld Gardens, Barnes, near the Colls family home on Castelnau Road. Katherine passed away in December 1921 leaving her small £1000 estate to Florence; and Harry Colls followed two years later in 1923. Florence and Augusta continued to share a house until their deaths in 1941: Augusta on 30 January at the age of eighty-six years old and Florence on 27 December at the age of ninety-one years old. Their nephew, Herbert Alfred Dickens, Edmund's youngest son, inherited £1948 and £3582, respectively, from his aunts.

Alfred and Helen's children Edmund and Florence actively took part in events celebrating their uncle, such as those organized by the Boz Club (begun in 1900) and the Dickens Fellowship (begun in 1902). Edmund, in particular, was a vice-president of the latter organization and through it became close friends with his cousin Kate Perugini, the daughter of Charles (Hawksley 328–29). Florence to the end of her life continued to attend Dickens-related and charity events, such as the Boz Club dinner, a bazaar for a children's hospital, and the Ladies' Association for the Princess of York hospital (*Times* 20 October 1938: 17; *Times* 12 May 1939: 19). According to a correspondent in 1936, Florence "is devoted to the memory of her uncle as the kindest and best of men" who made Dickens-inspired Christmas cards and wrote "pleasant verses about Dickensian subjects and characters" ("Our London Correspondence" 10). Katherine attended one Boz Club dinner in 1914 (*Times* 9 February 1914:8); Augusta attended one dinner of the Dickens Fellowship in 1931 (*Times* 9 February 1931: 7). Their mother, however, never attended any events or joined any organizations connected to her famous brother-in-law.

From what can be gleaned from archival materials, genealogical records, and existing correspondence, Helen Dickens, the widow of Alfred and the sister-in-law to Charles, lived a seemingly uneventful, retiring life. Her fourteen-year marriage produced five children and two grandchildren; her widowhood lasted forty-five-years. She maintained contact with her family in Yorkshire and the Dickens family, the latter mostly through her children. Her relationship with her famous brother-in-law began with his admiration of her (especially her tending to Alfred on his deathbed) and ended with little or no contact, which may explain Helen's absence from the Dickens Fellowship and other events. Though left nothing at the death of her husband, by the time of her own death she had accumulated a modest net worth, the source of which remains a mystery (presumably, her son Edmund may have helped support her). In the censuses she either lists no occupation or "living on own means" (a blanket term for annuities or investments). Nowhere in the record is there any reference or hint that Helen Dickens was or was not an author.

3. POSSIBLE CONNECTION?

Without definitive proof, we must examine the circumstantial evidence to see if there is a possible connection between Helen Dickens the novelist and Helen Dickens the sister-in-law of Charles Dickens.

First, the active years of Helen Dickens the novelist, 1872–1905, certainly fall within the life span of Helen Dickens. Most suggestive, however, the first novel is published within two years of Charles Dickens's death and the majority of them (five) within the first decade. Clearly, without the financial support of her brother-in-law and with dependent children, Helen Dickens might well have turned to writing fiction (a family trade of sorts) to eke out a living, finding in Newby a publisher keen to acquire an author named "Dickens." For a middle-class woman, writing fiction was a straightforward way to make money, where even a modest £30–50 per copyright would significantly help the family finances.[17] Her daughter Florence did write two anonymous children's books in the mid-1870s; as a witness to her daughter's contract and career (limited as it was), Helen did have some connection with at least one London publisher. The fact that Florence turned to literature surely increased the likelihood that the mother also may have embarked on a literary career in the wake of Charles's death.

The only drawback to this theory lies in the age of Helen Dickens; few Victorian women began literary careers at the age of forty-six years old and her last novel would have been written in her seventies. Though not unknown, authors rarely begin their careers in middle age; however, the threat of poverty may have served as motivation. As her few existing letters show, Helen Dickens certainly possessed the degree of literacy necessary to write a novel. On a few occasions, her brother-in-law sent copies of his books to Helen, suggesting Helen may have been a novel reader. Clearly the author of *Wild Wood*, and other volumes was familiar with *Jane Eyre*, sensation fiction, and popular poetry, and there is nothing to suggest Helen Dickens was not as well.

Second, the two other known biographical details about Helen Dickens the novelist do not preclude Helen Dickens being the author of the novels. The fourth novel (published in 1880) was dedicated to Marian Garling (née Newby): in the 1860s, the Newby family lived in Welbeck Street (south of Regents Park) and the Dickens family lived in Camden (north of Regents Park); in the 1870s, Garling married, lived in London, and then moved to Kent. Despite the geographical distance, they may well have met. The fifth novel was dedicated to "my one and only sister"; the year the novel appeared, 1881, Helen Dickens lived with her older sister Emma Dobson in London.

Third, the correspondences between the novels and the known life of Helen Dickens, perhaps, are most intriguing. The settings of the novels—mostly greater London and northern England—coincide neatly with the places Helen Dickens knew best, especially Yorkshire. By far, more specific places in Yorkshire are referenced than anywhere else in the fiction, the second being the London area.

In light of the experiences of Helen Dickens, the novel *Wild Wood* (1872) offers tantalizing parallels to the lives of the extended Dickens family. The fictional Drever family seems to conflate the John Dickens–Elizabeth Barrow and Charles Dickens–Catherine Hogarth families: both were large (eight and ten children, respectively) with a mix of the successful—those who made their ways—and the unsuccessful—those who suffered debts and failed careers. Invariably, the failures in the novel take after the mother, much like how Charles Dickens often blamed his father for affecting his siblings. For the Drever family, the parents cede control of the house to their eldest son Durill, an engineer, who manages the estate and finances of the family, in much the same role Charles was obliged to fill. The eldest daughter, Judith, remains a spinster as a result of "a [romantic] blight when young" (I.23) and similar to Charles's eldest daughter Mamie, she refuses to marry. The character of the debt-ridden alcoholic Gilbert has a potential antecedent in Frederick Dickens. In the novel, Gilbert "could not make anything for himself, though he had had every possible assistance rendered him" (I.25), he makes an unfortunate marriage with a low woman against his family's wishes, and the family disowns him because of his constant demands for money. Only Judith secretly aids the black sheep of the family—reminiscent of the assistance Helen attempted for her wayward brothers-in-law. Julius, another successful son in the fictional family, parallels Charles's son Henry, who at the time the novel appeared was entering his successful law career. Crispin, the youngest son in the novel, racks up debts before the family sends him to Australia much like Charles's son Alfred D'Orsay Tennyson Dickens who left unpaid bills when shipped to Australia in 1865. Though the parallels are not as pronounced as in *Wild Wood*, the novels *The Home of Faith* (1880) and *The Latch on the Door* (1905) also center on large families with two ne'er-do-well siblings. In the former novel, debts drive one son to India and he drowns on the way back to England; in the latter novel, alcoholism leads one son to be sent to South Africa.

Many of the women characters in the fiction of Helen Dickens have occupations, such as companion, governess, housekeeper, painter, musician, and actress. Of the former occupations, Helen Dickens served as housekeeper to her aged mother-in-law and one daughter, Katherine, worked as a companion. The extended Dickens family provides numerous examples of women painters, musicians, and actresses. By the time *The Mill Wheel* (1874) appeared (which includes a woman professional painter), Charles's daughter Kate was well advanced in her painting career, having just lost her painter husband Charles Alston Collins (she would later that year marry another painter Carlos Pergulini). Charles's and Alfred's eldest sister Fanny (d. 1848) was an academy-trained singer and musician who married another musician Henry C. Burnett. Both performed publicly. The younger sister of Catherine Dickens and the sister-in-law of Charles Dickens, Helen Hogarth Roney (1833–1891), became a professional singer and musician and later became a private teacher of music (Nayder 297–303). Roney also acted publicly, including in Charles's amateur productions. (Coincidentally, like the family in Helen Dickens's short story "Harvest Queen," Roney's husband Richard Cusack Roney and his siblings spent their childhoods in Demerara.) Her daughter May Roney Leon (b. 1865) also took to the stage, eventually performing in Gilbert and Sullivan's musicals in the 1880s (Nayder 307). Last, as Alfred's wife, Helen would have seen and heard much about Charles's dramatic productions because of Alfred's participation in them. It is no stretch of the imagination to see that Helen Dickens could have drawn on these examples to people her novels.

Only Helen Dickens's last novel *The Door on the Latch* (1905) includes characters who are authors. The narrator, Marjoriedel, before she inherits a fortune, reveals, "when I could find a quiet moment, wrote. That was my only recreation, my comfort. I could say whatever I liked to the paper, and, by relieving my pent-up feelings, saved myself from utter extinction. My success had been so far nil; but now and again I earned a few pounds by writing stories for a paper, and that gave me courage to persevere. . . . All I wanted was enough money to lift the dread of poverty-stricken old age off my mind" (54). Later, after she moves outside London, she meets Miss Lucas who, in answer to a question about her occupation, replies, "I write. It is slow, very dispiriting and disappointing, but fascinating. I have . . . very little money, so that I am obliged to live sparingly. I am hoping to make something for my old age. My little income has diminished terribly of late years" (213–214). She goes on to confess she uses a pseudonym, to which Marjoriedel responds, "I knew the name. . . . And to think this plain-looking, poorly-dressed, hidden-away woman should have written [those books]!" (214). Perhaps these characters speak for their author; the views expressed certainly conform to what we know of Helen Dickens the sister-in-law.

So was Helen Dickens the novelist related to Charles Dickens? Ultimately, no definitive proof for or against a connection has been found. Of course, the name on the novels could be a pseudonym. But Helen Dickens, the wife of Alfred and sister-in-law to Charles, could very well be the author of these seven works of fiction. The authorial name, dates, and subject matter of the novels certainly fit what we know of the sister-in-law of Charles. Clearly, after the death of her husband and brother-in-law, Helen may well have turned to fiction writing as a way to make money. What success she had, unfortunately, was small and quickly forgotten.

NOTES

The author wishes to acknowledge the generous help of Marie-Francoise Cachin, Cathleen Carosella, Mark Charles Dickens, Elizabeth James, Lucinda Hawksley, Robert L. Patten, Michael Slater, and John Sutherland during the researching and writing of this chapter.

1. Unfortunately, the financial records of these three publishers do not survive.

2. Longer summaries of all the novels can be found *At the the Circulating Library: A Database of Victorian Fiction, 1837–1901*, available at www.victorianresearch.org/atcl.

3. Newby's short-lived successors Morgan and Hebron published a short story "The Cuckoo's Call" by Helen Dickens in their quarterly *Mayfair* in July 1874. The story tells of the meeting between a simple country girl Cassey and Captain O'Ryan of Her Majesty's Dragoons. The two professed their love before the captain must go away; when he returns a year later he finds her on her death bed.

4. As a testament to her unpopularity, the copy of *The Home of Faith* in the British Library had uncut pages until 2012.

5. The contents are: "A Thousand Pounds," "Weeping Cross," "From the Silent Land," "On the Wings of the Wind," "For Ever and a Day," "The Welsh Harp," "Between the Lights," "When the Raven Dances with the Yellow Bird's Wife," "Greta," and "Gate Ahoy!" None seemed to have appeared in periodicals before publication.

6. Throughout the latter part of the essay, I relied on Ancestry.com for English census, birth, marriage, death, and probate records.

7. Charles Dickens agreed to be the boy's godfather (Pilgrim 5:160).

8. According to a newspaper account of the 1857 performance in the *Examiner*, a "Miss Helen Dickens" also took a role in the play. This could be an error for Alfred's wife or Helen Hogarth, the sister of Charles's wife Catherine ("Tavistock House Theatricals").

9. The editors of the Pilgrim edition of the letters imply a trust fund for the widow was also set up (9:280), though none of the letters refer to one.

10. The Free Library of Philadelphia holds a third undated letter from Helen to Frederick written before his death in 1868.

11. Parkinson (a friend of Alfred and himself an ardent Freemason) arranged for Augusta Maud to attend the Royal Masonic Institution for Girls at St. John's Hill (Viator 295). The school was originally founded to maintain the indigent children of Freemasons.

12. Woodhead's middle name was "Dobson" suggesting he was possibly a cousin or other relation.

13. Strangely, no probate or obituary has been found for Alfred Charles Dickens.

14. The contract is found in Agreements and Some Receipts, 1860s–1919, MS 5337, Archive of Frederick Warne, Special Collections, University of Reading, United Kingdom.

15. Katherine Louise has not been traced in the 1891 British Census.

16. Coincidently, Walter L. Colls contributed illustrations to the Nonesuch Edition of Charles Dickens, published in 1937.

17. An examination of records of the publisher Bentley around this same time finds new authors receiving payments in this range (Bassett 72–74).

WORKS CITED

Advertisement for Thomas Cautley Newby. *Athenaeum*, 7 March 1874, p. 313.

Arbuckle, Elisabeth Sanders. "Thomas Cautley Newby." *British Literary Publishing Houses, 1820–1880*. Edited by Patricia Anderson and Jonathan Rose, Gale Research, 1991.

Bassett, Troy J. "Living on the Margin: George Bentley and the Economics of the Three-Volume Novel, 1865–70." *Book History*, vol. 13, 2010, pp. 58–79.

Cooper, T. P. *The Real Micawber: With a Batch of his Remarkable Letters*. Simpkin, Marshall, 1922.

Dickens, Charles. *The British Academy Pilgrim Edition of the Letters of Charles Dickens*, 12 volumes. Edited by Madeline House, Graham Storey, and Kathleen Tillotson, Oxford UP, 1965–2002.

Dickens, Florence. *Nine Niggers More*. Frederick Warne, 1874.

———. *The Ten Little Niggers*. Frederick Warne, 1873.

Dickens, Helen [1]. "The Cuckoo's Call." *Mayfair*, July 1874, pp. 91–107.

———. *The Home of Faith*, 3 volumes. C. J. Skeet, 1880.

———. *Married at Last*, 2 volumes. C. J. Skeet, 1877.

———. *The Mill Wheel*, 3 volumes. T. C. Newby, 1874.

———. *Puffs of Wind*. Henry J. Drane, 1901.

———. *Wild Wood: A Novel*, 3 volumes. T. C. Newby, 1872.

———. *A Woman's Requital*, 3 volumes. C. J. Skeet, 1881.

Dickens, Helen [2]. Letter to Frederick Dickens. 23 May 1861. Charles Dickens Collection. Rare Book Department, Free Library of Philadelphia. DCL D556h 1861-05-23. 13 December 2012.

———. Letter to Frederick Dickens. 9 October 1861. Charles Dickens Collection. Rare Book Department, Free Library of Philadelphia. DCL D556h 1861-10-09. 13 December 2012.

Dictionary of Literary Biography, vol. 106. *Literature Resource Center*. 17 January 2013.

"Edmund Dickens." *Dickensian*, vol. 6, no. 7, July 1910, p. 189.

Ellis, Appleton [Helen Dickens]. *The Door on the Latch*. Henry J. Drane, 1905.

Hawksley, Lucinda. *Katey: The Life and Loves of Dickens's Artistic Daughter*. Doubleday, 2006.

"Latest Intelligence." *Standard*, vol. 6, August 1860, p. 5.

"Mr. H. B. Garling." *Times*, 9 December 1909, p. 11.

"Mr. Joseph Charles Parkinson." *Times*, 26 October 1908, p. 11.

Nayder, Lillian. *The Other Dickens: A Life of Catherine Hogarth*. Cornell UP, 2011.

Newbolt, Peter. *William Tinsley (1831–1902): "Speculative Publisher."* Ashgate, 2001.

"Our London Correspondence." *Manchester Guardian*, 30 March 1936, p. 10.

"Our Weekly Gossip." *Athenaeum*, 2 December 1865, p. 769.

"Queries." *Literary World*, 1 November 1895, p. 349.

Review of *The Door on the Latch* by Appleton Ellis. *Manchester Courier*, 2 March 1906, p. 3.

Review of *The Home of Faith* by Helen Dickens. *Atheneaum*, 17 January 1880, p. 84.

Review of *The Home of Faith* by Helen Dickens. *Literary World*, 13 February 1880, p. 109.

Review of *Married at Last* by Helen Dickens. *Academy*, 14 July 1877, p. 33.

Review of *Married at Last* by Helen Dickens. *Athenaeum*, 23 June 1877, pp. 795–96.
Review of *Married at Last* by Helen Dickens. *Standard*, 25 July 1877, p. 2.
Review of *The Mill Wheel* by Helen Dickens. *Athenaeum*, 28 March 1874, p. 424.
Review of *Puffs of Wind* by Helen Dickens. *Athenaeum*, 6 July 1901, p. 29.
Review of *Wild Wood* by Helen Dickens. *Morning Post*, 26 August 1872, p. 3.
Review of *Wild Wood* by Helen Dickens. *Spectator*, 31 August 1872, p. 1116.
Review of *A Woman's Requital* by Helen Dickens. *Spectator*, 23 July 1881, p. 967.
Slater, Michael. *Charles Dickens*. Yale UP, 2009.
Storey, Gladys. *Dickens and Daughter*. Haskell House Publishers, 1971.
"Tavistock House Theatricals." *Examiner*, 17 January 1857, pp. 38–39.
Viator. "Masonic Notes and Queries." *Freemason*, 18 June 1870, pp. 295.

TWO

Moonrise and the Ascent of Eve, the Woman Titan: Charlotte Brontë's Epiphanies of the Fourfold Elemental Feminine

Martin Bidney

My aim in this chapter is to determine the structural pattern of the literary epiphanies in Charlotte Brontë's *Shirley*, *Villette*, and *Jane Eyre* and to interpret their subversiveness in a context of present-day theoretical concerns. The method of analysis, based on the thought of philosopher-critic Gaston Bachelard, is systematized in my *Patterns of Epiphany: From Wordsworth to Tolstoy, Pater, and Barrett Browning* (Bidney 1997, 1–21 and passim). A literary epiphany is defined subjectively as a moment experienced by the reader as uncommonly intense, mysterious, and with implications that seem disproportionate to the brevity of the experience. Objectively, an epiphany is identified by three distinctive recurrent formal criteria: elemental focus (earth, water, air, and/or fire), pattern of motion, and shape(s). First I identify, as paradigm of the structure pattern, the epiphany that exhibits the features in fullest clarity; then other epiphanies are related to this pattern and their implications interpreted. I will find that the paradigm of the Woman-Titan Eve at Moonrise in *Shirley* aids in understanding more fragmentary epiphanies elsewhere in Brontë's writing; these include also parodic or nightmare variants that reveal unresolved psychological problems in the texts. Modern theorists and critics provide context for interpreting Brontë's achievement. In particular, Hélène Cixous and Mary Daly prove to be recent continuators of what I may well call a Charlotte Brontë tradition in subversive epiphany making.

In her three major novels, Charlotte Brontë offers epiphanies of Ideal Woman, and her epiphanic paradigm depicts the feminine sublime as maternal. But far from idealizing a vanished, mother-guided past, Brontë offers instead a new myth of possibility and the envisioned future. True, her epiphanies of moonrise as the ascent of Eve (a wordplay I base on Brontë's own allusions) do reveal a maternal link to both sea and night, to the womb and its darkness; but in Brontë's epiphanies, as the moon *rises*, transcending—though not abandoning—a lower world of water and earth, of tides and dark rifts, it moves into, and gradually encompasses, the traditionally "higher" elements of air and star-fire. The ascent of Eve becomes a vision of a fourfold plenitude, an elemental feminine cosmos.

Brontë's epiphanic paradigm requires the harmonious, lyrical-sublime *interplay of all four cosmic elements*. Brontë's ideal cosmic inclusiveness or elemental synthesis is embodied in a woman, called in the paradigm "Eve" (and, in a corollary epiphany, "Eva") but also "Nature" (as well as, in the corollary, "Humanity"). This Eve is our General Mother, yet more; she is a "woman-Titan." The Titans were sons of Gaia and Ouranos, earth and sky; they included Prometheus (fire) and Oceanus (water), and in Brontë they are elemental forces as well as masculine powers. So the "woman-Titan" in Brontë's epiphanic paradigm, combining (along with powers of water and earth) the skyey purity of Mary and the rebel fire of Prometheus, is *elemental and androgynous*.

A vision of the Feminine/Androgyne might seem a theophany, but there are no imputed deities involved; in fact, as just noted, in a variant of the paradigm Brontë calls her Fourfold Elemental Being "Humanity." Brontë's syncretic moments of visionary exhilaration become highly personal revelations, their lyric force and resonance entirely dependent on imaginative intensity.

Elemental inclusiveness is the boldest feature of Brontë's epiphanic paradigm, but a formal component will also recur. The form of motion in a Brontëan epiphany is a *luminous ascent*—the ascent of the moon, or of a woman deemed coessential with, or imaginatively linked to, the moon. Geometric shapes are not crucial to the paradigm or its variants, though the circularity of the full moon may appear, or the related circularity of a "crown," moonlight may occur simply in diffuse form or in a white patch on a wall. In incomplete versions of the epiphany pattern, imperfect epiphanies that may signify stages of visionary struggle undergone by Brontë's maturing female protagonists, elements strive in mutual conflict, or some elements may be missing. In negative epiphanies—nightmarish, parodic, or both—descent replaces ascent, and a fiery plunge may substitute for an ethereal and luminous rising.

Though Brontë did not know the epic poems of William Blake, her imagining of the fourfold elemental Universal Woman may be viewed as a welcome implicit rejoinder to Blake's conception, in *The Four Zoas* and elsewhere, of the four (masculine, elemental) Zoas that constitute Albion, Blake's "Universal Man." In Blake's myth, every feminine being is the "emanation" of a masculine one. But when Brontë's feminine "Humanity," epiphanically inspired, unites with masculine "Genius," it is less clear who emanates whom; the word "Genius," suggesting *either a higher power or one's own inward spirit*, is strategically ambiguous. In her paradigmatic epiphany of a Universal Self Brontë offers a feminist counterthrust to Blake's *Four Zoas*, and (in anticipation) to Whitman's universalizing but masculine-dominant "Song of Myself." Like these poets, but in feminist terms, Brontë creates an epiphany of a fourfold elemental unity as an inner cosmos mirrored in an outer one.

In her paradigmatic epiphany of a fourfold elemental unity, feminine yet implicitly androgynous in its inclusiveness, Brontë anticipates present-day feminist vision. More elementally inclusive than Luce Irigaray, whose *Elemental Passions* contains no fourfold vision or impulse toward androgyny, Brontë as epiphanic performer finds her closest contemporary analogues as epiphanic performer in Hélène Cixous and Mary Daly, theorists whose poetic prose is often inclusively "elemental" precisely in the Brontëan sense. After surveying Brontë's epiphanies I will compare her to these proclaimers and poetic exemplifiers of feminine elemental powers.

Although "elemental" language used in epiphanies might suggest a naturalistic or biologic bias, Brontë's elemental epiphanies are cultural constructions, projects that reshape language, myth, and poetry to create images not of a pre-given female sex but of a transvaluated feminine gender. Theorists such as Diana Fuss (n26) have shown how the rhetoric of nature is deployed for culturally transvaluative purposes. So I will be using "masculine" and "feminine" gender concepts instead of "male" and "female" sexual labels.

Shirley, though not Brontë's best novel, showcases her paradigmatic dreamlike epiphany—clearly singled out as such with the words *mystical, visions*, and *trance*—and also its equally elaborate variant or corollary, both to be studied in Part 1, along with a fragmentary epiphany, a nightmare epiphany, and a parodic one. *Villette* provides two epiphanies (one far more complete and powerful than the other, but both incorporating parts of the *Shirley* paradigm), examined in Part 2. *Jane Eyre*, finally, presents three fascinating epiphanies of high intensity, along with a couple of more attenuated or fragmentary visions that undermine the gathering triumphalism of the major epiphanic episodes. (*The Professor*, a fourth Brontë novel, lacks epiphanies and will not be treated here.) I alter the chronology of Brontë's three epiphanic novels (*Jane Eyre, Shirley, Villette*) for greater clarity. We must consider *Shirley* first if Brontë's epiphanic paradigm is to be made clear at the outset, and *Jane Eyre* should culminate the discussion because its three epiphanies form a psychologically instructive progression toward a dramatically appealing if not wholly satisfying climax.

My epiphanological analysis of Brontë will differ in focus from the work of critics who have studied Brontë's "Eve" and "Eva" visions in *Shirley* (Sandra M. Gilbert and Susan Gubar, Irene Tayler, Kate Lawson) but have not seen them, respectively, as the epiphanic paradigm and corollary of a recurrent pattern: fourfold elemental feminine; ascending moon. I will respond to these and other critics as occasion offers.

1

Charlotte Brontë presents her paradigmatic feminist literary epiphany in vivid contrast to traditional Miltonic vision, a contrast Gilbert and Gubar emphasize.[1] In Chapter VII of *Shirley*, the eponymous heroine tells her friend Caroline Helstone that she would just as soon skip the "pungent" sermon Caroline's reverend uncle would doubtless offer ("all sense for the Church, and all causticity for Schism"). A more appealing revelation beckons Shirley—better than Helstone's, far better even than Milton saw in *Paradise Lost*:

> "Nature is now at her evening prayers: she is kneeling before those red hills. I see her prostrate on the great steps of her altar, praying for a fair night for mariners at sea, for travellers in deserts, for lambs on moors, and unfledged birds in woods. Caroline, I see her! and I will tell you what she is like: she is like what Eve was when she and Adam stood alone on earth."

> "And that is not Milton's Eve, Shirley."

> "Milton's Eve! Milton's Eve! No, by the pure Mother of God, she is not!"[2]

Shirley's visionary Eve is the spirit of Mother Nature viewed at eve, praying for harmony and tranquility to pervade all the four cosmic elements of which she and all her incarnations are composed, for peace and succor to be visited on travelers at sea and in the fiery deserts, on beasts of the earth and birds of the air. Milton "tried to see the first woman" but sadly "saw her not"; "It was his cook that he saw; or it was Mrs. Gill, as I have seen her, making custards . . . for the Rectors,—preserves, and 'dulcet creams'—puzzled 'what choice to choose for delicacy best'" (*S* 320). Milton must be reminded "that the first men of the earth were Titans, and that Eve was their mother: from her sprang Saturn, Hyperion, Oceanus; she bore Prometheus—" (*S* 320). The Greek Titans were children of Earth and Sky, but for Shirley their mother Eve contains both elements; she also begets water-spirit Oceanus and fiery Prometheus. Eve is the inclusive begetter and originative encompasser of earth, air, water, and fire—the four elements that make up Nature, which she personifies and animates.

What Brontë calls the "mighty and mystical parent of Shirley's visions" (*S* 320) continues to grow in epiphanic power and promise as Shirley's astonishing prose poem continues:

> I say, there were giants on the earth in those days: giants that strove to scale heaven. The first woman's breast that heaved with life on this world yielded the daring which could contend with Omnipotence: the strength which could bear a thousand years of bondage,—the vitality which could feed that vulture death through uncounted ages,—the unexhausted life and uncorrupted excellence, sisters to immortality, which, after millenniums of crimes, struggles, and woes, could conceive and bring forth a Messiah. The first woman was heaven-born: vast was the heart whence gushed the well-spring of the blood of nations; and grand the undegenerate head where rested the consort-crown of creation. (*S* 320)

Because Adam remains unmentioned here, the "heaven-born" Eve wearing the "consort-crown of creation" no longer seems the wife of a mortal; rather, these magically ambiguous phrases transform her almost into a celestial kabbalistic Shekhinah, a divine consort (indeed, she is coessential with Virgin Mary, who "could conceive" a "Messiah"). "Undegenerate," untouched by original sin, she retains "uncorrupted excellence" along with Promethean daring and "unexhausted life" until, after showing her Promethean willingness to "contend with Omnipotence" (to struggle with God) for a thousand years, in the form of Mary she brings forth yet another fiery Deliverer.

The strategic slipperiness of Brontë's crafty rhetoric leaves it unclear whether Eve-Mary-Nature has "yielded the daring which could contend with Omnipotence" by begetting the vulture-defier Prometheus or by struggling against the Father-God in her own right; if she affirms her own "uncorrupted excellence," that affirmation in itself, as Gilbert and Gubar show, is sufficient Promethean challenge to any God-enforced conception of a female fall.[3] Eve's is not only the unblemished crown of creation; hers is also the "heart," which is the "well-spring of the blood of nations" and of the continuing life of Titans (equatable in mythic typology to the giant "Antediluvians" who, as William Blake said, "are our Energies"[4]). The heart of the Great Mother is as a burning fountain embodying eternal youth and perfection (contentment in herself), along with the unquenchable fire of rebellious "daring" (contention with all challengers).

But all this is too abstract, protests Caroline to Shirley; "You have not told me what you saw kneeling on those hills" (*S* 321). An epiphany must be a concrete vision. And that is what Shirley now offers in her poetic peroration—the ascent of Eve, an evening vision of a fourfold elemental feminine spirit that, rising like the moon, encompasses the cosmos and communes "face to face" with its heavenly source:

> I saw—I now see—a woman-Titan: her robe of blue air spreads to the outskirts of the heath, where yonder flock is grazing; a veil white as an avalanche sweeps from her head to her breast. I see her zone, purple like that horizon: through its blush shines the star of evening. Her steady eyes I cannot picture; they are clear—they tremble with the softness of love and the lustre of prayer. Her forehead has the expanse of a cloud, and is paler than the early moon, risen long before dark gathers: she reclines her bosom on the ridge of Stilbro' Moor; her mighty hands are joined beneath it. So kneeling, face to face she speaks with God. That Eve is Jehovah's daughter, as Adam was his son. . . . I will stay out here with my mother Eve, in these days called Nature. I love her—undying, mighty being! Heaven may have faded from her brow when she fell in paradise; but all that is precious on earth shines there still. She is taking me to her bosom and showing me her heart. (*S* 321)

This is indeed too "visionary" for diffident, conservative Caroline. But as Shirley, after the climax of her epiphany, fixes "her eyes on the deep burning west" she sinks "into a pleasurable trance" (*S* 321), cherishing the delights of contemplation and wonder.

It is fortunate that in *Shirley* Brontë has created, for once, a protagonist free of extreme socioeconomic constraints (though not free of mental obstacles, as the novel's plot shows), a heroine who need not fear a governess's life of subjugation, for only by transcending the customary economic servitude of a Victorian single woman can Shirley acquire the confidence for an empowering epiphany of the elemental, defiantly Promethean "woman-Titan." The androgynous nature of this visionary being mirrors and extends the androgyny of Shirley herself, a landowner and mill-owner who bears the "masculine" name her parents had intended for the son they had hoped to have; she calls herself "Captain Keeldar" and "Shirley Keeldar, Esquire"; Rector Helstone, who half-jocularly calls her "Mr. Keeldar," refers to her with masculine pronouns; and Shirley, who says she is "a woman, and something more," explains, "They gave me a man's name; I hold a man's position: it is enough to inspire me with a touch of manhood" (*S* 200–203). Blake's and Whitman's cosmicized mythic selves are androgynous, but with a masculine bias; Brontë's Shirley has the courage, as epiphanic poet, to counter such a bias in rectifying the subaltern status of Milton's Eve.

Shirley's epiphany of the Promethean Eve-Mary-Nature provides the paradigm for all of Brontë's epiphanies. Eve's robe of blue air, recalling the symbolic blue apparel of the iconic Mary, gives her the stature of a sky queen, whose sash has the purple hue of the horizon. Reclining her bosom on the moor, she is as an earth spirit, her veil white as a snowy avalanche. Her brow recalls the "risen" moon, and her purple sash leads the seer to recall the fiery light of the Evening Star at dusk. All elements combine in this ascent of Eve to the post- and contra-Miltonic heights, an ascent repeated in the epiphanies of her British daughters—Shirley, Lucy, and Jane.

Among critics, Gilbert and Gubar have best evoked the anti-Miltonic Prometheanism of Brontë's paradigm epiphany in *Shirley*. Kate Lawson, although noting the power of Brontë's feminist vision here as an alternative to the "dissenting" religion presented in the novel,[5] finds Shirley's "Eve" too "vast and impersonal, too removed from the lived experience of the particular and human."[6] For Irene Tayler, as for Brontë's Catherine Helstone, "Eve is too 'vague and visionary' a figure"—also merely "a female analogue not of God or the Savior, but of Adam," thus "not a goddess, but a creature."[7] Both critics find Eve too vague, but Lawson wants her more down-to-earth, whereas Tayler wants her nearer to divinity, more akin to the upper skies. In my view, a detailed study of Eve as inclusive Elemental Fourfold has shown that she concretely encompasses earth *and* air, and fire and water also.

Eve ascends again in Shirley's corollary to this epiphanic paradigm in a supposed translation of a homework essay Shirley had written previously for her former French teacher (who will eventually become her spouse), Louis Moore. This epiphany is stimulated by the Biblical verses, "And it came to pass when men began to multiply on the face of the earth, and daughters were born unto them, that the sons of God saw the daughters of men that they were fair; and they took them wives of all which they chose" (Gen. 6:1–2). The startling and traditionally problematic union of God's sons with humanity's daughters, which immediately preceded the biblical flood and may have helped arouse the divine anger causing that deluge, has been seen as impious, rebellious, tragic; Byron's play *Heaven and Earth*, based on the same Bible passage (part of which serves as its epigraph), epitomizes this tragic outlook—though with a sinister glamor suitable to his romanticism of doomed defiance. (For the seventeen-year-old Eliza Lynn Linton, later to become a well-known Victorian anti-feminist, the pagan presumption of the same biblical passage brought on a crisis: she fainted.)[8] But Brontë looks at the divine-human union differently. For her, the representative Daughter of Humanity is a variant of her epiphanic "Eve" (now "Eva"), and the Son of God who enters her is Genius—from one viewpoint, an aspect of herself.

Brontë pictures her new Adamless Eva not as the first woman but as an orphan, "bereaved of both parents," yet "the green wilderness nurses her, and becomes to her a mother," so she grows up healthy and attractive, her moonlike "form gleam[ing] ivory-white through the trees" (*S* 486). Eva feels "the world, the sky, the night boundlessly mighty," yet the (once again, Promethean) "flame of her intelligence" seems "a star in an else starless firmament," a "spark" of fiery light "burning unmarked," unrecognized (*S* 487). "She gazed abroad on Heaven and Evening; Heaven and Evening gazed back on her" (*S* 488). She is herself Eve; gazing on Evening, she seems to call on an image of herself, on some inner resource, to answer her want—and the reply she receives reflects her own spirit: "The Evening flushed full of hope: the Air panted; the Moon—rising before—ascended large, but her light showed no shape" (*S* 488). The spirit of this ascending moon of Eve[ning], *her* spirit but also that of a "Son of God," says, "Acknowledge in me the Seraph, on earth named Genius"; he calls to her, "Come again into the heaven whence thou wert sent" (*S* 489). The heaven-born Eve of Shirley's epiphanic paradigm reappears to us in this variant, and because a seraph is a burning angel, Eva's Seraph-Genius mirrors the Promethean "flame" of her own "intelligence."

As the new epiphanic Eve rises, moonlike, to unite with her Genius, once again the spirits of all four elements, combining, enter into her and seem to deify her in so doing:

> Her eye received no image; and yet a sense visited her vision and her brain as of the serenity of stainless *air*, the power of sovereign *seas*, the majesty of marching *stars*, the energy of colliding *elements*, the rooted endurance of *hills* wide-based, and above all, as of the lustre of heroic beauty rushing victorious on the Night, vanquishing its shadows like a diviner *Sun*. Such was the bridal-hour of Genius and Humanity. (*S* 489; emphases added)

In the postscript to this epiphany of the Fourfold Feminine Ascendant, we learn that, as Humanity, she is invincibly divine and immortal: the "faithful Seraph fought for Humanity a good fight through Time; and, when Time's course closed, . . . crowned her with the crown of Immortality" (*S* 490). Brontë's Shirley implicitly or proleptically counters the masculine bias of Blake's Albion and Whitman's Self (or, within the novel, of Moore) with a feminist re-envisioning of the spirit of Humanity as elemental fourfold harmony.

Can it be said that the previously composed "Eva" epiphany "differs drastically" from Shirley's later paradigm of a "Promethean titan-woman because this alternative myth countenances female submission"? Gilbert and Gubar support their claim by arguing that "Here in Shirley's homework for her teacher we find a hungry, cold orphan girl who is first fostered by the earth but who ultimately responds to a male master, called Genius, who finally takes his dying bride into 'his' home—Heaven, where he 'restored her, redeemed, to Jehovah—her Maker,'" a "child of physical maternal Nature" now "seduced or abducted into the Father's deathly realm of spirit."[9] Lawson elaborates on these ideas; for her, Eva the daughter of men is "feeble and secondary, and can only be restored and redeemed by the male figure," variously called "Jehovah," a "Son of God," or a "Comforter."[10] The most comprehensive critique of Eva is

Tayler's chapter "A Late Addition: 'The First Bluestocking,'" where the triumphant-sounding "bridal-hour of Genius and Humanity" is noted as "modeled on the marriage of the lamb and his bride in Revelation, which though spoken in the language of love, in fact figures the [asexual] mystical union in eternity of Creator and Creation, of God and his Church"; so Eva, like a "virgin nun" married to "Christ," is a woman indomitably overpowered by an all-subduing male.[11]

Though these are intelligent arguments for seeing Shirley's previous corollary epiphany of Eva as to some extent less bold than the paradigmatic Eve, they are seriously weakened by a shared and necessarily narrowing focus on sources, on traditional symbolic props or allusions, rather than on Brontë's transformative reshaping of her materials. Admittedly less defiant than Eve (and so, alas, more fitted to *Shirley*'s sadly un-Promethean plot and ending), Eva—by the time Brontë is done transforming this daughter of earth—pantheistically embodies all the elemental forces, the "serenity," "power," "majesty," and "endurance" of air, water, star-fire, and hills, plus the "energy" of "colliding elements," the dynamism of chaos allied to the grandeur of cosmos. Moreover, she has become identified with all-inclusive, bisexual, universal "Humanity"; and the delightfully crafty rhetoric of Brontë has "married" her at last to nothing more (nothing less!) than her own salvific, godlike Genius. From *this* point of view she is the Universe itself: elemental, human, and divine. In viewing Brontë as a shrewdly transformative feminist rhetorical prose poet, we ought to stress not her biblical starting points but her daring departures from them. True, "Comforter" (Greek "Paraclete") usually means the Holy Ghost, as Tayler says.[12] But the Comforter of fourfold elemental Eva is her own "Genius"—a burning angel, a Promethean fiery "Seraph."

In the same polemical-visionary mode, Brontë's parodic negative epiphany offers a vivid glimpse of the proud egotist Napoleon as a fake Titan, a Failed Fourfold. Childish Bonaparte can hardly control the elements either within or without; instead, they overcome his pride and teach him a lesson:

> The nineteenth century wantons in its giant adolescence; the Titan-boy uproots mountains in his game, and hurls rocks in his wild sport. . . . [Bonaparte] puts his trust in a snow-cloud: the Wilderness, the Wind, and the Hail-storm are his refuge: his allies are the elements—Air, Fire, Water. And what are these? (*S* 635)

They are spirits of "vengeance"; Napoleon is the anti-Humanity, with all the faults of which Eve is now absolved. Elementally incomplete, he is a mere thoughtless rock-thrower, thinking the earth is meant only to provide him with weapons. Air, fire, and water inflict on him an elemental retribution.

There are an additional fragmentary epiphany and a brief nightmare epiphany in *Shirley* that indicate recurrent problems for Brontëan heroines. The first is a vision of mermaids that Shirley recounts to Caroline, with ascending moon and triumphant affirmation of water, but without the other elements:

> I am to be walking by myself on deck, rather late of an August evening, watching and being watched by a full harvest-moon; something is to rise white on the surface of the sea, over which that moon mounts silent, and hangs glorious: the object glitters and sinks. It rises again. . . . I show you an image, fair as alabaster, emerging from the dim wave. We both see the long hair, the lifted and foam-white arm, the oval mirror brilliant as a star. . . . I see a preternatural lure in its wily glance; it beckons . . . . She comprehends our unmoved gaze; she feels herself powerless; anger crosses her front; she cannot charm, but she will appal us; she rises high, and glides all revealed, on the dark wave-ridge. Temptress-terror! monstrous likeness of ourselves! Are you not glad, Caroline, when at last, and with a wild shriek, she dives? (*S* 246)

Robert B. Heilman notes the "surrealistic" power of this epiphany.[13] When asked why she imagines such a "non-entity," Shirley says, "I don't know," but she also replies to Caroline's objection that women are "neither temptresses, nor terrors, nor monsters" with the reminder that "Some" women are said to be "all three" and that "There are men who ascribe to 'woman,' in general, such attributes" (*S* 246). Moments of fragmentary epiphanic imagery like this one signify for Brontë a vision of rebellion rather than of wholeness—psychologically needed but incomplete, less active than *reactive*, a stage on the way to something more inclusive and more salutary.

Similarly fragmentary but far more threatening is Moore's terrified epiphany of Shirley as a Semele-turned-Juno, an incendiary goddess whose fire is fatal to her adulating but unapproved worshiper, her presumptuous priest:

> A shock of heaven and earth is felt—not by the slumbering city; only by that lonely watcher, brave and unshaken in his fanaticism. In the midst of silence, with no preluding sound, he is wrapt in sudden light. Through the roof—through the rent, wide-yawning, vast, white-blazing blue of heaven above, pours a wondrous descent—dread as the down-rushing of stars. He has what he asked: withdraw—forbear to look—I am blinded. I hear in that fane an unspeakable sound—would that I could not hear it! I see an insufferable glory burning terribly between the pillars. Gods be merciful and quench it!
> A pious Argive enters to make an early offering in the cool dawn of morning. . . . No priest remains: he who watched will be seen no more. (*S* 526)

As elementally powerful but fragmentary as Shirley's mermaid vision, this nightmare-epiphany of descending fire also terrifyingly reverses the pattern of ascent that typifies Brontëan epiphanies of the fourfold elemental Eve.

Moore imagines Shirley-Juno as fatal not to himself but to a rival whose inadequacy he imagines her disliking. Yet the fiery Junonian descent is conveyed with a force suggesting genuine personal fear. We think of Bertha's comparable fiery fall in *Jane Eyre*, and we detect a recurrent subtext of negative epiphany in Brontë that can work powerfully against the redemptive vision of the paradigm.

Moore's vision of a fiery Junonian woman's fatal descent ends with asterisks, indicating a break after which he starts to work through the implications of his frightening epiphany, but this working-through is disturbingly inadequate. Moore plans to

> make privileges for myself; every feature of [Shirley's] face, her bright eyes, her lips, shall go through each change they know, for my pleasure: display each exquisite variety of glance and curve, to delight— thrill—perhaps, more hopelessly to enchain me. If I *must* be her slave, I will not lose my freedom for nothing. (*S* 527)

If this unhealthy reverie on power stratagems is not bad enough, Shirley herself avers, "I will accept no hand which cannot hold me in check"; "any man who wishes to live in decent comfort with me as a husband must be able to control me" (*S* 551). This from the temerarious epiphanist of the triumphant Titan-woman striving against Omnipotence with Promethean pertinacity for a millennium?

Brontë evidently wants to appease her reader's fears, and her own. It is hard for her to remain faithful to such a breakthrough paradigm as Shirley's epiphany of the ascent of Eve. As we shall see, the fears recur. In *Villette*, Lucy Snowe's astonishing epiphany of the fiery, stormy Vashti must work against her previous, regressive epiphany of Imagination as a mere consoling mother. Even the emancipation achieved in *Jane Eyre* is undermined when its final epiphany of triumph is counterbalanced by a sad extinction of Promethean fires.

2

In *Villette*, an ambivalent book like *Shirley*, and with a more melancholy mood and ending, Lucy Snowe fails to attain the triumphant elemental inclusiveness of Shirley's epiphany; instead, her two epiphanic visions embody contrasting values never integrated. (Susan Watkins, who does not mention either epiphany, finds others in *Villette*, but the brief passages she offers are in my view too insubstantial to convey intensity, mystery, and expansiveness.)[14] It is as if the elementally unified "woman-Titan" of *Shirley*'s epiphanic paradigm had been split, for what we have in *Villette* is a diptych—two epiphanies—both near the novel's cen-

                    Martin Bidney

ter and separated by only a few pages, one a regressive vision of consoling Imagination as a generously descending mother and the other a powerful apparition of tragic Drama as an ascending wild maenad. The first elemental vision is white, motherly and moonlike, a dispenser of manna from her sphere of air; the second Titan-like, a rising demon-queen, fiery in murderous rage, churning up the waters of destruction. As Shirley's androgynous mother-Titan mirrors her (temporary) aspirations to inclusiveness, the twofold epiphanic experience of Lucy Snowe reveals a not-yet-resolved duality in her nature—suggested also by her name (Lucy Snowe, light and coldness, ardent sensitivity and diffidence). Moreover, the two epiphanies are vastly unequal in power: the "heavenly" beneficent mother quickly yields in force and import to the "hellish" ascending rebel, mysteriously, unsuspectedly angelic and "glorious" in her own right—the true epiphanic power source of the novel.

If "Reason" has been a cruel "step-mother" to Lucy, "Imagination," by contrast, appears consolingly in the sky as

> a head amidst circling stars, of which the midmost and the brightest lend a ray sympathetic and attent. A spirit, softer and better than Human Reason, has descended with quiet flight to the waste—bringing all round her a sphere of air borrowed of eternal summer; bringing perfume of flowers which cannot fade—fragrance of trees whose fruit is life, bringing breezes pure from a world whose day needs no sun to lighten it. My hunger has this good angel appeased with food, sweet and strange, gathered amongst gleaning angels, garnering their dew-white harvest in the first fresh hour of a heavenly day; tenderly has she assuaged the insufferable tears which weep away life itself—kindly given rest to deadly weariness—generously lent hope and impulse to paralyzed despair. Divine, compassionate, succourable influence! When I bend the knee to other than God, it shall be at thy white and winged feet, beautiful on mountain or on plain. Temples have been reared to the Sun—altars dedicated to the Moon. Oh, greater glory! To thee neither hands build, nor lips consecrate; but hearts, through ages, are faithful to thy worship. A dwelling thou hast, too wide for walls, too high for dome—a temple whose floors are space—rites whose mysteries transpire in presence, to the kindling, the harmony of worlds!
>
> . . .
>
> This daughter of Heaven remembered me to-night; she saw me weep and she came with comfort: 'Sleep,' she said. 'Sleep, sweetly—I gild thy dreams!'
>
> She kept her word, and watched me through a night's rest; but at dawn Reason relieved the guard.[15]

The last clause quietly parodies the epiphany as a whole, its cloying sweetness disclosed as infantilism. This un-Promethean, elementally incomplete vision, with its fragrance of Edenic earth and purity of upper air but with no hint of passionate fire, drastically lowers the stature of the "daughter of Heaven" we saw in Shirley's epiphany of a heaven-born woman. The enervated vision is a retreat to innocence, as a starry, descending Mother replaces the paradigmatic rising, defiant androgynous incarnation.

For a Promethean ascent like those in *Shirley*, we must turn to the performance of an actress (based on Rachel[16]) playing rebel queen Vashti. Now, as a new and riddling planet rises, we enjoy the elevation of a more energetic—a truly Titanlike—Eve:

> She was a study of such nature as had not encountered my eyes yet: a great and new planet she was: but in what shape? I waited her rising.
> She rose at nine that December night: above the horizon I saw her come. She could shine yet with pale grandeur and steady might; but that star verged already on its judgment-day. Seen near, it was a chaos—hollow, half-consumed: an orb perished or perishing—half lava, half glow. (*V* 321)

Mystery pervades this apparition of perishing star and volcanic lava; heavenly and hellish forces contend in her:

> Behold! I found upon her something neither of woman nor of man: in each of her eyes sat a devil. These evil forces bore her through the tragedy, kept up her feeble strength. . . . They wrote HELL on her straight, haughty brow. . . . It was a marvellous sight: a mighty revelation.
> It was a spectacle low, horrible, immoral.
> . . . . Wicked, perhaps, she is, but also she is strong; and her strength has conquered Beauty, has overcome Grace, and bound both at her side, captives peerlessly fair, and docile as fair. Even in the uttermost frenzy of energy is each maenad movement royally, imperially, incedingly upborne. Her hair, flying loose in revel or war, is still an angel's hair, and glorious under a halo. Fallen, insurgent, banished, she remembers the heaven where she rebelled. Heaven's light, following her exile, pierces its confines, and discloses their forlorn remoteness. (*V* 321–3)

The "hell" written on Vashti's brow indicates no Miltonic darkness visible, for this daughter of Heaven remains an angel in her equivocal fall. Still angelic and haloed (recalling the sky-born Mother Eve of *Shirley's* paradigm), Vashti is majestic. Her every gesture ("maenad movement") is both fervent and sacred, impassioned and "upborne"; the light she has known belongs to her always; it still accompanies her, intent to pierce darkness. Impious according to one mythology, she is a pious worshipper of deity in another—a maenad or bacchante faithful to Dionysus.

This new ascending Eve is an androgynous elemental prophet; as her visionary sword recalls Moses' rod, drowning the unworthy in a Bacchic flood, Vashti takes on "masculine" qualities, acquiring the androgynous nature of *Shirley's* paradigm:

> Place now the Cleopatra, or any other slug, before her as an obstacle, and see her cut through the pulpy mass as the scimitar of Saladin clove

> the down cushion. Let Paul Peter Rubens wake from the dead, let him
> rise out of his cerements, and bring into this presence all the army of
> his fat women; the magian power or prophet-virtue gifting that slight
> rod of Moses, could, at one waft, release and re-mingle a sea spell-
> parted, whelming the heavy host with the down-rush of overthrown
> sea-ramparts. (*V* 323)

The word *virtue* (from Latin *vir*, cf. "virile") keeps the meaning of manly
power; Vashti has turned from a Satan-like rebel into Moses the deliverer. We recall Vashti as salutary defier of the pernicious Persian monarch
in Tennyson's *Princess*:

> O Vashti, noble Vashti! summoned out
> She kept her state, and left the drunken king
> To brawl at Shushan underneath the palms. (III.212–15)[17]

Lucy's epiphany of Vashti culminates:

> Vashti was not good, I was told; and I have said she did not look good:
> though a spirit, she was a spirit out of Tophet. Well, if so much of
> unholy force can arise from below, may not an equal efflux of sacred
> essence descend one day from above?
> . . . The strong magnetism of genius drew my heart out of its wonted
> orbit; the sunflower turned from the south to a fierce light, not solar — a
> rushing, red, cometary light — hot on vision and to sensation. I had seen
> acting before, but never anything like this: never anything which aston-
> ished Hope and hushed Desire, which outstripped Impulse and paled
> Conception; which, instead of merely irritating imagination with the
> thought of what *might* be done, disclosed power like a deep, swollen,
> winter river, thundering in cataract, and bearing the soul, like a leaf, on
> the steep and steely sweep of its descent. (*V* 323–4)

It is a "Pythian inspiration" (*V* 324), Vashti as serpentine-sibylline oracle
from below. Fires and waters of the underworld rise — for a moment — to
make their chthonic claims, just as Oceanus and Prometheus united in
Shirley's epiphany of Eve-Mary-Nature, in a spirit of lordly feminine
defiance. The chthonic contributions are the more remarkable when combined with halo, angel's hair, and Mosaic rod: *fire, water, earth, and air*
unite here as convincingly as they did in the paradigm of *Shirley*.

But heaven is still at a "forlorn" distance; Vashti's magnetic genius is
thought too eccentric, too "cometary," to serve as visionary center for
Lucy's life, so we wait in vain for consequences of this epiphany to illu-
mine her continued progress. Whereas Vashti's "unholy force" ascends
from below, Lucy willingly waits for a counterbalancing "efflux of sacred
essence . . . from above," as if dewy, snowy, descending Mother Imagination were obliged to revisit her from a hiding-place in Lucy's vanished
child-heaven. In the *Shirley* paradigm, by contrast, the sky-born mother-
Titan was herself raised upward; Shirley's epiphany focused on the *ascent*
of Eve.

The Vashti vision, combining halo and lava, comet and pythia, empyrean angel and swollen flood (Cixous would call this epiphany a "chaosmos"[18]), is a striking synthesis of elemental inclusion and feminist Titanism.

3

The three great epiphanies of *Jane Eyre* powerfully present the paradigmatic theme of luminous ascent. In all three, the ascending light is linked to the moon or to moonlight. Androgyny and the titanism of a feminine rebel are prominent in all three epiphanies. But the elemental synthesis of the *Shirley* paradigm is not wholly achieved in any of them, and by scrutinizing a couple of more attentuated or fragmentary epiphanic passages we find a clue to this lack of fulfilment.

Jane's first epiphany shows extreme elemental conflict but sets forth the elemental materials of later epiphanic victories. The vividness of her vision is famed worldwide; twentieth-century Russian poet Marina Tsvetaeva, praising the "indispensable tabletop reference work of all our mothers and grandmothers—*Jane Eyre*," evokes the "secret of the red room."[19] Jane is confined to this room for attacking, in desperation, her sadist cousin John. Nightmarish reds—"curtains of deep red damask," "red" carpet, "crimson" tablecloth—mirror the fires of Jane's own rage ("the mood of the revolted slave"), complemented by somber hues of "darkly polished" mahogany furniture.[20] But the theme of ascending whiteness is sounded early: "Out of these deep surrounding shades rose high, and glared white, the piled-up mattresses and pillows of the bed, spread with a snowy Marseilles counterpane" (*JE* 14). The glaring, rising whiteness becomes that of Jane herself as viewed in the looking-glass: "the strange little figure there gazing at me, with a white face and arms speckling the gloom, and glittering eyes of fear moving where all else was still, had the effect of a real spirit," "half fairy, half imp," like a will-o'-the-wisp "coming out of lone, ferny dells in moors" (*JE* 15). We move to a realm of ghostly fires in enchanted bogs; nature is invading—or bursting—the prison.

Because Jane thinks the spirit of her uncle, who had died in this room, may rise to haunt her, she is alarmed when a "light gleam[s] on the wall": "Was it, I asked myself, a ray from the moon penetrating some aperture in the blind?" She concludes later that it was likely the reflection of a lantern outside, but her earlier theory lets Brontë sound the epiphanic ascent-of-the-moon motif, to be developed later. For it is an epiphany that young Jane sees: "I thought the swift-darting beam was a herald of some coming vision from another world" (*JE* 17). She shakes the lock, then tries to explain her panic, but when thrust back and locked in by her despotic aunt, Jane has "a species of fit":

> The next thing I remember is, waking up with a feeling as if I had had a frightful nightmare, and seeing before me a terrible red glare, crossed with thick black bars. I heard voices, too, speaking with a hollow sound, as if muffled by a rush of wind or waters; agitation, uncertainty, and an all-predominating sense of terror confused my faculties. (*JE* 19)

Rising whites of pillows and counterpane, followed by the seeming moonbeam and "swift-darting beam" of vision from "another world," perhaps her uncle's ghost (androgynizing the moon-theme), lead to no elemental synthesis. But we see raw elemental power—the four elements in tension. Prophetic-sounding rushes of wind or water (cf. Ezekiel 1:24) combine with fiery perfusive glare and thick black iron-like bars to cosmicize Jane's prison, now containing powers of air, earth, water, and fire. Elemental harmony is not yet possible, but elemental grandeur concentrates Jane's vision. It is an epiphanic transition in Jane's life, preparing her for liberation from Gateshead.

The second epiphany in *Jane Eyre*, also a transition (it occurs after Jane has rejected Rochester's offer of mistress-hood on learning his insane wife is alive), presents the glorious ascent of Eve at moonrise with near-paradigmatic completeness:

> That night I never thought to sleep; but a slumber fell on me as I lay down in bed. I was transported in thought to the scenes of childhood; I dreamt I lay in the red-room at Gateshead; that the night was dark, and my mind impressed with strange fears. The *light* that long ago had struck me into syncope, recalled in this vision, *seemed glidingly to mount the wall*, and trembling to pause in the centre of the obscured ceiling. I lifted up my head to look: *the roof resolved to clouds, high and dim; the gleam was such as the moon imparts* to vapours she is about to sever. I watched her come—watched with the strangest anticipation; as though some word of doom were to be written on her disk. *She broke forth as never moon yet burst from cloud: a hand* first penetrated the sable folds and waved them away; then, *not a moon, but a white human form shone in the azure*, inclining a glorious brow earthward. It gazed and gazed and gazed on me. It spoke to my spirit: immeasurably distant was the tone, yet so near, it whispered in my heart—"My daughter, flee temptation!"
>
> "Mother, I will."
>
> So I answered after I had waked from the trance-like dream. (*JE* 336–7; emphases added)[21]

There is still a distance, and a big difference, between Jane and her vision of ascending Eve; the Great Mother ascends, whereas the still childlike Jane can only mirror her obsessive gaze and note the inclination of her "glorious brow earthward." But the epiphanic themes of elemental inclusiveness and androgyny are added to the vision in its briefly postponed sequel. Jane comes to realize (compare the *Shirley* paradigm) that the ascending Eve was none other than Nature Herself: "I have no relative," she thinks, "but the universal mother, Nature. I will seek her breast and ask repose" (*JE* 340). Viewing the Milky Way, Jane feels "the might and strength of God"; as the dew falls ("with propitious softness") and as she "nestle[s] to the breast of the hill," Jane puts into practice her new-found conviction that "Nature," her "mother," will "lodge" her "without money and without price" (*JE* 341–2). A masculine-feminine deity is evoked by earth, dew, and the fiery if distant lights of the sky.

In the third—attemptedly climactic but problematic—epiphany of *Jane Eyre*, Jane herself is the ascending Eve/Nature. Here the transition is Jane's narrow escape from the blandishments of St. John Rivers, who wants her to become his subaltern in evangelism and (in a cruel wordplay) temptingly makes her feel "pliant as a reed under his kindness" (*JE* 441). Just as she seems about to "rush down the torrent of his will into the gulf of his existence, and there lose" her own in a fatal descent, she feels the visionary equivalent of an "electric shock"—"quite as sharp, as strange, as startling"—when she hears an eerie voice crying, "Jane! Jane! Jane!" This, the voice of Rochester, is also, ambiguously and androgynously, "the work of Nature. She was roused, and did—no miracle—but her best" (*JE* 442). The disclaimer ("no miracle") keeps the episode an epiphany, not a theophany, but Nature's voice thrills Jane.

Nature calls, and Eve ascends, for, as we learned in the *Shirley* paradigm, Eve and Nature are one:

> I broke from St. John, who . . . would have detained me. It was *my* time to assume ascendancy. My powers were in play, and in force. . . . I mounted to my chamber; locked myself in; fell on my knees; and prayed in my way . . . . I seemed to penetrate very near a Mighty Spirit," and then she lies down "eager for the daylight," for this, too, is a nighttime epiphany—involving, as Heilman points out, a "room full of moonlight"[22] (*JE* 442–370).

In this final version Jane's ascending Eve/Nature does more than approach the Mighty Spirit; she seems to become, androgynously, that very Spirit. For when Rochester later tells Jane that in calling out her name he had been summoning "the alpha and omega" of his "heart's wishes" (*JE* 471), the reference to Revelation 1:8 shows Jane as Rochester's object of worship. Ascending Eve, no longer merely a rising moon, becomes for her epiphanic summoner the incarnation of a more elevated luminary: she is Rochester's god.

But even the bold scriptural allusion cannot create an apotheosis; two things are missing. First, though this epiphany is designed to be climactic, Jane-Eve-Nature is not endowed with the palpable supernal fire that animated the Promethean Eve of *Shirley* and could again offer a Promethean appeal. (The eerie voice crying, "Jane!" was attended by something like an "electric shock," but that quick touch of fire is soon gone.) Second, the elemental synthesis of the *Shirley* paradigm is absent. A previous passage in *Jane Eyre*—showing the book's epiphany pattern in troublingly attenuated form—offers a clarifying context. During her early days at Thornfield with Rochester, Jane makes three watercolors of things seen "with the spiritual eye." The first shows a cormorant holding a gem-set bracelet taken from a drowned female corpse; the third, a "colossal head" of Death as described by Milton in *Paradise Lost* II.266–73. The middle portrait epiphanically intimates the ascending Eve:

> The second picture contained for foreground only the dim peak of a hill, with grass and some leaves slanting as if by a breeze. Beyond and above spread an expanse of sky, dark blue as at twilight; rising into the sky was a woman's shape to the bust, pourtrayed in tints as dusk and soft as I could combine. The dim forehead was crowned with a star; the lineaments below were seen as through the suffusion of vapour; the eyes shone dark and wild; the hair streamed shadowy, like a beamless cloud torn by storm or by electric travail. On the neck lay a pale reflection like moonlight; the same faint lustre touched the train of thin clouds from which rose and bowed this vision of the Evening Star. (*JE* 131)

Eve rises into the heights; her portrait invokes hill, breeze, clouds, and "electric" fire (though a *vanished* fire)—the four elements—with moonlight and the moon-linked Evening Star, suggesting feminine immortality (for evening and morning star are Venus). Yet the vision is *misty, shadowy, dim*: the "lustre" is "faint," the "reflection" is "pale," the "cloud" is "beamless." The mournful picture, flanked by death scenes, *lacks fire*.

The gloom of this death-framed portrait of ascending Eve is prophetic; before Jane can unite with Rochester, his wife Bertha must die. In Bertha's last moments before her suicide, described by a butler, we see the fire we missed in Jane's watercolor self-portrait, now ready to flare out fatally: Bertha "had long black hair; we could see it streaming against the flames as she stood" (*JE* 451) above the battlements, before springing to her death. Gilbert and Gubar view Bertha as an irate double of Jane, who had first seen her in a *mirror* (*JE* 297).[23] But now Bertha's fires are extinguished, and in her suicide (cf. Louis's nightmare of descending Semele-as-fiery-Juno in *Villette*) the descending Bertha has also caused *the loss of other crucial vital fires*.[24] The fire of Rochester's eyes is almost quenched; his castle is burnt, and he is multiply maimed—a burnt-out case. All fire-force is gone from Rochester, and we are not convincingly shown any renascent fire in Jane, bound like Antigone to a prematurely aged unfortunate who "might almost" be her "father" (*JE* 277).

So after her third and final epiphany, Jane scarcely resembles Shirley's powerfully Promethean heaven-born Eve, an embodiment of fourfold elemental completeness who, contending with Omnipotence, could defeat the vulture Death, or Shirley's corollary epiphany of Eva-Humanity, a fourfold bisexual cosmos, rapt by her own perfect Genius. We miss in Jane the fire—as well as the elemental synthesis—of Lucy's Vashti, herself an apparition of genius. Despite Jane's and Brontë's insistence on a happy ending, there can be no elemental fullness, no fourfold elemental synthesis, in Jane's present or future—for no such synthesis appears in Jane's final epiphanic self-portrait.

If Shirley's paradigmatic Eve-Mary-Nature was Titanic and Promethean, Jane's epiphany of herself ascending is neither. The Promethean fire we saw in Vashti is gone. Jane's recurrent epiphanies of ascending Eve, at moonrise or by moonlight, reveal Nature as inspiring, comforting mother but not as woman-Titan. Brontë's epiphanic paradigm-and-corollary in *Shirley*, fourfold elemental and implicitly androgynous feminine Titan, is a performance she approximated in Vashti but never fully equaled.

4

Of the theorists of elemental feminine powers most influential in recent decades, Hélène Cixous and Mary Daly provide closer parallels to Brontë than does Luce Irigaray. In Irigaray's love monologue *Elemental Passions* a feminine voice affirms open-endedness, boundlessness, fluidity as opposed to all delimitation. Fluxile elements take priority over stable ones:

> If you are so afraid that I should love some other, is that not because you fear that it would make your world explode? Taking the ground from under your feet. And sweeping away what takes its place, the enclosure of the earth.
> Fire, air, water—are they thus to be dominated by the earth? The outline of a womb-like maternal body, based upon your need for solidity. For a rock-solid home.
> Is fire not joy? Is burning with you not grace?[25]

Irigaray opposes all who distrust "in-finity" because they are terrified by "lack of closure" (*EP* 71). Even the inclusive totality of a Brontëan elemental female fourfold would be paradoxically too constrictedly finite for Irigaray; in her ideal of Woman, what is fluid must rule, and all solidity is limited and limiting; "the id-is-flowing cannot be halted" (*EP* 89).[26]

By contrast, Hélène Cixous's "The Laugh of the Medusa" and Mary Daly's *Pure Lust: Elemental Feminist Philosophy* often sound like fantasias on themes from Brontëan epiphanies of the all-inclusive Fourfold Elemental Feminine. These theorists posit woman as the imaginative embodiment of elemental forces, and the way to prove such metaphoric claims about the feminine poetic spirit is to perform them imaginatively. Centos of excerpts from the two theorist-imaginers show the Brontëan way they do this. Note first, in Cixous as in Brontë, androgynous as well as feminist implications of the fourfold elemental vision:[27]

> Now it happens that at present, for historico-cultural reasons, it is women who are opening up to and benefiting from this vatic bisexual-ity which doesn't annul differences but stirs them up, pursues them, increases their number. In a certain way, *"woman is bisexual"*; man—it's a secret to no one—being poised to keep glorious phallic monosexual-ity in view. . . .
> *Flying* is woman's gesture—flying in language and making it fly. . . . It's no accident: women take after birds and robbers just as robbers take after *women and birds*. . . .
> A feminine text cannot fail to be more than subversive. It is *volcanic*; as it is written it brings about an *upheaval of the old property crust*, carrier of masculine investments; there's no other way.
> . . . If she is a whole, it's *a whole composed of parts that are wholes*, not simple partial objects but a moving, limitlessly changing ensemble, a cosmos tirelessly traversed by Eros, an immense *astral space* not orga-nized around any one sun that's any more of a star than the others.
> This doesn't mean that she's an undifferentiated magma, but that she doesn't lord it over her body or her desire. . . . Her libido is *cosmic*, just as her unconscious is worldwide. . . .
> Write! and your self-seeking text will know itself better than flesh and blood, *rising*, insurrectionary dough kneading itself, with sonorous, perfumed ingredients, a lively combination of *flying colors, leaves, and rivers plunging into the seas we feed*. . . . More or less wavily *sea, earth, sky*—what matter would rebuff us? We know how to speak them all.[28]
> (emphases added)

Even Brontë's epiphanic theme of ascent is here, along with her elemental inclusiveness, cosmicity, and insistence on wholeness, in an expansive neo-Brontëan performance.

Mary Daly, closely akin in spirit to Cixous, varies this vision as she rethinks world folklore. Her goal, like that of Brontë in amalgamating Genesis and Greek myth, is to systematize a new set of mythic categories for the study and performance of fourfold elemental feminine cosmicity of imagination:

> Since the symbolism of the earth is so totally female, there can be no doubt, despite later depictions of gnomes [earth spirits] as little old men, that the ageless wisdom that is Gnomic is also primordially fe-male and Elemental.
> . . . Undines [water spirits] are frequently identified with Mermaids [as] powerful symbols for Self-identified women, suggesting the buoyancy and freedom of movement in water. Moreover, the Mermaid's anatomy suggests that she cannot be raped.

> . . . As symbol, *Salamander* means "a mythical and not clearly defined animal having the power to endure fire without harm." . . . Elemental women move within a Salamandrous tradition, remembering in our own lives the nine million women who were massacred during the Witchcraze in Western Europe. Although their bodies were reduced to ashes, the spirits of the Witches have survived.
>
> . . . *Sylph* is defined as "one of a race of spirits or beings supposed to inhabit the air" (*O.E.D.*). . . . [Air] is associated with the creative breath of life, hence with speech. As inhabitants of the air, Lusty women are breathers/speakers of Radiant Words. Insofar as we are elemental, our speech releases words from the state of contamination. Like a sharp wind, it cuts through smog, clarifying, making it possible to breathe freely again.
>
> . . . Claiming that speaking Radiant Words has Angelic power is Naming/re-claiming primal force. It is overcoming the false dichotomy between spirit and matter, proclaiming Lust for that Integrity of be-ing from which we have been separated and which we have half-forgotten, but never lost.[29]

Like the Cixous cento, this poetic soliloquy with its elemental verve, its Genesis-recalling, Titanlike creative faith in the feminine will to embrace the powers of all the elemental spirits and so to embody an ascending force no more Marian or Eve-like than Promethean and bacchantic, makes a worthy antiphonal response, from a kindred sibyl of today, to the originative epiphanies of Charlotte Brontë.

NOTES

1. Gilbert and Gubar, *The Madwoman in the Attic*, pp. 194–195.
2. Brontë, *Shirley*, pp. 319–20 (hereafter *S* with page numbers in parentheses).
3. For the crafty rhetoric and implied Prometheanism of Eve see also Gilbert and Gubar, *The Madwoman in the Attic*, p. 194.
4. Blake, *The Marriage of Heaven and Hell* Pl. 17, p. 40.
5. Lawson, "The Dissenting Voice," pp. 729–743 passim.
6. Lawson, "Imagining Eve," p. 419.
7. Tayler, *Holy Ghosts*, p. 185, citing *S* 321.
8. Annan, *Leslie Stephen*, 202n.
9. Gilbert and Gubar, p. 394, quoting *S* 490.
10. Lawson, "Imagining Eve," p. 421, quoting *S* 488–90.
11. Tayler, *Holy Ghosts*, p. 198.
12. Tayler, *Holy Ghosts*, p. 189.
13. Heilman, "Charlotte Brontë, Reason, and the Moon," p. 292 for "revelatory" powers of Brontë's "lunar muse." Heilman examines the moon's role in two of our *Jane Eyre* epiphanies; see below.
14. Among the "many" epiphanies Watkins finds are a briefly recounted nightmare of drowning (340); an even shorter account of the Aurora Borealis (104); an "assertion," on board a ship, of Lucy's "mental and spiritual independence" (117); a vision of the moon (175); and an account of catalepsy with a reference to Jael and Sisera (175–6); see Watkins, "Epiphany and Subjectivity in Charlotte Brontë's *Villette*," pp. 49–57.
15. Brontë, *Villette*, pp. 287–8; hereafter *V* with page numbers in parentheses.

16. Stokes, "Rachel's 'Terrible Beauty'," pp. 779–83; Brownstein, *Tragic Muse*, pp. 216–218; "Representing the 'Latent Vashti,'" pp. 4–14 (excellent bibliography).

17. See *The Poems of Tennyson* ed. Christopher Ricks. Longman/Norton, 1969, p. 779.

18. Cixous, "The Laugh of the Medusa," p. 258.

19. Marina Tsvetaeva, "My Pushkin." *A Captive Spirit: Selected Prose*. Edited and translated by J. Marin King, Ardis, 1980, pp. 319–362; see p. 319.

20. Brontë, *Jane Eyre*, pp.14–15; hereafter *JE* with page numbers in parentheses.

21. For Heilman the moon is the "thrilling center" of this experience (298).

22. Heilman 299. Cf. Sandra M. Gilbert, "Plain Jane's Progress," p. 798: "That the pilgrimage of this 'savage, beautiful creature' must now necessarily lead her away from Thornfield is signaled, like many other events in the novel, by the rising of the moon, which accompanies a reminiscent dream of the red-room."

23. Gilbert and Gubar 360. Cf. Gilbert on Bertha as "Jane's dark double" (796).

24. The crippling loss entailed by this extinction of fires is clarified when their centrality to *Jane Eyre* is shown by Lodge and Carlton-Ford. In "Fire and Eyre." Lodge shows fire as embodying both Romanticist passion and the moderating influence of Christianity and reason. In "Intimacy Without Immolation," Carlton-Ford shows fire as embodying both intimacy and destruction.

25. Luce Irigaray, *Elemental Passions*, p. 80; hereafter *EP* with page numbers in parentheses.

26. Toril Moi, *Sexual/Textual Politics: Feminist Literary Theory*. Methuen, 1985, p. 139, thinks the fluidity requirement tends to "essentialize" woman. But in *Essentially Speaking: Feminism, Nature and Difference*. Routledge, 1989, p. 57, Diana Fuss praises Jane Gallop's view of Irigaray's poetics as "a *construction* rather than a *reflection* of the body," part of "a larger constructionist project of re-creating, re-metaphorizing, the body"; see Gallop, "Quand nos lèvres s'écrivent": Irigaray's Body Politic," *Romanic Review*, vol. 74, 1983, pp. 77–83.

27. Lawson, comparing Brontë to Cixous as visionaries of female cosmicity, does not note the elemental fourfold and finds Cixous's portrait of Woman to be as disappointingly "vast and impersonal" as Brontë's ("Imagining Eve" 419). But Lawson finds Cixous's version of bisexuality a healthy deconstruction of standard categories, whereas Brontë's is said merely to "invert" them (418).

28. Cixous, in Marks and de Courtivron eds., pp. 254–60.

29. Daly, *Pure Lust*, pp. 14–19. Cixous and Daly, like Brontë, are mythmakers, visionaries. My epiphanological investigative method, in contrast, aims to understand the imaginative uses of elements not by creating an inclusive scheme based on the accumulation of data drawn from many writers and traditions, but rather by analyzing the differing uses of elemental imagination by individual writers considered as unique imaginers, whose distinctive patterns of epiphany-making are to be considered in detail, one by one. See my "Fire, Flutter, Fall, and Scatter," p. 85 n16 for bibliography on the epiphanological method used here as applied to Bishop, Brooke, Dostoevsky, Frost, Larkin, Nemerov, Salinger, Edward Thomas, and Tolstoy.

WORKS CITED

Annan, Noel. *Leslie Stephen: The Godless Victorian*. U of Chicago P, 1984.

Bidney, Martin. "Fire, Flutter, Fall, and Scatter: A Structure in the Epiphanies of Hawthorne's Tales." *Texas Studies in Literature and Language*, vol. 50, no. 1, Spring 2008, pp. 58–89.

Blake, William. *The Marriage of Heaven and Hell* Pl. 17. *The Complete Poetry and Prose of William Blake*. Revised edition by David V. Erdman, commentary by Harold Bloom, Doubleday, 1988.

Brontë, Charlotte. *Jane Eyre*. Edited by Margaret Smith, Oxford UP, 1998.

———. *Shirley*. Edited by Herbert Rosengarten and Margaret Smith, Oxford UP, 1979.

———. *Villette*. Edited by Margaret Smith and Herbert Rosengarten, Oxford UP, 1998.

Brownstein, Rachel M. "Representing the 'Latent Vashti': Theatricality in Charlotte Brontë's *Villette*." *Victorian Newsletter*, no. 87, Spring 1995, pp. 4–14.

———. *Tragic Muse: Rachel of the Comédie-Française*. Knopf, 1993.

Carlton-Ford, Cynthia. "Intimacy Without Immolation: Fire in *Jane Eyre*." *Women's Studies*, no. 15, 1988, pp. 375–386.

Cixous, Hélène. "The Laugh of the Medusa." Translated by Keith Cohen and Paula Cohen, *New French Feminisms: An Anthology*, edited by Elaine Marks and Isabelle de Courtivron, U of Massachusetts P, 1980, pp. 245–264.

Daly, Mary. *Pure Lust: Elemental Feminist Philosophy*. Harper, 1984.

Gilbert, Sandra M. "Plain Jane's Progress." *Signs*, no. 2, 1977, pp. 779–804.

Gilbert, Sandra M., and Susan Gubar, *The Madwoman in the Attic: The Woman Writer and the Nineteenth-Century Imagination*. Yale UP, 1979.

Heilman, Robert B. "Charlotte Brontë, Reason, and the Moon." *Nineteenth-Century Fiction*, vol. 14, 1960, pp. 283–302.

Lawson, Kate. "Imagining Eve: Charlotte Brontë, Kate Millett, Hélène Cixous." *Women's Studies*, 24, 1995, pp. 411–426.

———. "The Dissenting Voice: *Shirley*'s Vision of Women and Christianity." *Studies in English Literature*, vol. 29, 1989, pp. 729–743.

Lodge, David, and Cynthia Carlton-Ford. "Fire and Eyre: Charlotte Brontë's War of Earthly Elements." *The Language of Fiction: Essays in Criticism and Verbal Analysis of the English Novel*. Routledge, 1966, pp. 114–143.

Stokes, John. "Rachel's 'Terrible Beauty': An Actress Among the Novelists." *ELH*, vol. 51, 1984, pp. 771–93.

Tayler, Irene. *Holy Ghosts: The Male Muses of Emily and Charlotte Brontë*. Columbia UP, 1990.

Watkins, Susan. "Epiphany and Subjectivity in Charlotte Brontë's *Villette*." *Subjectivity and Literature from the Romantics to the Present Day*, edited by Philip Shaw and Peter Stockwell, Pinter, 1991, pp. 49–57.

THREE

Condoning Adultery: Problems of Marriage and Divorce in George Eliot's Life and Writing

Nancy Henry

"[T]he thread which ran through the web of her life's history will never be truly told—for those who know it keep silent, and those who do not know it would deny it if they were told."[1]

Agnes Jervis Lewes, George Henry Lewes's wife, is a shadowy presence in Gordon Haight's *George Eliot: A Biography* (1968) and in virtually all biographical and critical accounts of Eliot's relationship to Lewes. She is known as the woman who committed adultery with Lewes's friend, Thornton Leigh Hunt, and is said to have begun bearing Hunt's children prior to Lewes's meeting Eliot in October 1851. The first of these children was a son named Edmund. Lewes, who was living with Agnes and their three sons (Charles, Thornton and Herbert), registered Edmund's birth on April 16, 1850, listing himself as father.

On October 21, 1851, Lewes also registered the birth of a daughter named Rose Agnes Lewes. After he moved out of the couple's London home at 26 Bedford Square, Kensington, in the summer of 1852 (*Letters of GHL* I:191; Ashton *GHL*, 333), Agnes would bear two more children: Ethel Isabella (October 9, 1853) and Mildred Jane (May 26, 1857). She registered both of these births, falsely naming Lewes as the father (Ashton *GHL* 122). Lewes and Eliot began living together in July 1854, and from that time until the end of their respective lives, they provided support for Agnes and what Haight calls her "illegitimate brood" (132).

Haight's use of the term *brood* is a good example of the way in which Agnes and her children have been characterized in biographies of Eliot.[2] Such language reflects an intention on the part of biographers to cast Lewes and Eliot's union in a particularly blameless light. The same intention seems to underlie a now-standard narrative about Agnes and Hunt's relationship that eliminates ambiguity when considering the paternity of her children and oversimplifies the circumstances that prevented Lewes from obtaining a divorce.

A set of unsubstantiated claims relating to the Agnes-Hunt affair and its impact on the Lewes-Eliot union have attained the status of unquestioned fact in biographies of Eliot as well as in literary criticism of her work. I will trace the genealogy of the notion—asserted but not documented by biographers—that Lewes could not divorce his wife because, by the act of registering Edmund as his son, he had "condoned" her adultery with Hunt and was therefore prohibited from even seeking a divorce. The story is important because it offers a particular interpretation of why Eliot and Lewes were unable to marry and thus continued in a union unsanctioned by the law. It makes the couple a victim of Lewes's generosity, a rigid and unforgiving legal system and Agnes's unrepentant ways, thereby shifting the emphasis away from Eliot and Lewes's adulterous relationship. Biographers and critics have failed to question this reduction of a complex legal problem to an act of good will and instead have repeated the claim so often that its truth seems beyond doubt.

Without impugning Lewes's good will, or the generous and dutiful way in which he and Eliot behaved toward Agnes and her children, I want to suggest that the story is more complicated than most biographies have led us to believe. There is no documented evidence in any existing biography to prove that registering Edmund's birth constituted "condonation" of adultery and thereby precluded his seeking divorce, especially when the alleged infidelity continued for years after Edmund's birth.

Many questions arise from the claims of biographers: Did Lewes "condone" Agnes's adultery before the birth of Edmund? Some biographers say yes, but only as long as she did not have a child (Hughes 141). How do we know that Lewes knew the infant Edmund was not his because Agnes became pregnant while Lewes was still living with her and his personal diaries from this time are presumed destroyed?[3] If he had a history of "sharing" her in a "free love" arrangement with Hunt, as many biographies contend, would there not be some doubt about Edmund's paternity? Biographies prior to Haight's raise this possibility. In these accounts, there seems to be some uncertainty about the paternity of several of the children, including St. Vincent Arthy Lewes, who lived from May 11, 1848, to March 23, 1850, dying two weeks before Edmund's birth. Anne Fremantle (1933) raises doubts about the paternity of Thornton and Herbert, whom Lewes fully accepted as his own, as does Blanche Colton

Williams (1936). As I will discuss, the rumors swirling around Agnes's children may be traced back to an article and fictionalized autobiography written by Eliza Lynn Linton in 1885.[4] If there is definitive evidence drawn from unpublished diaries or letters, it does not appear in any biography that I have found and certainly not in Haight's, which is the one to which most biographers and critics still return.

If I cannot definitively correct the record, at least I can complicate it on a matter that has implications for the study of Eliot's life, and also potentially for our reading of her fiction, which abounds in bad marriages ["Janet's Repentance," "The Lifted Veil," *Romola, Felix Holt, Middlemarch, Daniel Deronda*], secret wives and mistresses [*Romola, Silas Marner, Felix Holt, Daniel Deronda*], illegitimate children [*Adam Bede, Romola, Felix Holt, Middlemarch, Daniel Deronda*], and thoughts of separation on the part of wives contemplating the failings of their husbands [*Romola, Middlemarch*]. Perhaps the reason divorce never appears as an option or an issue in these works is that, with the exception of *Daniel Deronda*, they are all set before the Matrimonial Causes Act of 1857, which was a major step toward making divorce available to middle-class Britons.

The story of Lewes's condonation of Agnes's adultery as a permanent barrier to his seeking divorce, repeated in numerous contemporary biographies, guides, companions, and critical articles, also raises broad questions about biographies and the myths they perpetuate. By excavating the sources of this particular claim, and examining the repetition of language from biography to biography, we can see how rumor and inconclusive speculation can concretize into fact. By questioning such claims, we establish the necessity of ongoing biographical research as an aspect of historical inquiry and also as a complement to ever-richer interpretive literary analyses.

THE CLAIMS

Addressing the question of why Eliot and Lewes could not marry, Haight writes: "Lewes, having once condoned [Agnes's] adultery, was forever precluded from appealing for divorce" (*Biography* 132).[5] In her biography of Lewes (1991), Rosemary Ashton makes a similar assertion: "Lewes registered Edmund as his own child; when he met and fell in love with Marian Evans, he was debarred from seeking a divorce on the grounds— not changed under the partially liberating Divorce Act of 1857—that he had thereby condoned his wife's adultery" (99–100). In her biography of Eliot (1996), Ashton qualifies the claim: "There was no possibility of his ever getting a divorce, since he had under the law condoned Agnes's relationship with Hunt by registering Edmund and Rose as his own children" (102). The slight change from Haight's "forever precluded from appealing" and her own "debarred from seeking" to "no possibility his ever getting" might suggest a rethinking of the claim's validity on Ashton's part. Interestingly, in her later book, *142 Strand* (2006), she does not mention the notion of "condoning" and merely states parenthetically that the 1857 Divorce Act did not "allow Lewes to divorce Agnes and marry Marian" (235).

Other biographies since Haight's have also repeated the condonation theory without providing additional biographical or legal sources. Frederick Karl (1995) writes: "Lewes torpedoed any chance of divorce for adultery by accepting Hunt's child by Agnes as his own . . . " (160). Kathryn Hughes (1998) asserts: "As the law stood, by giving Hunt's child his name Lewes was condoning Agnes's adultery and relinquishing the right to sue at any point for divorce." She concludes dramatically: "By this one administrative act he would condemn Marian Evans to a life as a sexual and social outcast" (141). Because no legal documents, case histories, precedents, letters, diaries, or sources of any kind have ever been cited to support the notion that Lewes's registering of Edmund's birth represented a condonation of adultery "under the law," or that condoning adultery under these complicated circumstances *forever precluded* his petitioning for divorce, it will be useful to trace the origins of these claims in the various versions that appeared in biographies preceding Haight's.

The first full-length biography is Mathilde Blind's *George Eliot* (1884), which merely states that at the time Lewes met Marian Evans, he "found his conjugal relations irretrievably spoiled" (85). She continues: "Legal union, however, there could be none, for though virtually separated from his wife, Mr. Lewes could not divorce" (86). Following Blind came *George Eliot's Life as Related in Her Letters and Journals* (1885), written—or edited—by John Walter Cross, whom Eliot married just six months before she died on December 22, 1880.[6] Cross's *Life* was for many years the most influential treatment and was the primary target of Haight's revisionist biography, which was based on research for his edition of Eliot's letters. In his introduction and in the letters themselves, Haight revealed just how much censoring Cross did to retrospectively impose on Marian Evans's entire life the image of the sage and sober author that "George Eliot" became. On the subject of Eliot and Lewes's union, Cross is as reticent as Blind, and his language echoes hers when he explains that at the time of his meeting with Marian Evans, "not only was Mr. Lewes's previous family life irretrievably spoiled, but his home had been wholly broken up for nearly two years" (I:234).[7] Blind and Cross both approach the question of Lewes's marriage with ambiguous language: he was "virtually separated" and his home was "broken up." Because neither Blind nor Cross discusses Agnes, Hunt, or their children, and neither therefore mentions the condonation of adultery, we still need to seek the origin of this explanation for why divorce was impossible.

In 1886, the Reverend Charles Gordon Ames—an American Unitarian minister, well-known in mid-century suffragette and abolitionist circles—published a pamphlet titled *George Eliot's Two Marriages*. His primary intention was to defend Eliot's union with Lewes as a legitimate marriage from a specifically Christian perspective.[8] Lamenting "the absence of anything like a legal or other inquiry," as well as "the absence of sifted and recorded evidence," he nonetheless asserts that Lewes's "condonation of [his wife's] first offence worked a forfeiture of his right of divorce for the second," adding, "thus does the law punish the husband's magnanimity!" (8). Ames seems to be one of the first to suggest that it was Lewes's magnanimity that prohibited his ability to divorce. Intriguingly, Ames qualifies his condonation claim in a footnote, reading simply: "This statement is discredited by an American lawyer."

This cryptic footnote demonstrates that, as early as 1886, the notion of Lewes's condoning Agnes's adultery was a circulated—but also a dubious—theory. Ames disparages the anonymous 1885 article in *Temple Bar* that we now know was written by Linton. In fact, his pamphlet in defense of the morality of Eliot's "marriage" to Lewes might be seen as a refutation of Linton's attack on the myth of that union's moral superiority. In her article (a review of Cross's *Life*), Linton denies that there was anything admirable or extraordinary in the Eliot-Lewes "marriage": "It was a very simple, natural and commonplace arrangement between two people who loved each other and who could not marry by any law of any land" (521).[9] Linton is angry at the attempts of Eliot's admirers to sanctify a union that only Eliot's fame as an author made socially palatable. Linton's description of the Leweses' life is interesting when we consider some of the marital plots and triangles in Eliot's work: "She lived as his wife with a man whose name she bore, whose children called her mother, and whose wife, the mother of those children, was living almost within a stone's throw of her own home" (522). The phrase "mother of those children" living a "stone's throw" from Eliot's home echoes the "Whispering Stones," where Lydia Glasher confronts Gwendolen Grandcourt—insisting on the entitlements of her illegitimate children by Grandcourt. Linton, of course, had a thorough knowledge of Eliot's fictional plots at the time she contributed this sensational-sounding description of Eliot's personal situation to the history of her biography.

The *Temple Bar* article is not the source of the condoning adultery claims, but Linton's *Autobiography of Christopher Kirkland* (also published in 1885 but not mentioned by Ames) may be. Linton's published statements, even though under cover of fiction and even when discredited, have provided a source of information about Eliot, George and Agnes Lewes, and the Hunts—information that does not appear in Cross's *Life*, but which has worked its way into biographies since 1885. Ames's gesture in a footnote toward the legal dubiousness of the condonation claim—along with his recognition that there was no "legal inquiry" into the matter—have disappeared from modern biographies.

Even though the condoning theory was available as early as 1885, it was not always picked up by subsequent biographers. In *George Eliot* (1890), Oscar Browning writes merely that "circumstances which need not be here related had made a divorce impracticable" (39). Similarly, Leslie Stephen's *George Eliot* (1902) does not mention Agnes's affair with Hunt but moves beyond Browning's "impracticable" to assert vaguely: "A legal divorce was impossible. . . ." (47). It is interesting that within a decade "impracticable" has turned into "impossible" and that sources for the claims remain conspicuously absent.

Between 1902 and the1930s, new archival material was becoming available, specifically the diary of John Chapman, treated by Haight in his *George Eliot and John Chapman* (1940). Elizabeth Haldane (1927) offers an interesting version of the biographical story, which does not mention condoning, but rather states that Lewes's own actions were what precluded divorce after 1857. She notes: "Lewes had put himself out of court by his union with another" (92). Anne Fremantle's *George Eliot* (1933) perpetuates the theory that it was Lewes's as much as Agnes's behavior that was at issue, writing that Lewes could not divorce because "his own mode of life can hardly be called moral" (60). Anna Kitchel (1933) qualifies Haldane's notion that Lewes was at fault by resurrecting the still unsubstantiated condonation theory and noting that "even personal immorality on [Lewes's] part of a marked kind would not have prevented his obtaining a divorce if he had never condoned his wife's unfaithfulness" (152). Kitchel's important study, perhaps not sufficiently credited in Haight's biography, may be an authority for his assertions. In an appendix to her book, Kitchel acknowledges but discredits Linton's recollections of the Hunt-Lewes affair—the likely source of the condonation claim that she repeats.[10]

Even after Kitchel attempted to dismiss the notion that Lewes's sexual conduct was a barrier to his divorcing, questions persisted in biographies. Blanche Colton Williams (1936) claims that the fact that Lewes as well as Agnes, "had been false to earlier marriage vows, would have prevented his being freed" (102).[11] In *Marian Evans and George Eliot* (1952), Lawrence and Elizabeth Hanson give two reasons for the inability to divorce: "Lewes had condoned his wife's association with Thornton Hunt and had led too irregular a life himself to hope for a decision in his favor" (167). They do not say that the act of signing the birth certificate constituted condonation. Rather (following Linton) they argue that the previous, alleged "free love" arrangement prior to the birth of Edmund would put him out of favor in a divorce court. Ultimately, all of these attempts to provide a legal explanation for Lewes's inability to divorce are merely speculative about what a court of divorce might have concluded had the case come to trial.

I have found no single reason or act—such as registering a birth—that legally prohibited Lewes from petitioning for divorce, whatever he might have thought his chances of receiving one might have been. As far as I can tell, it was Haight's biography that finally put to rest any question of Lewes's "irregular life" as precluding divorce and instead emphasized and established—by sheer undocumented assertion—the notion of Lewes's signing Edmund's birth certificate as an act of condonation forever precluding divorce.

The only recent scholar to challenge the simple narrative of condoning adultery is Harriet F. Adams in an article (2000) focusing on the Deed of Declaration by which Marian Evans legally changed her name to Marian Evans Lewes following Lewes's death.[12] Adams refers to the irony that "Lewes's relation with Marian may have been a factor in his inability to divorce" (58). This idea, she writes, "has been obscured by the insistence by scholars that what prevented Lewes from divorcing Agnes was his 'condoning' that first Hunt baby . . . ." (58). Although her language somewhat misleadingly suggests that it was the baby itself that was "condoned" (the adultery was supposedly condoned by registering the baby), she rightly concludes that there is nothing to substantiate claims that "condonation" prevented divorce. She returns to previous, mostly forgotten suggestions that a man living in an adulterous relationship would have no grounds for establishing himself as a victim of his wife's adultery in a Victorian divorce court.

Most biographers recognize that before the 1857 Matrimonial Causes Act, divorce would have been impossible for financial reasons. It is from circumstances following the 1857 Act that questions arise. We can be certain that no one (Lewes, Agnes, Hunt, or Eliot) wished to be dragged through the courts and into the public limelight, exposing sensitive and ambiguous questions of sexual conduct and paternity that would be embarrassing to all parties and harmful to the children. Furthermore, Lewes may have decided not to pursue divorce because it would be damaging to the reputation of the famous author George Eliot with whom he was living. Lewes and Eliot demanded that the world call them husband and wife. The reason we refer to Marian Evans as George Eliot today is that she and Lewes knew that suspicions of sexual and social impropriety would affect the publication, reception, and sales of her novels. They succeeded in promoting the domestic fiction that she was Mrs. Lewes. But the legal Mrs. Lewes lived on, and I contend that the continued presence of Agnes Lewes as the "real," shadow Mrs. Lewes behind Eliot's assumption of this identity, inevitably influenced the sexual triangles and irregular and unhappy marriages throughout her fiction.

THE LAW

My research into legal cases of Victorian divorce following the 1857 Matrimonial Causes Act suggests that the condonation clause in the Act (statute 30) was open to debate and interpretation.[13] Lewes was not prohibited from "seeking" a divorce. After 1857, he, like many men, might have petitioned for a divorce on the grounds of his wife's adultery in the past. Cases heard after 1857 were for adultery committed as long before as the 1820s (Horstman 89). Had he chosen to petition, he would have been obliged to state that there was no "collusion or connivance" between husband and wife in seeking the divorce. And he would have been required to name the alleged adulterer (Hunt) as co-respondent. Despite the fact that Lewes quarreled with Hunt over the latter's failure to support Agnes and her children financially, his comments remained private, and he showed no desire to make Hunt's adultery and the moral failings of his wife public.

Had Lewes taken his case to court, Hunt would have had the option of counter-charging "condonation." In such a case, the adultery itself would have to be proven and then the charge of condonation would also have to be proven. Many of the judgments in cases that came before the newly established Divorce Commission disputed just what constituted condonation. Nothing I have read mentions registering a birth in itself as an act of condonation. Rather, condonation means forgiveness and reconciliation generally; specifically, it means returning to conjugal cohabitation. According to an 1858 pamphlet on the new law, *A Practical Treatise on Divorce and Matrimonial Jurisdiction* by John Fraser MacQueen, "when the injury is deliberately and knowingly condoned by the party injured, there is an end of all claim to redress, unless the injury be repeated, in which case the original offence will revive" (43). As we know, within Lewes and Agnes's marriage, the "injury" was repeated because Agnes continued bearing children even after Lewes had left his home and begun living with Marian Evans. Theoretically, he might still have petitioned for a divorce on the grounds of an injury that he had not condoned by resuming relations with Agnes. But as Agnes's adultery continued, he had begun a technically adulterous relationship with Eliot, and as earlier biographers note, this would have been a factor in a court's judgment on the worthiness of his suit for divorce.

We do not know whether Lewes knew for certain that Edmund was Hunt's child. We do not know that Edmund was Hunt's child. If Lewes knew of Agnes and Hunt's affair and continued living with her as man and wife, that (not the administrative act of registering births) would constitute condonation. But if he did take her back as his wife, resuming sexual relations, then it seems to me there would be ambiguity about several of the children involved—St. Vincent, Edmund and Rose. If, on the other hand, he was not having sexual relations with Agnes, then I wonder whether he can be said to have taken her back as a wife and condoned the adultery. Either way, he did not condone adultery that occurred after he left their home, and he had the legal right to pursue a divorce suit, but the fact that he was living with another woman and that the case would bring damaging publicity, would have been determining factors in his decision not do so.

All of this is speculation about what the court might have found had Lewes petitioned for divorce against Agnes. As it is, to say that condonation precluded him from appealing for divorce is to judge the case before knowing the facts—to reach a conclusion about a trial that never occurred. Such a conclusion is false and misleading, and until someone produces evidence showing that Lewes decided against petitioning because he knew he had condoned the relationship—instead of because he did not want to make a spectacle of himself, Eliot and his three acknowledged sons, or because he was himself living in an adulterous relationship with a woman and now-famous author whose career would be compromised—the validity of the claim that condonation was the sole reason for his remaining married is unsupportable.

Divorce laws in Victorian England were designed to encourage moral behavior, not to make unhappy individuals happy. Unlike today, divorce was awarded as a social gesture toward ensuring the health of Victorian marriages.[14] Condonation of adultery was considered as immoral as adultery itself. It is interesting that the modern story about Eliot and Lewes's relationship—which was transformed from speculation in the 1930s to fact after Haight's biography—turns Victorian morality on its head by representing an imagined condonation as a moral act. That would be fine, if only we could say that such noble sacrifice had occurred. But we cannot, and the details of the situation—unknown to us but known to George Eliot—worked their way into her representations of marital discord and infidelity. There is no need to oversimplify and cover up ambiguities in her life story, which might—when re-examined—reveal even more complexities in her fiction.[15]

MARRIAGE, SECRECY, AND TRIANGLES IN ELIOT'S FICTION

Long before entering into her relationship with Lewes and coming into contact and conflict with the conventions and laws of marriage, George Eliot had opinions about marriage and divorce. In 1838, she complained of the "marrying and giving in marriage that is constantly being transacted" as an example of earthly ties "so brittle as to be liable to be snapped asunder at every breeze" (*GEL* I:6). In 1848, she sympathized with the character of Rochester in *Jane Eyre*, referring the "diabolical law which chains a man soul and body to a putrefying carcase" (*GEL* I:268).

Once she became involved with Lewes, she defended her union in terms that reflect Feuerbach's notion of a higher ideal in marriage. Feuerbach (in Eliot's 1854 translation of the *Essence of Christianity*) writes, "for a marriage the bond of which is merely an external restriction, not the voluntary, contented self-restriction of love . . . is not a true marriage, and therefore not a truly moral marriage" (*Selected Critical Writings*, 70). Clearly, some version in this belief in a marriage above the law justified Eliot's actions and declarations of her identity as Lewes's wife. In a letter to her friend Cara Bray in 1855 about the seriousness of her attitude toward marriage generally and toward Lewes particularly, she wrote: "Light and easily broken ties are what I neither desire theoretically nor could live for practically" (*GEL* II: 213–14). She makes it known that the strength of the tie has nothing to do with the laws or ceremonies.

It was also in 1855 that Eliot wrote a revealing book review of Thomas Knightley's *An Account of the Life, Opinions, and Writings of John Milton*. She was helping the ailing Lewes meet his responsibilities to *The Leader*, which he was still editing with Thornton Hunt, and so her focus on Milton's views of divorce is particularly significant. She compares Milton's arguments to those of Caroline Norton — who was campaigning for women's marital and property rights — and refers to Norton's pamphlet *A Letter to the Queen on Lord Chancellor Cranworth's Marriage & Divorce Bill* (1855). Quoting Milton's pathetic portrayal of a man "bound fast to an uncomplying discord of nature" who sees that "his bondage is now inevitable," she writes: "a picture, alas! too often realized since the year 1644, when it was thus powerfully drawn. For want of a more modern pendant to Mrs. Norton's plea, it is worth while to take up Milton's, and consider what such a mind as his had to urge on the husband's side of the subject."[16]

And so we find that the binding nature of matrimony was very much on Eliot's mind early in her relationship with Lewes when she was preparing to begin writing fiction. Perhaps not surprisingly, she was particularly sympathetic to the husband's position. Despite her decision to call her own partnership a marriage, and the intellectual and domestic happiness she clearly enjoyed within that marriage, her fiction is, from the start, scathing in its representation of the various ways in which the marital bond might become destructive to the material and emotional lives of both husbands and wives. This impulse to critique marriage only intensified over the course of her career as a novelist.[17]

As I have indicated, we know a fair amount about the story (however full of gaps) of Lewes's marriage and his wife's affair with Hunt, also a married man. Too little attention has been paid to the force that Eliot's intimate knowledge of Lewes's marital irregularities may have had on her representations of marriage in her fiction. Patterns emerge that seem traceable (whether consciously or unconsciously) to the triangular sexual relations of Agnes Lewes-George Lewes-Thornton Hunt and Marian Evans-George Lewes-Agnes Lewes. No one-to-one relationship between life and art could ever exist in a writer as imaginative, accomplished and complex as George Eliot, nor could such reductive correspondences ever be pursued productively in biographically informed explications of literary texts. Yet I suspect that reading these recurring patterns of secrecy, lies, and triangulation in Eliot's fiction, together with the known facts of her own direct and indirect experience of Lewes's marital complexities, will result in a fuller understanding of the predominant representations and themes of marriage in her work.[18]

Ultimately, I want to focus on *Romola*, the only novel that treats the legal and sacred—as well as the psychological—bond of marriage outside of a nineteenth-century English context. First, however, it is worth reviewing the bad English marriages that characterize Eliot's fiction, all imagined after she had begun living with Lewes. Some of these marriages are taken up in medias res, whereas others are tracked from their inception. In *Scenes of Clerical Life*, Janet Dempster's marriage exposes the horrors of—and links between—physical and psychological abuse and alcoholism. In this story, sympathy for the husband is suspended more completely than it would be again until her last portrait of an abusive husband, Henleigh Grandcourt in *Daniel Deronda*. In *Silas Marner*, Godfrey Cass's secret marriage is succeeded by a socially and emotionally more appropriate second marriage made possible only by the suppression of public knowledge about the first. Before the opium-addicted Molly's timely death, Godfrey seems on the verge of bigamy as he courts Nancy Lammeter in the hope that his marriage to Molly will simply go away. Eliot's decision to make Molly a wife, rather than a mistress, not only ensures Eppie's legitimacy, but emphasizes the legal prison of a bad marriage for a man of social standing tied to a sinning (drug-addicted) woman. By doing the right thing (marrying Molly), Godfrey precludes himself from ever marrying the woman he loves, unless of course Molly dies. Although readers today may be inclined to focus on Godfrey's exploitation and abandonment of a lower-class woman, Eliot's narrator judges the woman harshly: "Molly knew that the cause of her dingy rags was not her husband's neglect, but the demon Opium to whom she was enslaved, body and soul. . . ." (107). Her bitterness toward Godfrey is presented as irrational, and it is clear that Eliot felt some sympathy with him—like the fictional Rochester and the factual Milton—as a man chained by an imprudent marriage to hopeless woman. When Molly dies, the child becomes the focus of the narrative and is adopted by a man who was himself betrayed by his fiancé and best friend in a scenario that seems to resonate with Lewes's betrayal by his best friend Hunt. As she avoided illegitimacy by making Molly a wife rather than a mistress, Eliot avoided the troubling subject of adultery by having Silas's friend William steal his betrothed, rather than his wife. She would eventually confront the subject of adultery—so much a part of her own domestic experience—directly and boldly, especially in *Romola* and *Felix Holt*.

The Mill on the Floss is ironic in its portrayal of the Dodson sisters' domination of their weaker mates and also makes clear that the Tulliver marriage, although not miserable, is unsatisfying to both spouses. *Felix Holt*'s plot turns on the mercenary marriage of Mrs. Transome to an imbecile husband and her affair with the lawyer Jermyn, which produces an illegitimate child who becomes the source of the unfaithful wife's hope and suffering. Most famously, *Middlemarch* is structured around two of the worst marriages in Victorian fiction as it parallels Dorothea's misguided marriage to Casaubon and Lydgate's misguided marriage to Rosamond. *Daniel Deronda*'s "English plot" is set in motion by Gwendolen's conflicted, money-driven decision to marry the sadistic Grandcourt, knowing that he has a hidden former mistress and four illegitimate children. The fact that Grandcourt's illegitimate son ultimately inherits his estate implies a kind of restitution of the disinherited, which parallels Deronda's restoration of his Jewish heritage, suppressed partly as a result of his mother's unhappy marriage to his father.

Although Eliot's narratives also offer examples of relatively successful marriages (for example, the Poysers, Garths, and Klesmers), the bad marriages are predominant, and patterns emerge that suggest a preoccupation with triangles of deceit, desire and blackmail. Godfrey conceals his marriage to Molly, leaving himself open to blackmail by his brother; Mrs. Transome bears the burden of the secret affair that irrevocably binds her to her former lover; Gwendolen keeps her husband's secret, exposing herself to moral blackmail by both him and his mistress.[19] When considered in the light of Agnes Lewes's existence as a background presence in Eliot's life—as at one level an open secret, but at another as the embodiment of a situation fraught with deceptions and psychological pressures still unknown to us—the sexual triangles that characterize her fiction become even more interesting and complicated. The challenge is to reconcile the relative importance of known (and partially known) biographical facts with the literary conventions of period: the marriage and adultery plots and the triangulations that distinguish Victorian fiction and grew ever more popular during the period when Eliot was writing.[20]

In this catalogue of marital unhappiness, secrecy and deception in Eliot's life and fiction, her historical novel of fifteenth-century Florence has a distinctive position. *Romola* displaces the specific discontents of nineteenth-century marriage onto its Renaissance Italian characters, rendering divorce—but not marital unhappiness and separation—historically unthinkable. Although the temporal and religious contexts of Romola and Tito's marriage may seem far removed from Victorian England, it is in *Romola* that we find Eliot's darkest meditation on secrecy, adultery, and illegitimacy. We also find a fictional marriage between Tito and the gullible, almost imbecile but fertile peasant girl Tessa.

Tito's flirtation with Tessa begins before he meets Romola, but his involvement with her deepens after he has fallen in love with Romola, who acts as an external moral conscience from which Tessa offers an escape. On a day in which he is expected at Romola's home, he encounters Tessa in the hands of a street conjurer, Vaiano, "who was making laughing attempts to soothe and cajole her, evidently carrying with him the amused sympathy of the spectators" (99). Tito extricates the confused girl from the conjurer's grasp, to the amusement and insinuating sneers of the crowd. In so doing, he intensifies her idealization of him as a beautiful, mysterious guardian angel.

The scene is a crucial preparation for the next chance encounter between the two at the peasant's fair. Vaiano has installed himself at a table in mock priest's attire and is offering marriage services: "Behold my children. . . . neglect not the Holy Sacrament of matrimony when it can be had for the small sum of a white quattrino—the cheapest matrimony ever offered, and dissolved by special bull beforehand at every man's own will and pleasure" (137). He appeals to the maidens: "Matrimony to be had—hot, eaten and done with as easily as *berlingozzi!*" (138). The joke, in the highly sexualized street life of Florence, irreverently mimics the granting of papal indulgences and pretends to provide unmarried couples a temporary license to have guilt-free sex. It also echoes the language of Victorian divorce debates because legislators wanted to be sure that divorce did not become merely the whim of every man's will and pleasure.[21]

Tessa is awed by the spectacle of the conjuror (whom she does not recognize) dressed in "sham episcopal costume." Carried away by the moment, Tito permits the mock-priest to perform "a mimic ceremony with a liberal expenditure of *lingua furbesca* or thieves' Latin" (144). Vaiano recognizes the couple and assumes that they have come for retroactive legitimation: "you are come to be married. I commend your penitence—the blessing of the Holy Church can never come too late" (144). But the savvy charlatan soon realizes his mistake and reinterprets the ceremony as a ploy on Tito's part to pursue sexual relations with an ignorant girl. Although Tito is initially "far from that understanding" (144), after the ceremony is performed and the conjurer paid, the fact of the sham marriage (which he intimidates Tessa into concealing), permits him to do exactly what the conjurer imagined—deceive Tessa into believing he is her husband as he proceeds to keep her as a mistress and father her two children. As the conjurer's knowing smile implies, seduction will be easier for the man if the girl thinks she is married.

This marriage which is not one in *Romola* that may be viewed as part of Eliot's thick description of Renaissance Florence, as an indication of the disrespect for the Catholic church and its teachings that co-existed with—and perhaps inspired—Savonarola's reform movement. But when viewed in the context of Victorian divorce debates, and her own marriage which was not one, it raises interesting questions. The conjurer is an unsavory character whose mockery of the wedding ceremony is not admirable. At the same time, the mockery of Papal "bulls" and pardons and the general corruption of the Church is deserved; as usual, there is truth in mimicry. The unlikely way in which this strange scene functions might be better understood in light of other doubtful offstage marriages that

Eliot used to avoid questions of illegitimacy, specifically that of Godfrey to Molly and perhaps of Harold Transome to his deceased Greek wife/slave.

Tito's fictional marriage is one of his gravest moral transgressions, a different kind of transgression from the young couples buying false marriages in the street. The mockery made of marriage (and the Church) at the peasant's fair finds its parallel in the profound explicit and implicit questioning of the marriage vow in the scene of Romola's flight from Tito and her encounter with Savonarola, who sends her back to her husband. The conjurer plays on the technicalities of marriage—the buying and selling of "lightly broken ties"—that Eliot found at once disturbing and absurd.

It is the lie of Tito's marriage to Tessa that highlights peculiarly Eliot's awareness of the dubiousness of such a pretend, mock ceremony and subsequent bond. Tessa is a victim of Tito's lie, but a victim who never knows or recognizes the deceit to which she has been subjected. At the same time, Tito's legal marriage to Romola is also a moral lie, emphasizing the irrelevance of legal bonds in human relationships, a position that Eliot held with respect to her own fictional marriage but serious moral commitment to Lewes. Romola's devotion to Tessa and her children after Tito's death has intriguing resonances with Eliot's own assumption of financial responsibility for Agnes and her children as a corollary to her "marriage" to Lewes.

Tessa is the "other woman" in Tito's legal marriage to Romola, but Romola is the "other woman" in his fictional marriage to Tessa. The same might be said of Molly in *Silas Marner*, a novel that came to Eliot as she was contemplating *Romola*. The two works have numerous structural and thematic similarities. Molly is both the wife and the other woman. Her offstage marriage to Godfrey seems no more real than Tito's sham marriage to Tessa. Gwendolen, though legally married to Grandcourt, may be said to feel like the other woman relative to the mistress who has produced a family and an heir and who makes her moral entitlement known to the legal wife. Godfrey, Mrs. Transome, and Gwendolen suffer emotional and psychological conflicts from keeping secrets related to the marriages. In *Romola*, it is partly the pressure of trying to hold together two "marriages" and be a husband to two wives that pulls Tito apart and plays a role in his psychological disintegration.

To say simply that Eliot felt guilty about Agnes is to underestimate the complexities of the situation. Despite her protestations of a higher bond than marriage with Lewes, she was still the other woman in his married life. Looking at it another way, as one of Eliot's narrator's might, she certainly sympathized with Lewes's position. He was the legal husband of Agnes but also the other man in her affair with Hunt. Did she also sympathize with Agnes who, from what biographers tell us, might be considered a sinner like Molly, a mindless breeder like Tessa, or a demanding, blackmailing other woman like Lydia Glasher?

The reason we have failed to sort out this entanglement of emotions in our narratives of Eliot's life has much to do with the reductive story that Lewes did not divorce Agnes because, having condoned her adultery, he was powerless to do so. Eliot willingly entered into a fictional marriage and insisted on her identity as "Mrs. Lewes" until the fiction became a fact in all but the legal sense. It is possible that she felt cheated out of the ability to marry and at the same time that she was cheating with the husband of another woman, who himself occupied a similar double position of betrayed and betrayer. Of course it is fruitless to speculate and impossible to know what she felt, but the challenge and the potential of integrating our interpretation of the biographical narrative with our interpretation of her fiction lies in allowing life and fiction to inform each other. The occurrence of fictional marriage in her life and art is an intriguing point of intersection that reveals the potential critical value of setting straight the historical record.

Eliot's conflicted attitudes about the bond of marriage in an age of divorce reform are evident in her fiction. Although her recorded comments about divorce indicate a theoretical approval, she and Lewes did not pursue this option for reasons that might never be known, but that certainly are more complicated than biographies have led us to believe. Her fiction upholds the supremacy of duty, vows, and promises.[22] She never created a fictional scenario to mirror precisely that of her own life situation, but the secrets, lies, triangulations, and betrayals that characterize the representation of marriage in her fiction seem to be informed by more than Victorian literary conventions, or even the broader ideological critiques that such dramatic devices serve. They seem to show a preoccupation that belies the confidence with which she asserted her position as the wife of George Henry Lewes and confided to Barbara Bodichon her preference for "excommunication" (*GEL* 3:366).

Whether or not Lewes "condoned" Agnes's adultery is a hypothetical legal question that can never be answered. Hence, the claim by biographers that condoning was the reason for their not divorcing must be discredited. This may seem like a technicality of interest only to biographers, but, as I hope I have shown, the persistent assertion of this explanation as a fact that transforms the legal fiction of declaring paternity into a virtuous sacrifice, raises questions about our knowledge and our understanding of an historical situation that has relevance for our interpretation of Eliot's fiction.

NOTES

1. Linton "George Eliot," p. 534

2. Bullett (1948) uses the term *brood* (94). Taylor (1989) refers to Agnes's "brood of bastards" (149). Karl remarks that Agnes and Hunt's "breeding season lasted over seven years" (61).

3. Lewes traveled a great deal in the months prior to Edmund's birth in April 1850, but in July and August 1849, he was writing letters from 26 Bedford Place, Kensington (*Letters of GHL* 109–111), suggesting that he was at home at the time of conception.

4. See *The Autobiography of Christopher Kirkland* (1885), "George Eliot," (1885), and *My Literary Life* (1899).

5. Haight continued to assert these claims, for example in "The Carlyles and the Leweses" (1976), in which the sources are gossipy letters written by the Carlyles.

6. This final chapter of Eliot's life, in which achieved legally sanctioned matrimony, has been the subject of much comment and commentary, but because it occurred after Eliot had finished her writing career, its details and implications fall outside the scope of this study.

7. Haight reveals that Cross also chose to cut what may be a reference to Lewes's desire to divorce from Eliot's 1860 letter to Barbara Bodichon: "By the way, we have consulted a barrister, very accomplished in foreign and English law, about the matter broached by your friend Mrs. Brodie. He pronounces it *impossible*. I am not sorry. I think the boys will not suffer, and for myself I prefer excommunication" (*GEL* 3:366).

8. In his analysis of obituaries of Eliot in the Victorian religious press, Collins observes: "Some religious papers . . . called Lewes her husband or said she had married him and left it at that. . . . Others did not mention it—but a few did, and to these it was a stumbling-block far more serious than any doctrinal enigmas" (67).

9. Linton does not mention condoning adultery; rather, speaking of Eliot's union with Lewes as a mistake, she writes that people "condoned that mistake and created it into a virtue" ("George Eliot" 523).

10. Kitchel traces these and other claims back to Linton in an appendix called "Mrs. Lynn Linton's views on Lewes's break with his wife." She discredits Linton's account (though not the condonation claim). Redinger (1975) cites Kitchel in tracing the condoning theory, as well as the idea that Lewes and Agnes practiced "free love," back to Linton's *The Autobiography of Christopher Kirkland*. Redinger (like Haight) doubts the validity of this claim. Linton's fictional narrator states that Lewes could not "go into Divorce Court for his personal relief because of that condonation and his own unclean hands. . . ." (Linton *Kirkland*, I: 280; Kitchel 313; Redinger 249).

11. Williams follows Fremantle in hinting that, although Lewes recognized Thornie and Bertie as his own, they may have been Hunt's children (95). The idea of Thornie, Bertie, or St. Vincent's illegitimacy not broached by Haight, but Redinger entertains it as a possibility (252–53).

12. Adams discredits Ashton's explanation in her biography of Eliot that Marian Evans changed her name to Marian Lewes by "Deed Poll" to gain access to her own fortune, arguing that as a single woman, Evans would have had access to her own money and would have been denied access to it only if she been married.

13. This research has been invaluably assisted by Claudia Martin, attorney and PhD candidate in the English Department at Binghamton University

14. On this particular aspect of divorce law, see Dowling.

15. Condonation remained an important factor in Victorian divorce law. In Thomas Hardy's *Jude the Obscure* (1895), for example, Phillotson offers to condone Sue's relationship with Jude by taking her back and undermining his grounds for divorce (which are ironically already unfounded).

16. *Leader*, no. 280, 1 August 1855, p. 750. Reprinted as "Life and Opinions of Milton" in Pinney (1963). In an interesting analysis of Eliot as "Miltonist," Dayton Haskin makes the biographical connection, noting: "The climactic work of the review was to present Milton not as the author of *Paradise Lost*, but as a stand-in for Lewes. . . ." (214). His account of Lewes's actual marital situation, however, is vague: "Lewes was unable to obtain a divorce from his wife, Agnes, who for some years had been bearing children to Hunt" (211). He does not cite a source and does not mention condoning.

17. Boone explores the ideological manifestations of the traditional marriage plot in the Anglo-British novel and identifies a countertradition, which reacted to the notion of a happy ending by making marital discord part of the structure of the novel. He includes *Daniel Deronda* as part of this counter-tradition. Certainly aspects of Eliot's critique of marriage are an indictment of gendered Victorian ideologies and power structures, but the form that her indictments take are distinctive to her.

18. Dowling's 1995 article, "The Other Side of Silence": Matrimonial Conflict and the Divorce Court in George Eliot's Fiction," examines Eliot's "texts" in the "context" of the "legal discourse of the first English Divorce Court" (322). His New Historicist focus on silence as a "rhetorical device" that intersects with Divorce Court proceedings following the Matrimonial Causes Act of 1857, overlooks the obvious biographical context and is thus an example of how poststructuralist criticism denies the relevance of biography as context. He writes that, although Eliot may have had a personal interest in divorce, "the general literary trend toward the subject of matrimonial misery can be best understood, I think, as a response to this wider social desire to know in greater detail the intricacies of a previously invisible topic" (329). His only mention of the Eliot's life comes in a footnote in which he cites the cryptic 1860 letter to Barbara Bodichon (*GEL* III:366). Dowling does not mention Agnes, adultery or any other biographical details.

19. On blackmail in Eliot's fiction, see Welsh.

20. Girard is the most powerful theorist of triangulated desire in European fiction, and Sedgwick modified his model to read Eliot's *Adam Bede*. Girard writes that a "vaniteux will desire any object so long as he is convinced that it is already desired by another person whom he admires" (7). The relationship created between the "mediator" and the "rival," imitative in nature, is the primary relationship, making the "object" of desire secondary. Although instances of such mediated desire occur in Eliot's fiction, such as William Dane's desire for Silas's fiancée or Hans Meyrick's desire for Mirah, more frequently and insistently, Eliot breaks this pattern with uniquely fluid triangulations that defy the literary conventions available to her.

21. Writing about the Matrimonial Causes Act, Poovey makes an interesting comparison between pre-1857 granting of divorce to aristocrats by private parliamentary bill, "a procedure more regular and less visibly corrupt than the late sixteenth-century practice of the Catholic Church's selling papal dispensations for absolute divorce in order to raise revenue" (55). Eliot seems to encode an analogy between Victorian divorce "reform" and the actions of Pope Alexander the Sixth, whom Vaiano says "intends to reform and purify the Church and wisely begins by abolishing that priestly abuse which keeps too large a share of this privileged matrimony to the clergy and stints the laity" (137).

22. On promising in Eliot's fiction, see Ganz.

WORKS CITED

Adams, Harriet. "George Eliot's Deed: Reconciling an Outlaw Marriage." *Yale University Library Gazette*, October 2000, pp. 52–63.

Ames, Charles Gordon. *George Eliot's Two Marriages*. G. H. Buchanan and Co., 1886.

Ashton, Rosemary. *G. H. Lewes: A Life*. Oxford UP, 1991.

———. *George Eliot: A Life*. Hamish Hamilton, 1996.

Blind, Mathilde. *George Eliot*. W. H. Allen & Co., 1884.

Boone, Joseph Allen. *Tradition, Counter Tradition: Love and the Form of Fiction*. U of Chicago Press, 1987.

Bullett, Gerald. *George Eliot: Her Life and Books*. Yale UP, 1948.

Collins, K. K. *Identifying the Remains: George Eliot's Death in the London Religious Press*. ELS Editions, 2006.

Cross, John Walter. *George Eliot's Life as Related in her Letters and Journals*. Blackwood's, 1885.

Dowling, Andrew. "'The Other Side of Silence'": Matrimonial Conflict and the Divorce Court in George Eliot's Fiction." *Nineteenth-Century Literature*, no. 50, vol. 3, December 1995, pp. 322–336.

Eliot, George. *The George Eliot Journals*. Edited by Margaret Harris and Judith Johnston, Cambridge UP, 1998.

———. *The George Eliot Letters*, 9 vols. Edited by Gordon S. Haight, Yale UP, 1954–1955, 1978.

———. "Life and Opinions of Milton." *Essays of George Eliot*, edited by Thomas Pinney. Columbia UP, 1963, pp. 154–157. Originally published in the *Leader*, no. 280, vol. 4, August 1855, p. 750.

———. *Romola*. Edited by Andrew Brown, Oxford UP, 1994.

———. *Silas Marner*. Edited by David Carroll, Penguin, 1996.

———. *Selected Critical Writings*. Edited by Rosemary Ashton, Oxford UP, 1992.

Fremantle, Anne, *George Eliot*. Macmillan, 1933.

Ganz, Melissa J. "Binding the Will: George Eliot and the Practice of Promising." *ELH*, vol. 75, 2008, pp. 565–602.

Girard, René. *Deceit, Desire and the Novel: Self and Other in Literary Structure* [1961]. Translated by Yvonne Freccero, Johns Hopkins UP, 1976.

Haight, Gordon S. *George Eliot: A Biography*. Oxford UP, 1968.

———. "The Carlyles and the Leweses" [1976]. *George Eliot's Originals and Contemporaries: Essays in Victorian Literary History and Biography*, edited by Hugh Witemeyer, Macmillan, 1992, pp. 91–116.

Haldane, Elizabeth S. *George Eliot and Her Times*. Hodder and Stoughton, 1927.

Hanson, Lawrence, and Elizabeth. *Marian Evans and George Eliot: A Biography*. Oxford UP, 1952.

Haskin, Dayton. "George Eliot as 'Miltonist': Marriage and Milton in *Middlemarch*. *Milton and Gender*. Edited by Catherine Gimelli Martin, Cambridge UP, 2004, pp. 207–222.

Horstman, Allen. *Victorian Divorce*. Croom Helm, 1985.

Hughes, Kathryn. *George Eliot: The Last Victorian*. Fourth Estate, 1998.

Karl, Frederick. *George Eliot: Voice of a Century*. Norton, 1995.

Kitchel, Anna. *George Lewes and George Eliot: A Review of Records* (1932).

Lewes, George Henry. *The Letters of George Henry Lewes*, 3 vols. Edited by William Baker, U of Victoria P, 1995/1999.

Linton, Eliz Lynn. *The Autobiography of Christopher Kirkland* [1885]. Garland Publishing, 1976.

———. "George Eliot." *Temple Bar*, vol. 73, April 1885, pp. 512–524.

———. *My Literary Life*. Hodder and Stoughton, 1899.

MacQueen, John Fraser. *A practical treatise on divorce and matrimonial jurisdiction under the act of 1857 and new orders. . .* W. Maxwell, 1858.

Poovey, Mary. *Uneven Developments: The Ideological Work of Gender in Mid-Victorian England*. U of Chicago P, 1988.

Redinger, Ruby. *George Eliot: The Emergent Self*. Alfred Knopf, 1975.

Sedgwick, Eve Kosofsky. *Between Men: English Literature and Male Homosocial Desire*. Columbia UP. 1985.

Taylor, Ina. *A Woman of Contradictions: The Life of George Eliot*. Morrow, 1990.

Welsh, Alexander. *George Eliot and Blackmail*. Harvard UP, 1985.

Williams, Blanche Colton. *George Eliot*. Macmillan, 1936.

Part II

Subversive Ideologies

FOUR

Unraveling Orientalism: Dawe's "Yellow and White"

James M. Decker

> The Orient at large, therefore, vacillates between the West's contempt
> for what is familiar and its shivers in delight in—or fear of—novelty.
> —Edward Said, *Orientalism* (59)

The idea of simultaneous repulsion and attraction stands among Edward Said's most prescient conceptualizations in his path-breaking *Orientalism* (1978). Bryan Turner glosses Said's point, noting that the "forbidden Other . . . is simultaneously repulsive, seductive, and attractive" (1). For Said, the discourse of Orientalism functions as a self-perpetuating rationalization that sets up the conflicting idea of a decadent, uncivilized East that is nonetheless exotic, inviting, in need of Western control. Said also notes that "Always there lurks the assumption that although the Western consumer belongs to a numerical minority, he is entitled to own or to expend (or both) the majority of the world resources" (*Orientalism,* 108). The East, this logic holds, fails to use its resources efficiently and is in need of assistance. Rather than reinforcing a self-conceptualization of a rapacious invader, the Orientalist views the process of colonization as both inevitable and necessary. Without the West, the East would waste its potential and descend further into moral turpitude, indolence, and ugliness. As Said writes, "colonial rule was justified in advance by Orientalism" (*Orientalism*, 39).

Said, of course, generally limits his discussion in *Orientalism* to the Near East, and Shanyn Fiske argues that Said's ideas "fail to account for Britain's problematic relations with a politically independent empire" such as China (222). Nicholas Clifford also suggests that Said's description of Orientalism lacks much usefulness for an examination of England's attitudes toward China (15). Subsequent commentators, however, extended Said's principles to the Far East, including China. Daniel F. Vukovich, for instance, argues for the application of Said's theories to China, claiming that "It is *not* an exaggeration to say that China and Islam share a certain discursive history in Western intellectual-political culture, as does virtually every national culture subjected to the forces and significations of imperialism and modern colonialism" (10). Another theorist, Ouyang Yu, also discerns the importance of Said's ideas for a study of China and argues that, with respect to representing China, the "Orientalist must establish a series of binary oppositions that hold up Europeans as superior, civilized, virtuous, advanced, rational, normal, sane, and strong, and Orientals as inferior, barbarian, evil, backward, irrational, abnormal, insane, and weak" (34–35). Although the particulars of *Orientalism* certainly avoid much discussion of China, the broad strokes of Said's theory definitely apply. Despite having an eminent civilization (which, Fiske and Clifford note, made it harder to depict China as backward), that achievement was largely perceived as being in the past, and as Susan Schoenbauer Thurin observes, "Victorians increasingly viewed China as a static society" rather than as a progressive one capable of controlling its own affairs" (6). Thurin continues in a passage that mirrors Said's principles of Orientalism: "[British] travelers treat[ed] the nation as a backward child who must be coached and patronized" (18). The attitude and tone identified by Thurin dovetails perfectly with the Orientalist concept of "arrested development" recognized by Said (*Orientalism*, 145). Elizabeth Hope Chang creates yet another parallel between British discourse about China and Said's thoughts on Orientalism with her observation that for the British, China is a "field of imagined visual possibility" (1), an idea that she suggests finds it roots in the type of replication that Said stresses in *Orientalism*: the Victorian "vision of China is in fact a reflection mirrored back to the European reader by a representation made by a Western writer" (22). Here, Chang epitomizes Said's conception of Orientalism as a practice wherein representations of the East "responded more to the culture that produced it than to its putative object, which was also by the West" (22). For Said, "It is Europe that articulates the Orient," and this seems to apply to China equally as well as it does to other areas of the East (*Orientalism*, 57).

Carlton Dawe's "Yellow and White," the first story in his eponymous 1895 collection, provides a nearly perfect example of an Orientalist representation of China, and it also serves as a demonstration of the binary that underpins Said's explanation of the Orientalist fascination with the Eastern Other. Dawe, an Australian who moved to England in 1892, authored more than seventy books, several of which capitalized on his travels in Asia. A writer of popular, rather than literary, fiction, Dawe abundantly employs the stereotypes of his Orientalist precursors, yet he draws heavily from his own observations of China and other Eastern nations. Although Dawe's travels give him a veneer of authenticity and verisimilitude, Said critiques the extrapolation of personal experience into authoritative statements about the East with his claim that "the problem with personal utterance was that it inevitably retreated into a position equating the Orient with private fantasy" (*Orientalism*, 176). As most of Dawe's readers would never visit China, the importance of Said's point becomes clear. Dawe's personal China—or the China of his characters—literally becomes China for his audience, collapsing nuance and complexity into a collection of yellow peril images and melodramatic plots that an early reviewer summed up as "passion, horror, and peril" ("Review of *Yellow and White*" 868). In "Yellow and White," Dawe intermingles images of ugly brutality and exotic danger to depict a China that never existed—save in the pages of Orientalist discourse—and vacillates between contempt and delight.

Given the relative obscurity of "Yellow and White," a brief plot summary is necessary. Simple yet sensational, "Yellow and White" recounts the story of Gresham, a colonist with unspecified business interests, as he attempts a tryst with the beautiful "half-breed" (7) wife of the "wealthy merchant Quong" (6). Told through a frame tale by an unnamed narrator, the narrative first describes Gresham's immediate fascination with the (silent) woman as well as portrays Quong's defensive and jealous reaction to inquiries about his wife. Gresham's interest is whetted further when the nameless woman uses a "little slop of a Chinese girl" (8) to arrange an intimate meeting. Intrigued at the possibility of an "adventure" (9) Gresham returns, and he implies that he sleeps with the woman. Later, Gresham meets with Quong, whom he feels "knew nothing of what happened" (11). When Gresham attempts to meet with his lover a second time, several of Quong's men surprise him in the dark, and while he fiercely struggles with them, he suspects that the merchant "had set a trap" (14). After a vicious fight, Gresham escapes, only to find himself accosted in an alley, presumably by another of Quong's servants. Dodging the attack, Gresham rushes to the harbor, where he boards a sampan that, unbeknownst to him, is piloted by yet another of Quong's employees. After being knifed, Gresham fights off the rowers (also Quong's men) and dives into the water to make his escape. Gresham adds that he went to Quong's the next day and acted as though nothing out of the ordinary had happened. The narrator further relates that Gresham believes the woman to be either exiled or dead.

As the histrionic plot suggests, Dawe employs numerous Orientalist conventions, from the silent, compliant, and exotic woman—who represents for Said "sexual promise (and threat), untiring sensuality, unlimited desire, [and] deep generative energies" (*Orientalism*,188)—to what Gresham views as Quong's brutish cunning and feral menace, the "violent, unbalanced" traits that Said identifies in many Orientalist descriptions

(307). Additionally, Gresham's focus on adventure and his barely concealed disdain for Quong's marital rights both reveal his unstated assumption that China represents a passive body for him to sate his desires on. As Said emphasizes, Orientalists such as Gresham think the "West is the actor, the Orient a passive reactor. The West is the spectator, judge, and jury, of every facet of Oriental behavior" (*Orientalism*, 109). For Gresham, Quong's status as the nominal "master" of both China's wealth and his wife is purely contingent and subject to usurpation by a worthier, civilized, and intelligent adversary. Gresham strains at the notion that someone like Quong, with his "smug, oily face" and "little black eyes" should somehow possess great fortune as well as marry such an "unnaturally beautiful" woman (10).

In writing of Dawe, Ross Forman observes that the author consistently posited "assertions of British superiority and masculinity," and "Yellow and White" certainly appears no exception (44). Throughout the story, Dawe presents Gresham as a self-assured colonist dealing with the contemptible Quong, a man who is undeserving of his status and ignorant of his wife's value. Gresham never doubts the propriety of his actions, and he never doubts his superiority as a white man in a "yellow" land. In short, "Yellow and White" appears nearly a textbook case of Orientalism in which the "yellow peril" meets its comeuppance in the form of a British gentleman who is superior both physically and intellectually. The story employs stereotype after stereotype to cast China as a land of potential wasted on the natives but appreciated by colonizers such as Gresham, and it uniformly adopts a tone of pure disdain toward Quong and his staff.

Gresham's role as an Orientalist mouthpiece becomes immediately clear with his description of the nameless woman. His portrait emphasizes the exotic, hybrid[1] nature of Quong's wife and stresses that she is "quite four inches taller than the ordinary Chinese woman," had a "face almost as fair as a European's," had "light brown" hair, and possessed eyes "though suggestive of the slant" that "were languorous and blue" (3). Clearly, Gresham finds himself repulsed by the woman's Chinese features and absorbed by her European ones. Indeed, Gresham later observes that he "doubted if the Chinese blood could wholly absorb the European" (6). The woman, a child of an interracial relationship, represents a physicality that, for Gresham, transcends its limitations and functions as a "mystery" that he must solve—and conquer, just as he attempts to overcome Quong at business (4). Yu rightly connects Gresham's impulse to "the imperialist desire for power [that] lays claim to anything it finds attractive and obtainable, particularly . . . in China" (93). Gresham's sense of entitlement and his need to possess all he surveys is such that he tries to follow the woman up the "greasy stairs" into the house's private quarters, only to be nonplussed by Quong's objections, which Dawe renders in Pidgin English.[2]

Gresham, oblivious to the irony in Quong's statement that "Englishy-man he no welly good behave. He led-hot debbil for girlee" (5), quickly becomes obsessed with the woman, whose "blue eyes . . . danced in the wine bubbles" (6). As a Chinese male, Quong, for Gresham, holds no status, has no rights, even in his own home. As Yu notes, Gresham's rhetoric "reduces [Quong] to the position of an utterly bad, an inferior, Other who must be overpowered and put under control" (94). Thus, Gresham's "colonizing male gaze," as Forman puts it, tries to subjugate all in its view, including Quong's own wife (47). Indeed, Gresham be-comes nearly apoplectic in his indignation that Quong married the (si-lent) object of his desires:

> As I looked at Quong I felt a mad desire to strangle him. What right had this distended Chinese pig to have in his keeping such a heavenly creature? His black slanting eyes, full of horrible cunning and satisfac-tion, his flabby yellow face, his massive flabby throat—everything about the man seemed intensified and aggressive to me that night.

Gresham seizes on multiple stereotypes to dehumanize Quong and strip him of even the basic right to marry whom he pleases. In distorting and devaluing Quong's physical features by juxtaposing them to an image of a pig, Gresham simultaneously attributes the marriage to cunning, the same quality that Gresham assumes enables him to accumulate his mon-ey.

Silent and objectified, the woman fares even worse than Quong, for own thoughts on her marriage don't even merit consideration by Gres-ham, and he remarks that her European blood "had not been strong enough to resist the overtures" of Quong (6–7). Gresham continues his marshal imagery as he fantasizes about the woman's sexual encounters with Quong: "I fancied that I could even see the love-making of that estimable creature; the glow of the beady black eyes as they looked into the pale sweet face of the girl. I almost hated him for the exultation he must have felt over his victory" (6). In a passage that glosses Gresham's attitude, Said writes that "In most cases, the Orient seemed to offend sexual propriety; everything about the Orient . . . exuded dangerous sex" (167). The idea that the woman might love Quong, or that she could prefer him to an Englishman, fails to cross the affronted Gresham's mind. Quite simply, the woman is a passive body first captured by Quong but soon to be wrested away by the superior Gresham. For Gresham, it is a matter of "rights," and he views his own case as superior to that of Quong's despite the sanctity of marriage or the fact that he doesn't even know the woman's name. Gresham's "wish" and "purpose" trump all, and thus the mere act of wanting something (someone) prompts him to ignore Quong's legal rights and familial bonds and pursue his efforts at colonization on a more personal level (7).

Inevitably, Gresham's anger toward Quong, a man whom he perceives as violating a European beauty, allows him to project his own
desire onto the woman. An Orientalist figure "static, frozen, fixed eternally," the woman represents the Celestial "creature of a male power-
fantasy" who "express[es] unlimited sensuality . . . and willing[ness]"
(Said, *Orientalism*, 208; 207). Although the woman neither says a single
word nor makes a single gesture to Gresham, the character imagines that
Quong's wife "returned [his] look of amazement with one of equal intensity" (7). He further claims that "by her manner she seemed to invite
[him] forward" (7). Gresham completes his rationalization by calling her
a "bewitching novelty" and arguing that the situation contains "a spice of
the devil," rhetoric that shifts responsibility to the woman and suggests
that Gresham is powerless under her spell (7). In a neat trick, Gresham
quickly manages to convince himself not only that the woman returns his
passion but that it is her idea in the first place.[3]

Of course, the woman (or, perhaps, Quong[4]) does send a girl to fetch
Gresham, and the two do meet in private, a phenomenon that lends some
credence to Gresham's version of events. Although Yu asserts that Gresham's lust represents "unrequited infatuation," further analysis suggests
otherwise (94). After being led by the girl, Gresham ascends the stairs
alone, where he meets the woman. Significantly, the woman's hair "was
down her back," and her "little hand . . . slipped into [Gresham's], where
it nestled lovingly" (10). At this point, Dawe inserts an ellipsis that stands
for the rest of their encounter. In the following paragraph, when Gresham leaves the house, he notices a change in the face that he "now knew
so well" (10). The woman's hair, the handholding, and the coded language suggest that the physical intimacy continued after the ellipsis, and
the woman's change in demeanor[5] as well as the "host of unpleasant
thoughts" that ran through Gresham's mind are suggestive of a stronger
sort of remorse than would seem to be warranted from an illicit conversation alone. Although Dawe fails to give voice to the woman—a fact that
at once invests her with "mysterious" power and robs her of autonomy—
he strongly implies that the relationship was consummated.

Of significance to Gresham's colonizing, Orientalist attitude is his behavior following the intimate encounter. Rather than expressing guilt or
shame, Gresham brazenly enjoys Quong's hospitality by drinking his
liquor and smoking his cigars. Gresham describes the man he just cuck-
olded as "wily," "smug," "oily," "sinister," and "unpleasant," all traits
that one could reasonably argue he himself had exhibited with his behavior toward Quong's wife. Nevertheless, Gresham, assured by what Said
deems the "self-containing, self-reinforcing character of a closed system,
in which objects are what they are *because* they are . . . for ontological
reasons that no empirical material can either dislodge or alter," views
himself as justified, even heroic, in taking what he feels should be his
regardless of any claim that Quong may advance (*Orientalism*, 70). For

Gresham, Quong cannot be anything other than inferior, cannot represent anything other than a degraded culture that requires a rescue by Englishmen. The woman's biracial character underscores Quong's inherent inadequacy and the need for Gresham to usurp the husband's role. Just as in his business dealings Gresham feigns respect for Quong while privately belittling his abilities, so too does he masquerade as an intimate companion while secretly pursuing his wife.

Gresham consistently underestimates Quong precisely because in his narrative a Chinese man cannot outwit—or out fight—an Englishman. Said points out that Orientalists "reduce the Orient to a kind of human flatness, which exposed its characteristics easily to scrutiny and removed from it its complicating humanity" (*Orientalism*, 150). That Quong, a successful and powerful merchant might possess traits that would make him a worthy adversary—or a worthy match for his wife (whom Gresham reifies in purely physical dimensions)—never crosses the Englishman's mind. Gresham essentializes Quong, flattens him to a series of animalistic qualities that repel him yet that he feels he can easily domesticate, dominate. Precisely for this reason, Gresham's confidence mushrooms, and he feels that Quong "knew nothing of what had happened" (11).

Quong, of course, does suspect Gresham and is ready when his business associate returns for another tête-à-tête with his lover. Again using the rhetoric of "adventure" Gresham experiences a "curious feeling of uneasiness," but, falling back on his ability to defeat Quong on any field of battle, he "was disinclined to turn back at the first obstacle" (12). From this point, the story pits Gresham against Quong and his men and follows Gresham through an action-packed series of violent predicaments and close escapes that ultimately lead him to a ship headed north away from Hong Kong. Owing much to the conventions of the potboiler, these scenes nevertheless continue the Orientalist bent of the previous half of the tale. Gresham describes his "pigtail[ed]" (14) opponents as "devils" (18), "treacherous brutes" (22), and "wretches" (23), whereas he characterizes his own efforts as what Yu calls the "superhuman capabilities" of the English Orientalist hero: "daring resolve" (14), "spirit" (15) and "the strength of two men" (18). Additionally, Gresham depicts Quong's men variously as "hissing and spitting like a wild cat" (17), "spitting, howling, cursing" (18), and possessing "little eyes that gleamed like coals of fire" (2)3. Quong himself, Gresham represents as "wily" (21) and "cunning" (24). Gresham seems vexed—and perhaps perplexed—that against Orientalist expectations Quong has "set a trap into which [he] innocently walked" (21).

That Gresham could view himself as innocent after acting on his desire for another man's wife speaks volumes about the Orientalist rationalization for rapacious behavior that could not be so archly justified in England. Gresham sees himself not as a blackguard but as an adventurer claiming what should be rightfully his: the rich and fertile body of the

East. Half-colonized at birth, the woman needs (so Gesham's behavior intimates) a man who can fulfill her potential, reap her bounty. Gresham tells the narrator, without irony, that he had evidently contemplated "lay[ing] the affair before the authorities" but chose instead to "present [himself] at [Quong's] house the next day" (24). Clearly, for Gresham, Quong's audacity in defending his family honor holds little institutional weight and would have resulted in punitive actions on the part of the "authorities." As Forman observes, "The fact that the mixed-race woman's purely Chinese husband seeks spectacular revenge is attributed more to his innate character as a Celestial than to any sense that he might have an actual grievance" (47). Quong, though, exemplifies Said's assertion that "Never was it the case that the imperial encounter pitted an active Western intruder against a supine or inert non-Western native; there was *always* some form of active resistance" (*Culture*, xii). He challenges Gresham's violation of trust and intrusion into his private sphere—and succeeds in expelling the colonist from his territory (and in so doing mirrors Gresham's treatment of his voiceless wife as a passive land to be conquered). Nevertheless, Gresham controls the narrative, and he clearly feels vindicated and victorious, if slightly troubled at the fate of his nameless paramour. Further, Forman points out that in such Orientalist texts, "the protagonists' escape asserts an overarching sense of British superiority" (25). In other words, by simply eluding capture or death, Gresham reaffirms the Orientalist narrative.

The ending of the tale, however, stymies Gresham's sanguine interpretation, for the narrator's attitude toward his friend appears anything but congratulatory. Far from endorsing Gresham's choices, the story's ending suggests an ironic distancing from the protagonist's derisive attitude toward Quong and a rejection of Gresham's behavior. After Gresham has related his "adventure," including the conjecture that his erstwhile lover is dead, the narrator bluntly remarks, "And all for a moment's folly," to which Gresham, with a "sudden, startled expression in his eyes," responds, "Yes . . . all for a moment's folly. Good God, just think of it" (25).

Multiple possibilities exist for interpreting the narrator's comments and their implications. Certainly, the comment might simply express distaste for what David Martin Jones refers to as the "fear of racial degeneration and the dangers associated with miscegenation (81). Forman confirms this idea with his assertion that miscegenation "was despised by East and West alike because [it] signified the rejection of two powerful paradigms of purity" (91). Using this construal, the narrator would reject not Gresham's treatment of Quong but his liaison with a woman of mixed race. Indeed, upon learning that Gresham has fallen in love, the narrator immediately asks, "What colonist had ensnared the heart of the redoubtable Gresham, and without my knowledge?" (2). The narrator thus defaults to a "paradigm of purity" and cannot imagine that Gresham might desire a Chinese woman. This line of reasoning would also scrutinize the narrator's use of the word "folly" as it pertained not to the general situation of Gresham pursuing a married woman, but of him lusting after a racially mixed woman in particular. In this interpretation, the narrator might empathize somewhat with Gresham's attraction to the exotic woman yet reject his attempts to act on that desire. Nevertheless, the "folly" comment occurs immediately following Gresham's disclosure that Quong probably killed the woman, which suggests more empathy for the woman than it does for Gresham's boorish behavior.

The statement might also chastise Gresham for throwing away a prime business opportunity—and one that could hold national significance—for personal lust. As a reviewer in the *Atheneum* wrote, "It is not a volume to be recommended to those who cherish a patriotic belief in the nobility of the Englishman abroad" (868). The reviewer views Gresham (and other of Dawe's characters in *Yellow and White*) as a "mere hunter" and emphasizes his "profound selfishness" by noting that the woman (and other female characters in the collection) "pays the penalty . . . with her life" (868). Such an attitude would perhaps align the narrator's sympathies for the woman with his sense of duty as a colonial representative. Gresham relates his actions without any sense of remorse and would have ended his tale with his embarrassment of Quong had not the narrator inquired about the woman. Gresham's surprised reaction to the narrator's statement—his "sudden, startled expression"—suggests that Gresham had literally not thought about his behavior in the context of weak impulse control. The colonial's task is to milk the potential out of the underused land for the greater good, not to elevate personal desires above duty to country. The narrator expresses that "to be more correct" he should call Hong Kong Victoria, an offhand remark that might reveal his allegiance to his country and his disdain for Gresham's inability to behave properly.

A third possibility raises the idea that the narrator sympathizes not with his countryman but with the natives. In first referring to the town as Hong Kong rather than as Victoria, the narrator may reveal an attitude far more sympathetic to China than that of Gresham. Victoria is not the natural, native name of the island, and the narrator has not internalized it, preferring the phonetic approximation of the Cantonese. In this context, the narrator's statement about folly contains more of a rebuke. Not only has Gresham caused the woman to be punished, but he has also betrayed his "friend" Quong, a man who, even when Gresham is hurling his worst insults, is never cast as deceptive in business, domineering toward his wife, or cruel in general. Rather, an objective party such as the narrator can see—despite his initial affection for the "pronounced misogynist" Gresham with his "large heart and large limbs, his handsome, melancholy face" (2)—that his friend acted like a rogue and invited Quong's retribution. With a single sentence, the narrator destablilizes

Gresham's comfortable Orientalism and shocks him into recognizing that his loutish behavior affects actual people with complex emotions and needs. Gresham's self-enclosed world eschews the type of self-interrogation prompted by the narrator, but he at least temporarily shakes Gresham out of his self-absorption and forces him to consider the fate of his lover and, perhaps, Quong as well. In this view, the narrator's admonition serves as a corrective to the stereotyped attitudes represented by Gresham and perhaps shared by the reader. The O-Henry-like twist thus transforms Gresham from a heroic figure full of derring-do into a vulgar, petty creature with no self-control.

However one interprets the ending, "Yellow and White" ultimately exemplifies Said's ideas about the Orientalist's conflicting attitudes toward the East. With a complete lack of self-consciousness (save, perhaps, for the epiphany prompted by the narrator's remark), Gresham at once views China as an ugly, backward land full of vicious, conniving people that brings danger and as an inviting and enthralling space that suggests unimaginable treasures and pleasures. Said reconciles this binary by arguing that "the space of weaker or underdeveloped regions like the Orient was viewed as something inviting . . . interest, penetration, insemination—in short, colonization" (*Orientalism*, 219). Gresham, the colonist, pursues his "adventure" no matter what the cost in human lives and dignity precisely because he perceives of China and its denizens as already read projections of Orientalist discourse. Said points out that such discourse primarily reflects an "internal consistency of Orientalism . . . despite or beyond any correspondence, or lack thereof, with a 'real' Orient" (*Orientalism*, 5). In "Yellow and White," Gresham, the brutish, prurient, egotistic aggressor ever stands the aggrieved hero beset by barbarians yet ready to invigorate the fallow but promising land and thus "*confirm* the Orient in his readers' eyes" (*Orientalism*, 65).

NOTES

1. Forman remarks that one may find an "overwhelming preponderance" of hybrids in Orientalist narratives of China (50). He also notes that while such racial hybridity is often "erased under the sign of cultural hybridity," it is frequently punished as well (50). Quong, of course, attempts to punish Gresham for his interest in a married racial hybrid, and the fate of the woman herself—according to Gresham, at least—seems bleak.

2. All of the Chinese characters in the story speak a Pidgin English that transposes "l" and "r" sounds. In one significant passage, Quong explains to Gresham that, as a "China woman welly patricu'lar," his wife cannot communicate with him: "China woman no can pidgin to Englishyman" (4).

3. Forman again makes an excellent observation when he argues that "rampant masculinity . . . remains unchecked in the isolated environment of the outport and gives [such men] free rein to act in excess" (57). Gresham certainly provides a model of such "rampant masculinity." Dawe also ponders such an idea in the book's opening

poem, which contemplates interracial love and suggests that "Where, rid of convention, a fellow / Does everything right."

4. An alternative, and cynical, interpretation suggests that Quong—whatever the motivation—forced his wife to meet with Gresham so that Quong could attempt to kill his business associate. Gresham's second attempt at a rendezvous illustrates Quong's extensive investment and planning in punishing Gresham, and Yu argues that in "Yellow and White" Dawe "strongly suggests detestation on the part of the Chinese half-caste" (94). One could reconcile the evidence that the woman does commit adultery (see above) with Gresham with the detestation that Yu notes if the tryst were planned by Quong rather than by his wife. One might also explain the little girl's trembling fingers, given that she might know that Gresham is going to be attacked. In this scenario, the woman is victimized twice and castigated or killed for her compliance with Quong's wishes that she sleep with someone to whom she is not attracted. Of course, a weakness in this theory concerns the need for the woman to sleep with Gresham at all. Quong could have easily arranged for the child to tell Gresham to appear the next night, when he could have sprung his trap without forcing his wife to have sex with Gresham.

5. The woman's altered disposition is somewhat at odds with the fact that she "graciously granted" Gresham another assignation. Her "suddenly withdrawn" appearance denotes sadness or, perhaps, remorse, yet she allows Gresham to return (10). In any event, Gresham himself ultimately laughs at the prospect that the woman could have changed her attitude.

WORKS CITED

Chang, Elizabeth Hope. *Britain's Chinese Eye: Literature, Empire, and Aestheticism in Nineteenth-Century Britain*. Stanford UP, 2010.

Clifford, Nicholas. *"A truthful impression of the country": British and American Travel Writing in China, 1880–1949.* U of Michigan P, 2001.

Dawe, Carlton. *Yellow and White.* J. Lane, 1895.

Fiske, Shanyn. "Orientalism Reconsidered: China and the Chinese in Nineteenth-Century Literature and Victorian Studies." *Literature Compass*, vol. 8, no. 4, 2011, pp. 214–226.

Forman, Ross. *China and the Victorian Imagination: Empires Entwined.* Cambridge UP, 2013.

Jones, David Martin. *The Image of China in Western Social and Political Thought.* Palgrave, 2001.

Review of *Yellow and White,* by Carlton Dawe. *Atheneum*, 21 December 1895, p. 868.

Said, Edward. *Culture and Imperialism.* Vintage, 1993.

——. *Orientalism.* Vintage, 1978.

Sutherland, John. *The Stanford Companion to Victorian Fiction.* Stanford UP, 1989.

Thurin, Susan Schoenbauer. *Victorian Travelers and the Opening of China, 1842–1907.* Ohio UP, 1999.

Turner, Bryan S., ed. *Orientalism: Early Sources.* Vol. I. Routledge, 2006.

Vukovich, Daniel F. *China and Orientalism: Western Knowledge and the PRRC.* Routledge, 2012.

Yu, Ouyang. *Chinese in Australian Fiction, 1888–1988.* Cambria, 2008.

FIVE

"A familiar kinde of chastisement": Fasting in the Nineteenth-Century

Joseph Lennon

Before the hunger strike emerged as a modern practice, fasting had long drawn audiences and been the subject of debate. In 1841, London's *Literary Gazette* noted that "Mr. Bernard Cavanagh, the fasting-man, has issued an advertisement to say that he *'receives company'* at a shilling a head. Pretty entertainment is to be expected from acknowledged starvation!"[1] In European capitals from the 1880s to the 1920s, hunger artists fasted in glass boxes to entertain spectators, sometimes while diners milled around them. When they performed hunger amid plenty, they presented extreme hunger as curious and exotic as this extract about a 1926 Berlin restaurant suggests:

> The attraction of the restaurant Zurn Goldenen Hahn is the hunger artist, who in the middle of the hall under a sort of glass bell can be gazed at by visitors; a kind of human skeleton in dress-jacket, smoking cigarettes, with a glass of water in front of him on a little marble table. His achievements are announced on a blackboard: the hunger artist had not eaten for 28 days. Around him corpulent gentlemen and fashionably dressed ladies are consuming Wiener Schnitzel with fried potatoes. They are discussing whether the hunger record will be broken this time.[2]

The contrast of a fashionable "human skeleton" on display amidst corpulent diners "consuming" fried veal and potatoes is a peculiarly modern aesthetical complex of anonymity, hunger, and celebrity—with conspicuous abstention encouraging consumption. Such audiences, here at the tail end of the practice, gathered to witness hunger as a spectacle, hermeneutically (more than hermetically) sealed away from the consumption, where thinness could be a spur to gorge or a prick to one's conscience.

Fasting as a religious practice had also long held fascination across Europe. A divide existed in the representation of fasting in nineteenth-century English language texts. Fasting could promote spiritual humility and fasting could be done in the name of a cause or against a group. An article published in 1834 contrasts two enduring positions. The anonymous author compares an English religious tract on fasting with President James Madison's 1812 call for a public fast at the declaration of war against Britain. The first, written near London by a Baptist minister, Rev. James Hargreaves, argues that "Our fasting is vain if we cannot sincerely say to the Searcher of hearts, 'Forgive our trespasses, *as we forgive them that trespass against us.'* If we have bitter envyings and strife in our hearts, let us not glory in our fasting, nor lie against the truth."[3] Fasting here signifies the emptying of strife, done in the spirit of forgiveness. The second position points to another kind of fasting:

> The preacher that I heard on the day of the war fast took his text from Judges v. 23 "Curse ye Meroz, said the angel of the Lord: curse ye bitterly the inhabitants thereof, because they came not up to the help of the Lord, to the help of the Lord against the mighty. . . . He called on all the men, women and children to do their utmost to prosecute the war."

The author of the article, favors the first of the two "notions of fasting," and sees the second, which aligns fasting with cursing, as an aberration, but this second definition has a long history. Such fasting not only temporarily endures hunger, it also claims to wield a power, whether seen in terms of public opinion or divine favor depends on the fast.

Hunger bundles many associations and meanings, both as a noun and verb ranging from deprivation to desire, and its felt sense differs depending on the individual and context. Since the earliest Latin texts in the British Isles, hunger has had a spiritual dimension, and both Old English and Old Irish contain references to spiritual hungers as well as fasting as a power. Among these meanings hunger has also generally connoted a lacking, emptiness, weakness, or torpidity on the part of the hungering person. In contrast to this sense, the word in later times also suggested a mobilizing agency associated with mass rebellions—of workers, peasants, slaves, soldiers, or natives. Maud Ellmann in *The Hunger Artists: Starving, Writing, and Imprisonment* (1993) comments on this aspect of hunger's meaning: "in a unified collective, like a regiment of soldiers, or the workers in a factory . . . the experience of hunger sheds its intonations of submission and clarifies itself as solidarity or insurrection" (6). Ellmann's work on hunger has inspired a good deal of research across a range of disciplines on twentieth-century representations of anorexia nervosa, hunger, and fasting. In considering the history of self-willed hunger, she also considers the hunger strikes of nationalists in Ireland and

India, as well as those of the women's suffrage movement, as a kind of "individuals starving in the name of a collective." She distinguished these fasts, however, from other "ascetic forms of self-starvation, which extend from the medieval saints to modern slimmers" (7), but, as she also demonstrates, continuities exist between fasting and twentieth-century hunger striking. Both blend persistence and denial into a kind of performance of strength and endurance, whether as prayer, petition, plea, or protest. Both evoke the connotative freight of hunger—the Old English word *fæst* has a Germanic root and signifies the sense of fastening oneself solidly to a pledge. Ironically, the weakened, fasting body exhibits (and connotes in English) that kind of solid determination.

This chapter delineates and examines representations of fasting in a group of texts, primarily focused on fasting in Ireland, published in the second half of the nineteenth century, which mostly focus on ancient, medieval, and early modern fasts. The power of this kind of renunciation is often suggested in the commentaries of these medieval texts, however without its modern application as an appeal to public opinion in the case of the hunger strike. Nevertheless, in the representations of fasting as a transitive action, that is, fasting on, against, or for something, we see its nascent potential. In Ireland, fasting and hunger have had a particular history. Fasting for religious, ethical, or legal reasons had existed long before written records, and more obviously, memories of famine shaded both Irish history and conceptions of Irishness. By the twentieth-century, hunger and fasting remained familiar and less exotic in Ireland where "living skeletons" connoted famine and emigration more than spectacle or performance. Following the Irish Famine of 1845–1850, ancient and medieval Irish fasting became a topic of discussion although usually without reference to that catastrophe in which more than one million people died and between one and two million emigrated. Texts such as William Maunsell Hennessy's translation of *Aislinge Meic Conglinne* (1873), Whitely Stokes's edition of *The Tripartite Life of St. Patrick* (1887), and Rev. Evelyn Baring-Gould's address on Celtic Saints (1900) all attempt to reconcile perceived contradictory aspects of fasting, in part by distancing fasting as an ancient practice.

These texts and others were indebted to a series of publications of medieval Irish legal texts, translated and published over four decades as the *Ancient Laws of Ireland* (1865–1901). In a sense these texts were part of the publishing boom of the nineteenth century, particularly in the second half, when editors, translators, scholars, and publishers made medieval and ancient texts available to the reading public for the first time. Periodicals such as *Fraser's Magazine* and *Dublin University Review* brought out oft-cited texts for the first time, as well as newly rediscovered texts. Often the editorial apparatuses of these texts engaged in the cultural politics of the day, and authorities from long ago were pressed again into new service. Source criticism helped diminish the abuses by historians, antiquarians, and editors; nevertheless, publishers could not control how the texts were read. The related topics of fasting and hunger in the British Isles, as with so many other cultural practices, reappeared as modern curiosities with enduring messages.

Outside observers of Ireland had long noted how fasting was one distinguishing trait of Gaelic culture. Edmund Campion's 1571 *A Historie of Ireland* (republished in 1809 and cited often afterward) contrasts the virtuous Irish in the first paragraph of his section, "Disposition of the People," with their immoral counterparts:

> the lewder sort both Clarkes and Laymen, are sensuall and loose to leachery above measure. The same being vertuously bred up or reformed, are such mirrors of holinesse and austeritie, that other Nations retaine but a shewe or shadow of devotion in comparison of them. As for abstinence and fasting which these dayes make so dangerous, this is to them a familiar kinde of chastisement. (19)

Fasting—dangerous at the time likely because of food shortages but also perhaps because of hunger's mobilizing connotation—primarily demonstrates virtue here and works as a type of self-willed, God-directed, chastisement that brings an individual to virtue.

Notably, both chasten and chaste stem from *castus*: moral purity. A related Latin word for abstinence and fasting, *castimonium*, or the more common plural form, *castimonia*, illustrates the close connection conceived in religious texts between virtue and hunger, restraint and deliverance. A more common Latin noun for fasting, suggests a kind of boundless hunger, emptiness, or esurience—*ieiunium* or *jaiunium* (or *ieiunus* as an adjective) from which English also derives words that both carry connotations of emptiness: jejune and jejunum (the part of the small intestine that connects the duodenum and the ileum, frequently empty during autopsies because peristaltic motion continues after death). Although *castimonia* suggests moral restraint and fasting, both types of fasting were used to signify religious fasting, one suggesting deprivation and humility, the other a moral force. In Campion, Irish abstinence and fasting, as *castimonia*, counter the sensual and loose sexuality of the less devout Irishry. Hunger functions against sensual desire here, not as in later modernist texts where hunger frequently signifies, rather than chastises, desire. Moreover, if hunger often suggests desire for the modern, hunger for the medieval and early modern often suggested the emptying of earthly desire.

In medieval Irish-language texts, feasting, famine, and fasting were also closely bound. Perhaps the most representative text of its kind, *Aislinge Meic Conglinne*, focuses on the feasting-famine-fasting dynamic and its moral dimensions of hospitality/gluttony, punishment/corruption, and austerity/cursing. In the late eleventh- or early twelfth-century text, a king of Munster, Cathal mac Finguinne, has ingested a demon of gluttony, which causes him to devour enormous quantities of food. When we first hear of him, he is rapidly and perilously depleting his kingdom's food and hospitality, moving the kingdom toward famine. A low-ranking poet-satirist, Anér Mac Conglinne, comes from distant parts and ends up saving the king. On his way he relays his vision of a place made of food (a Land of Cockayne) where "your hunger will disappear and your tongue will tingle."[4] The first version of the text translated and printed in English was written by William Maunsell Hennessy, a native-speaking Irish language scholar, and printed in *Fraser's Magazine* in 1873. In his version of the text, he translates the legal practice of medieval Irish fasting, *troscud*, as "a practice that seems to have obtained among the ancient Irish, of fasting *against* a person from whom something was sought to be extorted."[5] This (here misunderstood) form of ritualized fasting both signified the justness of a suit and forced the defending party to respond. Hennessy recognizes the power of this kind of fasting, which he calls extortion, but clearly does not endorse it. This Irish verb that signifies this type of fasting (*troscud*) is distinct in Middle and Old Irish from another kind of fasting, *óine*, which is derived from the Latin, *ieiunium*, described previously, *óine* signifying a spiritual connection to God, and that serves as the root of the fast days, Wednesday and Friday, in the Irish language. *Troscud* (similar to the medieval Irish word for lepers *troscu*, associated with Jesus at the time), suggested both a legal practice and a moral, ethical imperative.

In 1892, Kuno Meyer published another fuller and more authoritative version of *Aislinge Meic Conglinne*, drawn from two distinct redactions; notably the translation is dedicated to Whitely Stokes, another leading scholar of medieval Irish works and a colonial legal scholar. In both late-nineteenth-century versions of this parody of Land of Cockayne and religious vision stories, excessive hunger and gluttony are linked to sin, particularly original sin—in this context, Eve and Adam broke a fast (or pledge) when they ate the fruit of the Tree of Knowledge, forbidden by God. Significantly, in the text, fasting, followed by a show of feasting, ultimately became the method Mac Conglinne uses to force the demon of gluttony to leap from Cathal Mac Finguinne's gullet.[6] Fasting and feasting become the moral antipodes with which to pinch the devil. At variance to this text and Campion's which both suggest the moral efficacy of fasting, other texts on Irish hunger convey the destructive power of hunger and famine.

Written not long after Campion's text, another sixteenth-century British text, this one only first published in the late nineteenth century, displays the punishing, brutal side of hunger in Ireland. In a one-page document addressed to Queen Elizabeth, now associated with but no longer attributed to Edmund Spenser (whose 1596 *A View of the Present State of Ireland* is a vicious example of anti-Irish vituperative), a "Briefe Note of Ireland" conveys another genus of sentiment about Irish hunger in a military recommendation. In 1882 Alexander Grosart first published this note in the *Complete Works in Verse and Prose of Edmund Spenser*, vol. 1. Since that time, readers have read the words as a kind of foreshadowing of Ireland's worst famine, that of *An Gorta Mór* of the mid-nineteenth century, even though famines had wracked Ireland for centuries. The note has now been attributed to the little-known English diplomat, Dudley Carleton. The most quoted line of the text has been: "Great force must be the instrument but famine must be the meane for till Ireland be famished it can not be subdued."[7] Famine and hunger would subdue the Irish, "be the meane" of lowering them into subjection. Hunger seemed fit punishment for Campion's chastising Irish fasters. Moreover, as a late nineteenth-century text, it seemed to offer evidence of a history of malign English designs on Irish hunger. Hunger had already accumulated a complex bundle of connotation by the nineteenth century, one that reflected broad cultural divides in the British Isles.

Hunger's associations, whether as subduer, extorter, or chastiser, developed further associations during British and French Enlightenment culture, when its instinctual animal was asserted, contrasting hunger's pull with the beneficence of reason, and diminishing hunger's associations with virtue. For instance in Adam Smith's *The Theory of Moral Sentiments* (1759), hunger is treated as an "original and immediate instinct" that prompts us "without any consideration of their tendency to [the] beneficent ends" of the "great Director of nature." Smith later groups hunger with thirst, pleasure, and pain, all of which "may be considered as lessons delivered by the voice of Nature herself," lessons resembling the ones children are taught: "Their principal object is to teach [one] how to keep out of harm's way."[8] From the rationalist's point of view, not eating goes against reason because it put oneself into harms way; moreover it put one out of dialogue with the great Director of nature.

Perhaps the most influential promoter of mechanistic sciences and the mind–body duality, René Descartes, maintained a special provision for hunger, pain, and thirst in his *Meditations*. In *Meditations on First Philosophy*, published in Latin in 1641 — and first published in an English translation by the intuitionist philosopher John Veitch in 1852 — Descartes comments on how the mind and body remain conjoined through pain, hunger, and thirst:

> There is nothing which that nature teaches me more expressly [or more sensibly] than that I have a body which is ill affected when I feel pain, and stands in need of food and drink when I experience the sensations of hunger and thirst, etc. And therefore I ought not to doubt but that there is some truth in these informations.
> Nature likewise teaches me by these sensations of pain, hunger, thirst, etc., that I am not only lodged in my body as a pilot in a vessel, but that I am besides so intimately conjoined, and as it were intermixed with it, that my mind and body compose a certain unity. For if this were not

the case, I should not feel pain when my body is hurt, seeing I am merely a thinking thing, but should perceive the wound by the understanding alone, just as a pilot perceives by sight when any part of his vessel is damaged; and when my body has need of food or drink, I should have a clear knowledge of this, and not be made aware of it by the confused sensations of hunger and thirst: for, in truth, all these sensations of hunger, thirst, pain, etc. are nothing more than certain confused modes of thinking, arising from the union and apparent fusion of mind and body. [Brackets in original][9]

For Descartes, hunger is a confused sensation in opposition to explicit understandings; fasting, by extension, initiates confusion, not a show of determination or a union with the divine. Although Descartes privileges the thinking mind in this union, he positions hunger as a kind of body thinking, one that is inherently not trustworthy.[10] Later he notes that the "the nature of man, in so far as it is composed of mind and body, cannot but be sometimes fallacious" (87).[11] Instead of clarifying thought and purpose, hunger, thirst, and pain, all bewilder. Here the teachings of nature, and hunger in particular, did not bring one closer to God's truth, rather they misled. For the rationalist, hunger exists to be dispatched.

Another group of texts published in the nineteenth century point to a more particular interest in the "ancient" practice of fasting of medieval and early modern culture. In contrast to the Enlightenment view, fasting was both a virtuous form of supplication and a route to divine grace. In Ireland, the two words for fasting, *troscud* and *óine*, suggest that one form existed before the introduction of Christianity. *Troscud*, as is widely acknowledged, long existed as a social and legal practice, as part of Early Irish or Brehon Law. The early Irish legal code, legendarily brought into accord with Christianity by St. Patrick in the fifth century, had existed before writing in Ireland, but with the introduction of Christianity, and thereby Latin, it was soon codified into a civil law. To make certain suits valid, a plaintiff would be required to fast at the threshold of the defendant's home from dawn to dusk—notably fasting was only necessary when the defendant was of equally rank or of higher social status.[12] In other words, fasting was not used against those with less power but could be used against the powerful in society, even kings. For three days, the defendant was required to offer food, and the plaintiff was required to abstain from accepting it.[13] The practice has been detailed by contemporary scholars and is referenced by many more.[14] Moreover, its later influence on Irish nationalist hunger strikes, even if often ahistorical, was enormous.

Brehon law existed well into the early modern period in Ireland and had application in the least Anglicized areas until as late as the sixteenth century when Queen Elizabeth's forces defeated Gaelic leaders. By 1612, James I had established English common law throughout Ireland, and the English assize circuit system began to hold courts across Ireland, eliminating what institutional aspects had remained of Brehon law. References and allusions to fasting as a legal practice as well as the links between hunger and ethics, however, endured. In the decade that followed the famine, and the near eradication of the Irish language, Irish scholars began to translate and comment with greater focus upon Irish-language texts, long unexamined outside of antiquarian and philological circles. Dozens of legends, histories, and hagiographies appeared, in part the result of official British government support of scholarship. In 1852 the government, responding to a proposal by Irish scholars, appointed the Commission for Publication of Ancient Irish Laws, which included established scholars such as George Petrie and James Henthorn Todd. The commission hired editors who, in turn, hired two renowned Irish language scholars, John O'Donovan and Eugene O'Curry to organize, transcribe, translate, and publish the myriad Irish medieval law manuscripts, collectively known as *Senchas Már* (Great Tradition). O'Curry and O'Donovan did not live to see the full publication of the *Ancient Laws of Ireland* (1865–1901), and four other editors built on their work and saw the project through to publication: William Nielson Hancock, Thaddeus O'Mahony, Alexander Richey, and Robert Atkinson.[15] The translations and commentary appeared in several volumes as *The Ancient Laws of Ireland* (1865–1901) and had great influence on Irish intellectual circles, including Whitely Stokes, Lady Speranza Wilde, and W. B. Yeats, whose *The King's Threshold* reimagined medieval fasting as an ethical protest.[16]

The publication of the first volume in 1865 contained dozens of references to fasting as part of the law of distress, in which debts or property is recovered. The main section on fasting describes how fasting must accompany the suits of members of the large noble class, who included *filid* (or early Irish poet, historian, genealogist) to small landowners to scholars and kings. Ritualized fasting forced Gaels to act in accord with law or established practice, and at times ethical and divine causes, as suggested by many hagiographies, particularly *The Tripartite Life of Patrick*. As these texts suggest, if a fast was ignored, the full force of condemnation of the Brehons could apply, which ranged from seizing titles and property to taking away legal status and banishment. The defendant who was fasted upon had to follow another set of rules: "If food be not offered to him he is entitled to double the food and double the debt."[17] The plaintiff's fast or *troscud* existed in part as a sign of the commitment of the suit, in effect making the plaintiff's suit de jure regardless of its eventual outcome. In a sense fasting and hunger demonstrated the plaintiff's commitment and, when described in legends and hagiographies, the divine justness of the suit.

A host of writers, cultural nationalists, and scholars referenced and represented the laws and legends in poems, plays, and books about Ireland. The Brehon laws, in particular, were cited in dozens of biographies of Saint Patrick that appeared in Ireland and around the world in the

Irish diaspora—particularly in Britain, the United States, and Australia—as a way of explaining Patrick's supernatural fasting. Although many writers, including Samuel Ferguson, Aubrey de Vere, James Henthorn Todd, William Hennessy, and Mary Cusack (the "nun of Kenmare") all portray St. Patrick's fasting as both extraordinary and belonging to the medieval laws in their works on Patrick, many other nineteenth-century biographies entirely avoid the topic.[18] Fasting was a side issue to most of the debates about St. Patrick at the time, who was claimed for both the Anglican and Catholic traditions in part because of his identity as a Briton as explained in the only document given historical credence, Patrick's autobiographical *Confessio*. Debates about his birthplace continued throughout the first much of the nineteenth century, despite the fact that his *Confessio* clearly places his birth in northwest England. Texts that avoided discussing his fasting, however, tended to argue for inclusion of St. Patrick in the Anglican tradition; unsurprisingly, those who highlighted his fasting tended to belong to (or sympathize with) the Catholic tradition. Differing opinions on the nature of Irish medieval fasting in this period reveal more than political sympathies, however. English scholars like Henry Maine emphasized how fasting was a premodern practice beholden to superstition and ancient religion; Irish writers and cultural nationalists such as James Kerr and Laurence Ginnell (later an Irish M. P.), as well as W. B. Yeats, saw it as an ancient ethically based practice, which depended on commitment and a unified culture, could potentially be revived, at least in representation. Indeed, Yeats later claimed his play was a precursor to the modern hunger strike,[19] as many scholars have explored.[20]

Henry Maine, the Law Member of the Council of Governor-General of India until 1869, argued how fasting could not function in modern times like the Roman-based British law could. Significantly, both he and Whitely Stokes—the translator and editor of the most authoritative and exhaustive edition of *The Tripartite Life of St. Patrick* (1887)[21] —worked in Calcutta to rewrite and modernize Indian law.[22] The crossover of scholarship and legal practice in colonial law is evident also in Stokes's *Tripartite Life*, which cites Maine's work on Irish and Indian law in reference to Brehon/Brahmin fasting traditions.[23] In *Ancient Law*, Maine dismissed fasting as a legal protest, treating it as an ineffective and pre-modern. Actions such as fasting only worked in lieu of modern legal sanctions, forms of distraint, and methods of compulsion such as that of another nineteenth-century British innovation: the modern prison. Stokes finds much more complexity in Irish law than Maine, however, and he analyzes St. Patrick's fasting, treating it as a relic of an earlier age but one loaded with powerful associations for the community.

Public fasting had another distinct history in social and religious contexts throughout in the British Isles (and North America), where public fasts were instituted to "dramatiz[e] social power" (to borrow Crawford

Gribben's phrase about Cromwellian fasting in Ireland).[24] Public fast days, where the public was asked to refrain from food in addition to work, alcohol, and festivities, were declared by leaders in a top-down fashion in Great Britain, Ireland, and the United States, among other countries, across the Christian religious spectrum whether Catholic, Anglican, Presbyterian, Quaker, or Puritan. But as Patrick Collinson reports in *The Elizabethan Puritan Movement* (1967) even by the sixteenth century, Protestant fasting was not as frequent as Catholic fasting, but it certainly suggested human dalliance with divine powers:

> One of the commonest complaints of catholic controversialists was that protestants did not fast. The protestants retorted that on the contrary they alone fasted in the spirit of the New Testament by joining fasting to prayer and the preaching of the word in public assemblies, and by proclaiming a fast only for a particular purpose. . . . Fasting in this sense was the practice in all the reformed churches, . . . from the early years of Elizabeth occasional fasts were called for by episcopal injunction; and even by royal command, on such occasions as unseasonable weather, and the plague brought back from Le Havre by the English expeditionary force in 1563. . . . In the early 'seventies fasting was probably an occasional function of the association for prophesying, the ministers of Ashby-de-la-Zouch [in central England] speaking of "public praying, fasting and prophecy." (214–15)

By the eighteenth century most public fast days had fallen away, however, if the associations with prophecy, religion, and penitence continued and, at times, even overshadowed other connotations. In this sense, fasting as prophesy may have retained a sense of occult magic in Protestant mystical circles. But clearly the nineteenth-century public fasts had also become more closely associated with Roman Catholicism, the dominant religion of Ireland, and was critiqued by Protestants as both not being vigorous enough (that is, only excluding meat) and for going too far.[25]

Individual extended fasts also had appeared for centuries, and were particularly associated with women. In the nineteenth century, they began to suggest either mental problems, fraud, or religiosity;[26] religious fasting was often seen as a kind of perversion of the body, inflicted in the name of a misguided notion of devotion.[27] In the first decade of the nineteenth century a celebrated religious faster was debunked by medical doctors. Ann Moore of Tutbury purported to live on water and air and was viewed "with a sort of religious awe" (according to Alexander Henderson, M.D.) but she was shown to be a hoax who hid her bodily evacuations and secretly ate.[28] Alexander Henderson, who visited Ann Moore, noted that her fasting "was a mere fabrication, which she had contrived with a view to excite wonder and compassion."[29] In the fine history, *From Fasting Saints to Anorexic Girls: The History of Self-Starvation* (1994), Walter Vandereycken and Ron Van Deth discuss the transition from fasting as religion to fasting as performance, arguing that as post-Enlightenment fasting drew more skeptics than believers, spectators grew curious in both witnessing and debunking the dubious feat: "With the decline of the miraculous maidens as a result of their medicalization, self-inflicted starvation as a spectacle did not completely disappear."[30] Fasting and emaciation began to be included in freak shows, where the public could view "living skeletons": "The fast of the former was a wonder of God, the latter's an extraordinary achievement" (76). Franz Kafka's famous short story, "The Hunger Artist" (1922), alternately translated as the "fasting artist" or "starvation artist,"[31] fictionalized the last hey-days of these performers with a protagonist who went on his long fasts not for any religious reason but because he saw fasting as an art. The hunger artist is dismayed that the public doubted the veracity of his fasts. The story concludes with the hunger artist's apologetic admission as he dies that he could fast so well because he never found a food he liked. In the end, he had become a great faster beating all the records, but unlike other great fasters, Kafka's hunger artist's fast—and death—goes unnoticed. Alone, he dies, lacking an audience, divine or human.

For Kafka, the hunger artist had become his own spectator, and his fast endured without social purpose and audience. Twenty-five years previously, however, in the hey-day of professional fasting, the best fasters toured Europe and America, making a handsome living by performing starvation. As Vandereycken and Van Deth note: Professional fasters followed the achievement of Henry Tanner, a fifty-year-old man "who undertook a fast for forty days in the Clarendon Hall in New York City in 1880. . . . They all sought publicity with their fasting and tried to exploit the commercial possibilities, created by the fascination of the crowd for long fasts" (84–85). Fasting had grown from Mr. Bernard Cavanagh's strange attraction in 1841 to become a modern curiosity, holding the interest of fin-de-siècle masses who sought to find the trick to the hunger artist's fast. Moreover, by the turn of the century in Great Britain, fasting as an ancient practice had become an intellectual curiosity within more elite and intellectual circles, where its contrasts with modernity were even more evident.

On May 23, 1899, at the outset of their spring meeting, the Royal Institution of Cornwall sent a wireless telegram to their patron, Queen Victoria, to congratulate her on the eve of her eightieth birthday. The immediacy and newness of the technology contrasted pointedly with the antiquarian topic of the president's address that day—"Celtic Saints." Only two months previously, on March 27, Guglielmo Marconi had sent a wireless telegraph across the English Channel from Wimereux France to South Foreland Lighthouse atop the Cliffs of Dover, impressing the world with the long-range capabilities of this new technology. The investigations of the RIC's president, Reverend Sabine Baring-Gould spanned another great distance, into the past and across an ideological chasm from modernity to Celtic antiquity. Baring-Gould, best known for writing the lyrics for "Onward Christian Soldier" (1865) spoke on "Celtic Saints" to the gathering of sixty-three members, including the Mayor of Truro, the Chief Constable of Cornwall, members of Parliament, and the local gentry. The *Journal* of the RIC printed his address, along with motions and remarks, the following year in its fourteenth volume (1900). Baring-Gould began by delivering a standard truism for Celticists of the day: "The organisation—political and social, and ecclesiastical,—of the Celt seems to have been much the same everywhere" (11). The lost Celtic culture was to be imagined as not only unified but also homogenized— neither of which seems to have been actually the case.[32] Through an examination of medieval Irish, Welsh, and Breton texts, he aimed to "reconstruct the political, social, and ecclesiastical life of the Cornu-British before they were subdued." For Baring-Gould, and doubtless many in his audience, the pre-conquered British Celts presented an unspoiled, premodern culture in silhouette, against which they could mark the glowing achievements of the present day. For Baring-Gould fasting signified a curious ancient practice, one that certainly went against reason.

Although Baring-Gould does not comment on his rationale for his study of Celtic Saints, his lecture seems in line of his larger body of work on curiosities. His career wove together arguments based on fantasy, folklore, fiction, and fact. His first book on folklore, *The Book of Were-Wolves, Being an Account of a Terrible Superstition* (1865), both debunked the existence of werewolves and showed the story's enduring (if unholy) interest. He moved from there to explore *Curious Myths of the Middle Ages* (1866) and Catholic saints in his sixteen-volume *Lives of the Saints* (1872 and 1877). Afterward, he wrote fiction and returned to study the folk songs, ghost stories, and enduring signs of Celtic antiquity, along with oddities and anecdotes, in Cornwall. His last book was called *Cornish Characters and Strange Events* (1909) and portrayed notable individuals (more than seventy men, six women, and several families) and their adventures; it begins: "Cornwall, peopled mainly by Celts, with an infusion of English blood, stands and has always stood apart from the rest of England."[33] The Celt was not a denigrating ancestry, rather an amusing one that distinguished the modern Anglo-Saxon-Celtic amalgam, which Matthew Arnold had famously praised in his lectures as the chair of poetry at Oxford.[34]

Directly after Baring-Gould's address, Sir Edward Durning-Lawrence, a member of Parliament, pointed to same dichotomy that modern fasting spurred—modern bounty versus premodern hunger. At the early dawn of the twentieth century in Great Britain, hunger was generally imagined to be exotic—that is, as a temporally or spatially distant problem—further away in time (because unreachable) than even distant colonized lands where famines recurred. Durning-Lawrence seconded a motion of thanks for the president's lecture and noted that "the old days were not altogether happy times, [we] must remember the people lived in the midst of great barbarism" (46). He said that he had attempted to "study ancient literature, and tried most to learn from what writers did not tell him —to read between the lines," but he had not succeeded. What he did discern, however, was a dichotomy that pitted hunger and barbarism against modern education and mechanical technology. The *Journal's* editor summarized his remarks as such:

> This was the age of mechanical knowledge, the age in which, for the first time in the history of humanity, man had powers of nature in his hand, so that almost daily some new power was given to man and turned to his service. To-day it was wireless telegraphy; what it would be to-morrow it was almost impossible to say. This was the result of education and the training of thought.
>
> Anyone who wandered through the streets of great cities would see scarcely a child who looked starved, and so, while man was getting more education, the very poorest were not being crushed down. In the ancient days the serf was ground still lower to enable men to carry on their work. It might in those days have been necessary, for the only slave was the living slave, but now they had the dead slave of a mechanical power. They now ground this slave and relieved men from the toil. (47)

To relieve hunger, humanity took control of nature's power. No longer, Durning-Lawrence's remarks suggested, would populations be subject to climate issues, growing cycles, and animal labor. His remarks could have illustrated Bruno LaTour's argument in *We Were Never Modern* (1993), which suggests that modernity has been ideology more than reality, that climate and nature have never really been in our hands, that such beliefs were more ideology than reality.

Durning-Lawrence's comments also suggest that hunger and starvation existed far away. Because it stretched beyond the origins of written texts in Britain, it exceeded both memory and history, if it still resonated for some with memories of hunger and famine across the British Empire. Generally, however, either suspicion or an intransigent backwardness accompanied the hungry; criticism could analyze the failings of modern states or colonial administrations as well as blame the distant culture itself. In Durning-Lawrence's formulation, starving children emblemized a time of "great barbarism," not the time of successful modern, urbanized societies. As James Vernon and others have suggested, when and where hunger persisted in the world in the British Empire, it challenged the success its modernity. Hunger when not fleeting, belonged to a more primitive, slavish, and animal past, which only reached the present where modernity had not yet succeeded.[35]

When Baring-Gould turned to the premodern Gaelic practice of fasting to prove a suit's legitimacy, he informed his audience, that the Celts used fasting for "levying a distress" or for exacting a fine from a "wrong-doer" (25), and he typified fasting, along with strange practices such as building dolmens, as something that "completely . . . affected the minds of the early Celtic Christians" (29). Never mind the fact that the dolmens greatly predated Christianity (and Celtic influence) in Ireland, Baring-Gould both dismissed the potential of a fast's ethical and affective suit and grouped all types of fasting together. His dismissal of it is a rationalist one which collapses the distinction between legal and religious fasting, suggesting that fasting was a "legal notion of transacting business with the Almighty" (29). Religious fasting and ethical, legal fasting certainly color one another in Irish hagiographies, such as *The Tripartite Life of Patrick*, but on close inspection, even these medieval texts make clear distinctions between these forms, despite the fact that both *óine* and *troscud* were translated as fast.

Penitence and cursing, two functions of medieval Irish fasting, have distinct passages in the hagiography, which also found full publication in English, albeit gradually, in the late nineteenth century. In 1877 William Maunsell Hennessy, in addition to rediscovering *Aislinge Meic Conglinne*, published a source text for the *Vita Tripartita* in English for the first time, translating it as *The Tripartite Life of St. Patrick* and including it as an appendix to a biography of three Irish saints by Mary Cusack: *The Trias Thaumaturga; or, Three Wonder-Working Saints of Ireland, St. Patrick, St. Bridget, and St. Columba. With "The Tripartite Life of Saint Patrick" Translated from the Irish of Saint Evin by William M. Hennessy*. As Kuno Meyer had done with Hennessy's *Aislinge*, Whitely Stokes then built on Hennessy's translation of *The Tripartite Life* and published a more complete and influential scholarly edition a decade later in 1887. The original medieval text, *Vita Tripartita*, seems to have first been written by clerics, borrowing from oral sources, and then copied and recopied over the centuries. It was composed in both Latin and Irish, and its framework is a "monastic *triduum* of readings in preparation for the saint's feast day," meant to be recited (or read) over the three days of the annual festivities.[36] Scholars agree that it was composed sometime in the ninth century by hagiographers, centuries after Patrick's death, and is a hagiography rather than a history. As Máire Johnson notes, "In such texts, early elements mingle with accretions and alterations from throughout the medieval period, mirroring, in a sense, the hagiographical genre's development."[37] The text survives in several seventeenth-century copies of older lost manuscripts dating back to the ninth century called *Vita Tripartita*—tripartite also because it came from three sources, covered the three days of readings, and also perhaps because triads figure prominently in Patrick's stories, emphasizing the Catholic trinity, and the triads of Gaelic culture.

The publication helped shift the conversation at the time around St. Patrick away from his English or Irish (or French) origins—and therefore Anglican or Catholic affiliations—and deepened a discussion on fasting traditions in Ireland. Patrick fasted to compel conversions, right injustices, and punish sinners, and in the text his fasting and hunger signaled his both a link to divine strength and a tradition of legal fasting, usually distinctly portrayed, though not always. Notably, the text mostly avoids mention of his starving and weakened body, except in reprinting the *Confessio*. As with other vengeful and holy saints in Ireland, Brigit, Columba, Ciarán, and Énda, Patrick used hunger in his fasts to wield God's power, similar to how he used cursing.[38] The hagiographers who wrote about Patrick, as Máire Johnson argues in "'Vengeance is Mine': Saintly Retribution in Medieval Ireland" (2010), textually melded Ireland's social and legal fabric with Christian tradition through his miraculous and vengeful fasts. To medieval audiences, his *troscud* or fasting as a legal maneuver signaled that he participated within the early Irish Gaelic tradition. In other words, he was not an outsider entirely rewriting legal code to fit with an imperial code, rather he was only adjusting legal tradition to accord Christian and canonical law. He is depicted as God's instrument, and he uses fasting, along with curses and blessings, to work wonders across Ireland.

The most well-known instance of Patrick's religious fasting is included in *The Tripartitie Life*, but it is from an earlier text. It is the earliest and most historically accurate version of Patrick's story, the *Confessio,* or the *Confession of Saint Patrick* (also included in Stokes's *Tripartite Life*). A copy of Patrick's Latin letter is found in the Book of Armagh, compiled in the ninth century, and most authorities accept its validity as being originally written sometime before his death in 461. The Latin letter was first printed by James Ware in 1656, and the first edition in English appeared in 1868 as an appendix to a polemical sectarian work on the saint.[39] An overview of the letter written to his religious superiors helps show the significance of fasting for his faith. He opens by giving us his name, Patricius (Pater Civilius), meaning father of the people, son of Calpornius. He was from Banna Venta Berniae, near the present-day city of Carlisle in northwestern England. The letter shows us Patrick as a boy living with his family at the edge of Roman England in the waning days of the Roman Empire. He belonged to a noted Christian family; his grandfather had been a priest, and his father was a deacon. But he was not particularly religious at that point in his life. Notably, they lived near the western coast of the land, which would have been near the great Hadrian's wall that stretched for 117 kilometers to the eastern sea. The Roman Emperor Hadrian had ordered the wall built in 122 A.D. as a protection from the Scots and Picts. It had long prevented raiding parties from descending from the Scottish lands in the north. This wall, both symbol and boundary of the empire, had been built nearly three centuries before and stood 6 meters wide and 3 1/2 meters tall. An enormous ditch fronted it and fortifications dotted it. Nevertheless, the border remained dangerous in the declining days of empire, and Irish and Scottish marauders could approach by sea.

When Patrick was sixteen, pirates entered their cottage and seized him. He and many others were carried across the sea to Ireland where they were kept as slaves. His captors were not Christian, spoke another language, and cared little for his well-being; he was only wanted for work. For six years, he tended sheep in the mountains and woods and lived outdoors, away from the comforts he had known. After some time, he reports that he began to pray in earnest the prayers he had learned as a child and began to distrust the empires of men and to seek out an eternal one. He learned to fast, going without food partly from deprivation, partly as a spiritual practice. One night, six years after his abduction, he heard a voice in his sleep: "You have fasted well. And, fasting, you will soon go to your country."[40] Then soon after the voice spoke again: "Behold, your ship is ready." The young man, now twenty-two followed this new authority. He left his master's flock and walked two hundred miles to the coast, where he found a ship willing to take him back over the sea. When he arrived home, he was welcomed with open arms, and they begged him to remain there forever. Patrick joined a religious order on his return and eventually became a bishop. Years later, he followed another dream and returned to Ireland to convert the Irish to Christianity.

In the *Confessio* the voice prompting his liberation from slavery, notably, first praises his fasting. Fasting functions both as an illustration of his suffering as well as the source for his spiritual calling and strength; it emblemizes his triumph over his suffering and his symbolic release from slavery. Throughout *The Tripartite Life* text, Patrick's fasting has two dimensions: a spiritual fasting that connects him to God and a forceful practice of punishing sinners that connotes legal fasting. Indeed, Patrick's fasting appears and reappears many times in the stories of his life. Following the publication of the *Confessio* and the *Tripartite Life*, more biographies of Patrick came into print in the second half of the nineteenth century. Many biographies blend the legendary tales with details from the *Confessio* and include stories from the more apocryphal body of writings including Patrick's banishment of snakes from Ireland, his use of the shamrock, and the most well-known instance of Patrick's fasting, his forty days without food and drink on Mount or Croagh Aigle, now Croagh Patrick.

In *The Tripartite Life* Patrick ascends the mountain and begins his fast. After some time, God tries to force Patrick to leave the mountain, sending a flock of black birds, often foreshadowing death in Irish legend, to harass him. He refuses to go and refrains from eating, however, until his prayers are met by God. Although *troscud* is used several times elsewhere in the text to describe Patrick's fasts against wrongdoers, words with the Latin root of *ieiunium* are generally used to describe Patrick's various spiritual fasts, most notably in the Book of Armagh, written mostly in Latin with some Irish. The Irish version of the story on Mount Aigle from the *Lebar Brece* only states that Patrick went to stay there without food and without drink for forty days and forty nights, and intriguingly, avoids using either *troscud* or *óine*.[41] Lisa Bitel highlights that this particular story was more spiritual than legal:

> the scene was no secular corruption of a spiritual fast by the tradition of *troscud*, as some historians have claimed. The hagiographer placed Pátraic's fast securely in a spiritual context. The writer compared the saint to Moses and assumed that a forty-day fast endowed Pátraic with extraordinary grace. Like all fasting, this *troscud* brought Patraic enhanced spiritual status in the eyes of his Patron, God.[42]

Despite Bitel's use of the word *troscud*, however, no version of the story of Patrick's time on Mount Aigle in the *Tripartite Life* appears to use the verb.

Confusion over whether Patrick's fasting was religious or legal has permeated the scholarship, even with Whitely Stokes, whose masterful scholarly edition in 1887 remains the standard edition. Scholars and readers have, for well more than a century, suggested that Patrick fasted against God, suggesting the verb *troscud* was used. In fact, only the Latin versions from the Book of Armagh include a direct reference to "fast" at all: "*Et perrexit Patricius ad montem Egli ut* ieiunaret *in illo .xl. diebus et .xl. noctibus, Moysaicam tenons disciplinam et Heliacam et Christianam* [emphasis added]."[43] Similarly, the Latin summary of the four ways in which Patrick resembles Moses likewise uses *ieiunium* (never *castimonia* which may be a more appropriate translation for *troscud*) when referencing both of their forty days and forty nights in the wilderness: "*quadraginta diebus et quadraginta noctibus* ieiunauit [emphasis added]."[44] And, the word is also used in the Harleian 3359 as well.[45] All of the references to his spiritual fasting emphasize his religious calling in Latin, whereas the Irish references to spiritual fasting almost entirely use *óine* or *áin* when any mention of a fast is used. This is not to say that the text does not play on the overlapping kinds of fasting, only that the text remains clear when Patrick fasts before God and when he fasts against someone with a clearer legal connotation. It may be more accurate to say that Patrick fasted on the mountain until God acquiesced and answered his prayers.

A clearer case of Patrick fasting against someone is seen where the Irish-language text actually uses *troscud*. The story takes place years after Saint Patrick returned to Ireland to convert the Irish. Walking through the woods one day with his followers, he encountered a group of slaves chopping down yew trees. Their hands were bleeding from their work and because their master refused to let them sharpen their axes. Feeling for them (and seemingly identifying with them as a former slave), Patrick blessed their axes, thereby sharpening them, and went to confront their master, Trían (a name resembling *trian* in Irish, meaning "a third") and fast against him. Here is how Whitely Stokes translated the passage:

> Patrick blessed the irons [axes] so that they became the more easily
> used, and he went to the king, to Rath-Tréna. And Patrick fasted
> against him. Trían did nothing for him. Patrick turned on the morrow
> from the fortress. He cast his spittle on the rock which lay on his road,
> and the rock broke into three. A third part [*trian*] was then flung a
> thousand paces. Patrick said: "Two thirds of the fasting on the rock, a
> third on the king and on the fort and on the district. There will be of
> Trían's children neither king nor crownprince. He himself shall perish
> early and shall go down into bitter hell."
>
> Trían himself went to bind and beat the slaves who had given an
> account of him. His horses drag[ged] him and his charioteer off in his
> chariot, and went into the lake. Lock Tréna is its name; that was his last
> fall. He will not come out of the lake until the vespers of Doomsday;
> and it will not be for happiness even then. [46]

Patrick's fasting "against" Trían uses *troisciss*, a verb form of *troscud*, to
show how Patrick wields early Irish law in a miraculous fashion. The
comment "Trían did nothing for him" suggests that Trían did not offer
Patrick food or fast with him, in other words, that either Trían did not
recognize Patrick's position in society (he was foreign-born) or that Trían
ignored the legal requirement to offer food to the plaintiff faster. Doris
Edel comments on this usage:

> This coercive fasting was called *troscad*, as opposed to the Christian
> fasting, *aín*, from Latin *ieiumium*. Whatever the earlier history of *troscad*,
> at the time of the redaction of the texts, the procedure implied a ritual
> hunger strike from sundown to sunrise outside the *nemed*'s [a person
> with legal status] house. If the latter held out against a justified and
> properly conducted fast, he was deprived of his legal rights in society
> or boycotted, to use a modern term. [47]

In the story, Patrick does more than boycott or press a legal suit against
Trían. He deals out divine power against Trían when he does follow the
Brehon code and respond properly. The result is that Trían not only
drowns, but also he is eternally damned. Clearly the text suggests that
Patrick fasts to right wrongs and to mete out retribution. Patrick turns the
legal practice of fasting against someone into a supernatural curse, and
his fasting (like his ability to break rocks by spitting on them) demonstrates the supernatural powers of saints in the medieval imagination.

The practice of fasting against someone—*troscud*—however, was not
normally an appeal to the Almighty (to borrow from Baring-Gould's lecture) so much as a textual signifier of a legally binding redress. If the fast
was not responded to properly, it could lead to loss of status and banishment. It did not seem to resonate spiritual fasting as the Latinate word
óine does. Significantly, in a rare oversight, Whitely Stokes also collapses
the distinction between these two forms and inserts the word "fast,"
presumably for clarity's sake, into one of his facing-page translations of
Patrick's fasting on Mount Aigle. In the Irish-language passage neither

troscud nor *óine* appears. The original authors of the *Lebar Brece*, perhaps intentionally creating an ambiguous space, do not use any word for fast but just note that he went without food and water. Although Stokes is normally faithful to the original in his translations, Stokes does not allow the absence of *troscud* and *óine* to stand in his English version.[48] Like both Henry Maine and Evelyn Baring-Gould do, the distinctions between fasting as a legal practice and as an antiquated religious "conduit to the Almighty" fade in the text, both translating into fast, both suggesting that the Celts believed fasting was an irrational, premodern belief that hunger could telegraph the Divine.

The idea of fasting for rights against the powerful, however, had also begun to be reconsidered—and fasting's sense as both *troscud* and *castimonia* reinvigorated. In 1894, for a different audience than Baring-Gould, Laurence Ginnell published *The Brehon Laws: A Legal Guide* (1894) and focused on presenting fasting as a legal practice. The following year, the English mystic poet and friend of W. B. Yeats, Edwin Ellis, composed a verse drama—"Sancan the Bard" (1895)—based on another translation of an early modern text: a fourteenth-century saga about public fasting, *Immtheacht na Tromdáimhe*, translated alternately as "The Proceeding of the Burdensome Company" or "The Proceeding of the Great Bardic Institution." The saga was first translated and published in 1857 in an issue of the *Transactions of the Ossianic Society* and reprinted three years later on its own.[49] But it did not attract much attention until Lady Speranza, Oscar Wilde's mother, translated and published much of the medieval manuscript in 1887.[50] Ellis's version, however, provided the structure for Yeats's own version of the story, the short play, *The King's Threshold* (1904), where Seanchan, the chief poet, fasts in protest of being asked to leave the King's table of advisors. For Yeats, the loss of the practice of fasting symbolized how Irish art, culture, and civility had been lost in modern times and he too sets it in an antiquated past, although one with important parallels to the present. The play was first performed in Dublin in 1903 and published in 1904 (revised and republished in 1922[51]). An early draft of the play, depicts King Guaire trying to persuade his pupils to convince Seanchan to break his fast. The King laments, "I thought that hunger and weakness had been enough, / But finding them too trifling and too light / To hold his mouth from biting at the grave I called you hither."[52] The King had thought Nature would persuade the bard to stop fasting—the king reasoned that hunger, as an instinct, would overrule Seanchan's fast. But that bard seemed to have a different conception of hunger and fasting in mind—one that aligned hunger with agency and hunger with a human audience.

The King's Threshold was performed in Dublin in 1903, years before the hunger strike had an international audience, as Yeats himself later pointed out.[53] The play appeared six years before the first hunger strike in 1909 London by Marion Wallace-Dunlop of Women's Social and Political Union, ten years before the first Irish nationalist strike in 1913 by James Connolly, and fourteen years before Mohandas Gandhi's first strike in 1918. But as Bernard Cavanagh the "fasting-man" must have known long before Yeats, "acknowledged starvation," draws a crowd and begs questions.

NOTES

1. "Mr. Bernarnd Cavanagh" *The Literary Gazette and Journal of the Belles Lettres, Arts, Sciences, &c,* no. 1293, 20 Oct 1841, p. 708.

2. From Bouman, P. J., Revolutie der Eenzamen: Spiegel van een, Van Gorcum, 1976, p. 249, quoted in Vandereycken, Walter, and Ron Van Deth, *From Fasting Saints to Anorexic Girls: The History of Self-Starvation.* NYU UP, 1994, p. 89.

3. "Pacificator" [Anonymous], "Public Fasting at the Declaration of War." *The Calumet,* vol. 2, no. 4, November and December 1834, pp. 13–14.

4. Preston, Aislinge Meic Conglinne, p. 42.

5. Hennessy, W[illiam] M[aunsell], "MacConglinny's Vision." *Fraser's Magazine,* vol. 8, no. 45, September 1873, pp. 298–323.

6. Preston comments on this argument in her excellent introduction to her translation of Aislinge Meic Conglinne: "Gluttony was commonly linked to original sin, which was itself an act of consumption and an abrogation of restraint in Christian doctrine (1998, 56)" (xlv).

7. Spenser, *The Works of Edmund Spenser,* p. 244. For an overview of the mistaken attribution to Spenser of "A Briefe Note on Ireland," now attributed to Dudley Carleton, an English diplomat, see the Edmund Spenser page on the Catalogue of English Literary Manuscripts: http://www.celm-ms.org.uk/introductions/SpenserEdmund.html.

8. http://www.econlib.org/library/Smith/smMS6.html, accessed July 14, 2015.

9. Veitch, *The Meditations, and Selections from the Principles of Philosophy of Descartes.* John Cottinham's more contemporary translation follows:

> There is nothing that my own nature teaches me more vividly than that I have a body, and that when I feel pain there is something wrong with the body, and that when I am hungry or thirsty the body needs food and drink, and so on. So I should not doubt that there is some truth in this.
>
> Nature also teaches me, by these sensations of pain, hunger, thirst and so on, that I am not merely present in my body as a sailor is present in a ship, but that I am very closely joined and, as it were, intermingled with it, so that I and the body form a unit. If this were not so, I, who am nothing but a thinking thing, would not feel pain when the body was hurt, but would perceive the damage purely by the intellect, just as a sailor perceives by sight if anything in his ship is broken. Similarly, when the body needed food or drink, I should have an explicit understanding of the fact, instead of having confused sensations of hunger and thirst. For these sensations of hunger, thirst, pain and so on are nothing but confused modes of thinking which arise from the union and, as it were, intermingling of the mind with the body. (René Descartes, René Descartes: Meditations on First Philosophy: With Selections from the Objections and Replies. Edited by John Cottingham, Cambridge UP, 2013, p. 113.)

10. Dalia Judovitz points to this passage of Descartes, noting that although "Descartes will stress the substantial union and intermingling of mind and body, this effort to reintegrate the two remains unconvincing" (*The Culture of the Body: Genealogies of Modernity.* U of Michigan P, 2001, p. 103).

11. Cottingham (2013) translates the passage as: "the nature of man as a combination of mind and body is such that it is bound to mislead him from time to time" (123).

12. For discussions on how the grades of plaintiffs and defendants used fasting in Irish laws of distraint see: D. A. Binchy, "A Text on the Forms of Distraint." *Celtica,* vol. 10, 1973, pp. 72–86; D. A. Binchy, "Distraint in Irish Law." *Celtica,* vol. 10, 1973, pp. 22–71; and Kelly, *A Guide to Early Irish Law,* vol. 3, pp. 9 and 182–183.

13. Kelly's A Guide to Early Irish Law, vol. 3, provides an overview on legal fasting for those "of full nemed rank":

> [E]arly Irish law uses the practice of fasting (troscud) against a person of high status to pressurize him into conceding justice. . . . The fast probably takes place outside the nemed's house. The text does not say how long it normally lasts, but later commentators take it to be merely from sundown to sunrise (thereby missing the main evening meal) rather than a fast until death or settlement.
>
> When a plaintiff fasts against a nemed, the latter must guarantee to concede justice to the plaintiff either by appointing a surety (ráth) or by giving a household article in pledge. If the nemed eats during the fast without having made any guarantee, he must pay twice the amount originally owed. On the other hand, if the plaintiff persists in his fast even though the nemed has offered to settle, the case automatically lapses. It is unclear from the text how soon after the fast the plaintiff may distrain the nemed's property. Later commentary allows the nemed a three-day respite before distraint is permitted. . . . A nemed who holds out against a justified and properly conducted fast (presumably by opposing the subsequent attempt at distraint) loses his entitlement to be paid for any offense committed against him. In effect he is deprived of his legal rights in society.
>
> The shorter text on distraint (see above) provides more information on the use of fasting as a means of securing redress from sóernemed persons such as poets, churchmen (óes ecalso) or kings. For example, a plaintiff who wishes to sue a churchman must fast against him and give notice (apad) that he is not to recite his pater or his credo or go to the sacraments or Mass. If he is an ordained cleric or a monastic superior (airchinnech), which is tied around the tongue (?) of his bell or the foot of his altar, and notice is given that the bell may not be struck nor Mass said until he has conceded justice. If he ignores these formalities, his cattle may be distrained. (182–83)

14. For more on early Irish law, also see Kelly's A Guide to Early Irish Law, vol. 3, as well as essays by D. A. Binchy, "A Pre-Christian Survival in Mediaeval Irish Hagiography." *Ireland in Early Mediaeval Europe: Studies in Memory of Kathleen Hughes,* edited by in Dorothy Whitelock et al., Cambridge UP, 1982, pp. 165–178 and Doris Edel's "An Emerging Legal System in an Embryonic State." *The Law's Beginnings,* edited by Joseph Di Ferdin and Maria Feldbrugge, Brill, 2003, pp. 59–76.

15. *Ancient Laws of Ireland* edited by William Nielson Hancock, Thaddeus O'Mahony, Alexander Richey, and Robert Atkinson, 6 vols. (1865–1901).

16. I have written previously on this and related topics in "Fasting for the Public: Irish and Indian Sources of Marion Wallace Dunlop's 1909 Hunger Strike." *Enemies of Empire: New Perspectives on Imperialism, Literature and History.* Four Courts, Winter 2007; "The Starvation of a Man: Terence MacSwiney's Hunger Strike and Famine Memory." *Memory Ireland: The Famine and the Troubles,* vol. 3, edited by Oona Frawley, Syracuse UP, 2014, pp. 59–90; and in *Irish Orientalism: A Literary and Intellectual History.* Syracuse UP, 2004.

17. *Ancient Laws,* p 117.

18. The Saint Patrick's Confessio Hypertext Stack Project hosted by the Royal Irish Academy has a bibliography of most of the published biographies of St. Patrick in their annotated bibliography of secondary literature on St. Patrick. They do not list

every popular biography or text on St. Patrick published in English but all of the significant appear to be listed. http://www.confessio.ie/more/bibliography_full#

19. In his note for the publication of the revised version of *The King's Threshold*, Yeasts claimed: "When I wrote this play neither suffragette nor patriot had adopted the hunger strike, nor had the hunger strike been used anywhere, so far as I know, as a political weapon. I have given the play the tragic end I would have given it at the first, had not a friend [Lady Gregory] advised me to 'write a comedy and have a few happy moments in the theatre.' My friend meant that tragic emotion, depending as it does upon the gradually deepening reverie, is so fragile, that it is shattered by a wrong movement or cadence, or even by a light in the wrong place" (W. B. Yeats [1904]. *The King's Threshold. Plays in Prose and Verse: Written for an Irish Theatre and Generally with the Help of a Friend*, 63–114. Macmillan. 1922, 315–316).

20. See Anthony Bradley, "Nation, Pedagogy, and Performance: W. B. Yeats's *The King's Threshold* and the Irish Hunger Strikes." *Literature & History*, vol. 18, no. 2, 2002, pp. 20–33; Kiely, The King's Threshold; Lennon, "The Starvation of a Man."; and Tom Paulin, "Yeats's Hunger-Strike Poem." *Minotaur: Poetry and the Nation State*. Harvard UP, 1992, pp. 133–150.

21. Whitely Stokes, ed. *The Tripartite Life of Patrick with Other Documents Relating to That Saint*. Eyre and Spottiswoode, 1887.

22. For more on Whitely Stokes see the fine collection of essays: *The Tripartite Life of Whitley Stokes (1830–1909)*. Edited by Elizabeth Boyle & Paul Russell, Four Courts, 2011.

23. See Lennon, Irish Orientalism for more on this history.

24. Crawford Gribben (God's Irishman: Theological Debates in Cromwellian Ireland. Oxford UP, 2007) comments on how public fasts "dramatiz[ed] social power" in the seventeenth century, citing the Westminster Assembly's Directory for the Public Worship of God in the Three Kingdoms (1647):

> But the demand for fast-day duties did not stop with the end of the congregational meeting. Religious fasting required "totall abstinence, not only from all food . . . but also from all worldly labour, discourses and thoughts, and from all bodily delights . . . rich apparel, ornaments and such like." In a situation where clothes marked their wearer's social status, public fasts had significant social and political, as well as economic, repercussions. Their disruption of the normal patterns of daily life meant that fasts could be proclaimed only by those invested with proper authority-those who had, effectively, the authority to shut down normal life. At both national and local levels, the public fast was a powerful tool in the dramatizing of social power.

25. A variety of texts concerned themselves with the benefits and illusions of fasting, particularly in the 1830s and 1840s. A few titles here will suggest the range: a Protestant debunking of superstitious fasting, *Fasting, Fasts and Fasters; or, A Sketch of the Rise, Progress and Results of Fasting in the Christian Church*. Nisbet, 1845; on discovering deceptive fasters, Hector Gavin, *On Feigned or Factitious Diseases, Chiefly of Soldiers and Seamen*. J. Churchill, 1843; a defense of religious (Catholic) fasting, Simon Patrick, *A Treatise of Repentance and of Fasting*. J. H. Parker, 1841.

26. See William Alexander Hammond, *Fasting Girls: Their Physiology and Pathology*. G. P. Putnam's Sons, 1879.

27. See Walter Vandereycken and Ron Van Deth, *From Fasting Saints to Anorexic Girls* for a much fuller discussion of these connections.

28. See Alexander Henderson's pamphlet: *An Examination of the Imposture of Ann Moore, Called the Fasting Woman, of Tutbury; Illustrated by Remarks on Other Cases of Real and Pretended Abstinence*. Underwood and Blacks, 1813, p. 2.

29. Ibid., p 10.

30. Vandereycken and Van Deth, *From Fasting Saints to Anorexic Girls*, p. 74.

31. See Julian Preece's *The Cambridge Companion to Kafka*. Cambridge UP, 2002, p. 92, and Richard T. Gray's *A Franz Kafka Encyclopedia*. Greenwood, 2005, p. 131.

32. Chapman's *The Celts*, has made some of the most enduring arguments about the construction of a Celtic identity based on La Tène culture. More recently the work of John Koch has furthered our understanding of the spread of an Atlantic Bronze Age culture. Although some debate remains about the Celtic origins of the Irish, few would agree today with the Celtic invasion theory supported by Celticists of the nineteenth century.

33. Baring-Gould, *Cornish Characters and Strange Events*, p. vii.

34. See Arnold, *On the Study of Celtic Literature*.

35. James Vernon has charted some of the movements in the late nineteenth-century associated with eradicating hunger, particularly the discovery of vitamins and dietary recommendations in *Hunger: A Modern History*. Harvard UP, 2007.

36. Binchy, "Distraint in Irish Law," p.70.

37. Johnson, "'Vengeance is Mine'," p. 8.

38. For an illuminating, broad study of saintly retribution and vengeance as textual devices in medieval hagiographies, see Johnson's study, "Vengeance is Mine."

39. The first publication in English of the Confessio appears to have been as an appendix to a second edition of a polemical biography of St. Patrick by Steele, *Saint Patrick: Apostle of Ireland in the Third Century*.

40. Cusack, *The Life of Saint Patrick*, p. 588.

41. Stokes, *The Tripartite Life of Patrick with Other Documents Relating to That Saint*, pp. 474–475.

42. Bitel, *Isle of the Saints*, p. 215.

43. Stokes, Part 2, *The Tripartite Life of Patrick with Other Documents Relating to That Saint*, p. 322. "Patrick went to Mount Egli to fast for fortty days and forty nights, after the manner of Moses, Christ and Elijah."

44. Ibid., p. 332.

45. Ibid., p. 500.

46. Ibid., pp. 219–220.

47. Edel, "An Emerging Legal System in an Embryonic State," p. 70.

48. Stokes, *The Tripartite Life of Patrick with Other Documents Relating to That Saint*, pp. 474–475.

49. Originally contained in the Book of Lismore, a fourteenth-century manuscript, it was translated and published by Owen Connellan in the *Transactions of the Ossianic Society*, vol. v, 1857, republished as *Transactions of the Ossianic Society*, vol. v. Dublin, 1860.

50. Lady Francesca Speranza Wilde, "Seanchan the Bard and the King of the Cats" in *Ancient Legends, Mystic Charms, and Superstitions of Ireland*. Ward & Downey, 1887.

51. Yeats, *Plays in Prose and Verse*.

52. Yeats, *The King's Threshold*, pp. 12–13.

53. Yeats, *Plays in Prose and Verse*, p. 423. Yeats's note to the reprint of the play makes his claim clear: "When I wrote this neither suffragette nor patriot had adopted the hunger strike, nor had the hunger strike been used anywhere, so far as I know, as a political weapon."

SELECTED WORKS CITED

Arnold, Matthew. *On the Study of Celtic Literature*. Smith, Elder, 1867.

Baring-Gould, Evelyn. *Cornish Characters and Strange Events*. John Lane, 1909.

Bitel, Lisa. *Isle of the Saints: Monastic Settlement and Christian Community in Early Ireland*. Cornell UP, 1990.

Boyle, Elizabeth, and Paul Russell, eds. *The Tripartite Life of Whitley Stokes (1830–1909)*. Four Courts, 2011.

Chapman, Malcolm. *The Celts : The Construction of a Myth*. St Martin's Press, 1993.

Cusack, Mary. *The Life of Saint Patrick, Apostle of Ireland.* Longmans, 1871.

Hancock, William Nielson, et al., ed. *Ancient Laws of Ireland.* 6 vols. 1865–1901.

Johnson, Máire. "'Vengeance is Mine': Saintly Retribution in Medieval Ireland." *Vengeance in the Middle Ages,* edited by Susanna A. Throop and Paul R Hyams, Ashgate, 2010, pp. 5–50.

Keily, Declan, ed. *The King's Threshold: Manuscript Materials.* Cornell UP, 2005.

Kelly, Fergus. *A Guide to Early Irish Law,* vol. 3. DIAS, 1988.

Lennon, Joseph. "Fasting for the Public: Irish and Indian Sources of Marion Wallace Dunlop's 1909 Hunger Strike." *Enemies of Empire: New Perspectives on Imperialism, Literature and History.* Four Courts, Winter 2007.

Lennon, Joseph. "The Starvation of a Man: Terence MacSwiney's Hunger Strike and Famine Memory." *Memory Ireland: The Famine and the Troubles,* vol. 3, edited by Oona Frawley, Syracuse UP, 2014, pp. 59–90.

Lennon, Joseph. *Irish Orientalism: A Literary and Intellectual History.* Syracuse UP, 2004.

Preston, Lahney. *Aislinge Meic Conglinne: The Vision of Mac Conglinne.* Syracuse UP, 2010.

Spenser, Edmund. *The Works of Edmund Spenser: A Variorum Edition.* Johns Hopkins Press, 1949.

Steele, R. Nicholson. *Saint Patrick: Apostle of Ireland in the Third Century: The Story of His Mission by Pope Celestine in A.d. 431, and of His Connexion with the Church of Rome Proved to Be a Mere Fiction.* M'Glashan and Gill, 1868.

Veitch, John. *The Meditations, and Selections from the Principles of Philosophy of Descartes. Translated from the Latin, and Collated with the French; with Preface, Appendix, and Notes.* Sutherland and Knox, 1853.

Yeats, W. B. *The King's Threshold: And on Baile's Strand: Being Volume Three of Plays for an Irish Theatre.* A. H. Bullen, 1904.

———. *Plays in Prose and Verse. Written for an Irish Theatre and Generally with the Help of a Friend.* Macmillan, 1922.

SIX

The Effect of Emerging New Media on Book Publishing: Lessons from the Origins of Cross-Media Storytelling in the Early Twentieth Century for Contemporary Transmedia Researchers

Alexis Weedon

One advantage of the study of the history of the book is the light it can shed on present-day publishing. In this chapter I want to draw out some of the parallels between the early days of the crossover of film, radio, and publishing, focusing on the beginning of the twentieth century, when new practices were emerging in comparison with specific examples of current trends in the digital book and reading.

Putting the two periods side by side can give us a framework to understand the complexity of contemporary trends in media publishing. There are obvious reasons for choosing the 1910s and 1920s because it was a period of emerging cross-media business practices, changing labor markets, and it witnessed rapid technological advancement and a global economic upheaval. Such themes are consonant with the forces that have directed the form of the current digital publishing revolution.

The early twentieth century saw a move to a more audiovisual culture that opened avenues for storytellers to write for textual, aural, and visual mediums. The change in authorship, increasing professionalization, led businesses to adapt their practices. Media theorists see this period as the rise of the mass audience with potentially subversive implications for the

101

social construction of notions of nationhood and citizenship mediated through regulated channels of communication.

There are parallels in the twenty-first century as media convergence based on digital and then mobile communications technologies has led to creative content being adapted across different platforms. Authors are more exposed to readers' or viewers' reactions to their work through public Internet forums, and authorship itself has become embedded in the practices of reading and consumption of the media. The digital media has led to a more openly visible process of production; however, arguments that the subversive implications of media convergence has led to a democratization of the production process need to be interrogated. In this chapter I will look at parallels with the business practices in the 1910s and 1920s, how this evidences both the changing relationship between audience and producers and the effect of innovation in audiovisual technology on the mechanisms that drive the market.

The past emergence of a mass audience is well documented but how this audience worked in creating market demand across media needs to be understood both then and now because today the trend has been reversed. Digital television and radio has led to diversification and smaller audiences. This is niche programming, what in the 1990s was called *narrowcasting* as broadcasters looked to the music and publishing industry for models. Similarly, we need to understand the interrelationship between movie and radio audiences and novel and story readerships and how cross-media audiences stimulate ongoing interest in the franchise or brand.

Unpicking this history, it is easy to overstate the intentionality of publication in multiple forms. The popularity of a work may simply give rise to isolated, individual initiatives in the publishing and performance of that work, even the reinterpretation, retelling, and reproduction of the stories as the work becomes part of a public domain. Studies of fandoms today recognize this as a process, and for many fans it is a conscious appropriation of the story. Although fandom is not a term that applies historically, there are historical antecedents in the subversive appropriation and repurposing of a title by readers that can be evidenced in the documented reading experiences in the nineteenth century and previous periods.[1]

CASE STUDY: 1912 MULTIPLE FORMS OF STORYTELLING: *THE PILGRIMS' PROGRESS*

In 1912 Canon Henson dedicated a window in Westminster Abbey to John Bunyan, preacher and author. Bunyan's tale of a Christian family's spiritual journey through the moral temptations of life, *The Pilgrims' Progress* had been republished in many and various editions since 1678, the window being one visual realization of the allegory.[2] The dedication of the window in the foremost Anglican Abbey in England is testament to the importance the tale in the religious and literary culture of its home country. As an uplifting religious text, it was a staple of Sunday family reading. This shared experience was acknowledged by the Canon in speech as he reminisced of his own childhood:

> I am a little boy again. In a country parsonage in Suffolk, on a winter Sunday evening my father and my mother and five children are gathered round the fire. Each has in his hand a cherished copy of the 'Pilgrims' Progress'. We read aloud from it: each reads a paragraph, turn and turn about: even the youngest can read the words with a little help and all, both senior and junior, have very happy moments while they read the story 'mid smiles and tears, and discuss familiar characters, and try to realize the meaning of the episodes.[3]

Taking this year in history, 1912, we can examine a cross-section of the multiple forms in which the story was being retold.

The evidence we have comes from the publication records, newspaper reviews and adverts, and artifacts that have survived the years. They are witness to the qualitative—and potentially subversive—engagement of readers and audiences with the range of texts and adaptations whereby they are "no longer consumers but producers of the text," and are indicative of the popularity of *The Pilgrim's Progress.*[4] The market extended into foreign language publication as evidenced by the Gaelic, Swedish, and Yiddish translations that came out in 1912 published by Grant in Edinburgh, Bonnier in Stockholm, and the SPCK in London. Newspapers also reviewed two books on Bunyan's tale showing its attraction as a text for devotional reading: Rev. Robert Stevenson's *Exposition of* The Pilgrims' Progress and John Kelman's *The Road: A Study of John Bunyan's* "Pilgrims' Progress."[5] The work also appeared in schools as Emily Rudd and Joseph Cox Bridge's *Dramatised scenes from* The Pilgrim's Progress, in George Allen's *Standard plays for amateur performance in girls' schools* series testifies.

The publication records show George Cruikshank's illustrated edition was republished that year. Many famous illustrators had imagined ("produced") the perils of Christian, Christiana, and her two sons in wood cuts, etchings and lithography in editions that were given out at Sunday schools or as prizes or gift books. Dickens's famous illustrator had started this prestigious project and produced twenty-five drawings but never finished it, so its publication in 1903 by Henry Frowde and its reprinting in 1912 was proof of the attraction of illustrated editions of the work. Such illustrative material was used by the Lantern slide companies who made colored or monotone glass plates to accompany published lectures, readings, and songs. These were popular evening entertainments put on within communities, led by the vicar or local notable and accompanied by amateur choirs and school children and the local newspapers reported on the size of the audiences and the scale of the shows. For example, at Battle, East Sussex in the south of Britain, lantern slides of illustrations from the works of Harold Copping, Arthur A. Dixon, Gustave Doré, and James Tissot accompanied an evening of recitation and song, and in Torry, Aberdeenshire in the north, a "large audience" appreciated the "singing, speaking and pictures" that formed a "unique illustration of Bunyan's masterpiece." Such interpretive license, of course, could both endorse and subvert Bunyan's theological message. Other lantern slide shows were given in Devon at Hemyock—"greatly enjoyed" by the audience—and at Torrington where "notwithstanding the very boisterous weather there was a very good attendance," as well as in Collompton, Thrapstox, Falkirk, and other places during that year.

The *Yorkshire Evening Post* spotted this early example of cross-media publication that year and commented:

> Apparently, ere long, instead of reading the classics, we shall see them. Following Victor Hugo's "Les Miserables", we shall have Bunyan's "Pilgrim's Progress" adapted for the cinematograph, along with scenes from the author's life. Well, Mr Bernard Shaw holds that John Bunyan had a higher dramatic reach than Shakespeare, and every schoolboy knows that Lord Macaulay thought that the dialogues in the "Pilgrim's Progress" were better than in most plays. The Late George MacDonald, the novelist, once toured the provinces in a dramatized version of the book; and a very interesting performance it was.[6]

George MacDonald's family had performed their dramatization in Italy from the late 1870s to the end of the 1880s as well as in the United Kingdom and the film was Italian made. "The Life of John Bunyan" (Il Pellegrino, Caserini 1912) was in three parts showing Bunyan's conversion, his vision in prison, and the story of Christian's family.[7] Famous for adapting Edward Bulwer-Lytton's *The Last Days of Pompeii* in a short film (Ambrosio and Maggi, 1908), Societo Anonimo Ambrosio had had other success with literary adaptations that they sought to repeat. The *Hull Daily Mail* reported positively on the film "the representation of the defeat of Apollyon is a remarkable piece of realism" and reassured their readership that "The production as a whole is handled in a most reverent manner, though some may think the introduction of devils shooting arrows and ghostly figures swathed in long white draperies savours somewhat of the grotesque," adding "[i]t would have been better if any reference to Catholicism had been omitted."[8] Note the subversive possibilities of such adaptation. As adaptation theorist Brian McFarlane observes, written narratives and films employ different signifying systems (conceptual for the former and perceptive for the latter), which creates a hybrid system for films adapted from books.[9] The director and screenwriter will inevitably impose their own vision on the text (via both emphasis and omission) and subtly subvert the narrative, intentionally or not. The film was distributed by North British Animated Pictures and exhibited across the country Exeter and Plymouth, Folkestone, Sheffield, Hull, and elsewhere from September.

Other forms of (decontextualized) storytelling in 1912 included a musical interpretation and a play: Earnest Austin's specially arranged narrative tone poem of *The Pilgrims' Progress* was performed at Tewkesbury Abbey Festival on two organs in September. This unusual work is divided into twelve parts, each is accompanied by an explanation of the section of the story read aloud by a narrator, and the final movement of the about 160-minute piece included a choral section. Austin's work was not the only classical interpretation of Bunyan's story, Ralph Vaughan Williams wrote incidental music for two dramatizations in 1906 and later a play. A further form was Mrs. Duncan Pearce's play adaptation of Part 2 of *The Pilgrims' Progress*, featuring Christiana and her boys' vision and journey that afforded "a rare treat according to the *Sussex Agricultural Express* on 12 March stating that "[p]ublic taste is evidently favourable to such productions for there were large and appreciative audiences for both performances." The newspaper went into a detailed description of her play, and asserted that "Mrs Duncan Pearce has achieved distinct success as a play writer, and apart from its spectacular beauty her production aims at a high purpose." Part of the Lewes Women's Suffrage association and wife of the vicar, Mrs. Duncan Pearce (Lillian Ann Donovan) was a local luminary and her work was performed elsewhere. An edition of her play with twenty-one photographs of scenes from a performance at Holyhead in aid of the Stanley home for sailors was published in 1914.

These examples of multiple storytelling of a well known and popular text in 1912 demonstrate some of the tendencies we would associate with transmedia stories today. We can see the importance of the anniversary and the event in providing a focus for associated performance and publishing activities. Audiences were familiar with the tale, and retellings brought reinterpretations to readers who had read the text intensely – a "knowing" audience. Additionally, they were engaged at a particular time and place because Bunyan's piece was acceptable for performance in church halls and on the Sabbath when other works that might have competed with it for attention were not. So it had a market space. Significantly it provided a range of kinesthetic forms of entertainment for the audience being performed through live readings, *tableaux vivant*, music, dramatization and, of course, rich colorful projected illustrations. And it traded in word-of-mouth recommendation and personal social relationships to the extent that audiences often knew the singers or actors in the drama through their community or church networks.

So both commercial and noncommercial interests drove this market in Bunyan's tale: amateur and professional. Enthusiasm for the text and its (alleged) purpose enabled readers to appropriate it as theirs and recreate, extend, enhance, and subvert the story world. Here, the message of the text was endorsed and favored by its readers and as with religious, charity, and not-for-profit groups today; it was published by organizations who sought to propagate it. The SPCK and the Religious Tract Society had a mission that took it outside purely commercial endeavor. Yet the commercial opportunities attracted companies: publishers such as A&C Black and the lantern slide manufacturers such as Riley Brothers[10] recognized a market, as did the producers of the film, Societo Anonimo Ambrosio of Turin.

In 1912, the way the audience drove market demand seems more innocent, less consumerist, more to do with being part of a local community and less to do with distinctions of lifestyle and socioeconomic status we now associate with brands. The popularity of the multiple forms of Bunyan's tale and the subversive processes of meaning-making through adaptation illustrate the social construction of citizenship at that time. Participation in the story retelling of Bunyan's tale demonstrated affiliation to the specific notion of citizenship bound up with duty and commitment to spiritual progress and nationhood that was expected of the respectable British public in 1912 but was to change with the war. Yet even this early key factors of cross-media storytelling can be identified: the new opportunities for story retelling afforded by innovative audiovisual technologies; the "knowing" audience enthusiastically adopting the role of producers; the powerfulness of vocal word-of-mouth recommendations at this time in the form of commentaries and readings that through missionary and not-for-profit organizations propagated the story beyond the United Kingdom and the English language.

EMERGING CROSS-MEDIA BUSINESS PRACTICES THAT HAVE SHAPED THE FORM OF THE DIGITAL PUBLISHING REVOLUTION NOW

The growth of audiences out of the late nineteenth-century mass market for print led, in time, to the cinema culture of the 1930s and the building of glittery "picture palaces." Marshall McLuhan viewed the electronic media as revolutionary, liberating the text from the page.[11] Certainly the technological innovation of film from the 1900s, then radio in Britain from 1922, and television experimented on before the Second World War were milestones in the development of mass audiences. With cinema culture came Hollywood celebrity and stardom generated by the international magazine companies such as Hearsts' and newspaper chains led by Northcliffe and Beaverbrook. The periodical industry not only told stories about film and media personalities, they published letters, queries, and questions from their readers. However artfully manufactured these texts might have been, they constructed an intimacy between the celebrity or star and the reader or viewer, making a fan. Articles with titles such as "Rudolph Valentino as I knew him," or Elinor Glyn's justification for her scandalous novel "Why I wrote *Three Weeks*" exposed authors and actors to readers' and audiences' reactions to their life and work albeit in a carefully moderated forum. Although this was not new — many Victorian novelists published in parts and received feedback from their readers, Dicken's *Pickwick Papers* being the prime example — the swiftness of feedback and review could be fast with daily or weekly periodical publication, allowing in the case of *The Radio Times*, comments and speculations on plot and character development between broadcast episodes. Radio and television broadcasters took the performance into the home of the listener and viewer, as the *Radio Times Supplement* proudly announced on 11 January 1937. The distinction in Britain between a public and private life that had been so marked under the monarchs Victoria and Edward, had to be renegotiated in the 1920s and 1930s. Within three generations the chaperone had given way to the flapper, the letter to the telephone, and stories about well-known personalities including authors had become common in the periodical press. This social change toward the greater public exposure of private lives has parallels with that brought about by the social media in the twenty-first century. Not all authors could cope under this media spotlight, then as now; but those that could were in a better position to exploit the financial rewards of the multiple outlets that were opening up for their work.

The rise of the Hollywood star machine and media celebrity can be seen in the changing attitude to authors, although this was not without resistance from theatrical folk who thought movies would diminish their audiences.[12] Writers who had an eye to movie and radio adaptation, however, drew on their experience of recitation or the theater. As actors or performers they had received top billing and knew about the draw of a known name, so it was not a great stretch to consider how cross-media publication could give rise to the celebrity branding of authors and authorial personas. British studios saw the possibilities and adapted popular authors giving them prominence in their credits; Stoll for example announcing *The Strand* authors series and drawing a mise-en-scène for the film from the illustrated magazine,[13] while Samuel Goldwyn announced an Eminent Author's series of films and invited Somerset Maugham and Elinor Glyn among others to Hollywood. Hugh Walpole and Glyn traveled and gave lectures, names in their own right, and their performances, not worlds away from Dickens's theatrical performances, were for an international audience. Glyn also participated in celebrity construction taking control of her appearances before audiences, on screen and in magazines and especially in her own photographic portraits using the proliferation of half-tone photography in an international magazine industry to promote celebrity.[14]

Glyn was one author who took more readily to writing for cross-media publication. The popular British romantic novelist and Hollywood icon told her readers in her *System of Writing* in 1922:

> Not only is it wise to study the policy of different magazines or studios but it is well to have a general knowledge of the different classes of markets, so that we may know at once where an experience, an anecdote, a write-up, a story, or a photoplay will likely find a welcome.[15]

Those who had some experience of the stage or theatrical adaptation had an advantage in the dramatic requirement of picturization of their novel or short story. Former actors and actresses Clemence Dane, A. E. W. Mason, and authors familiar with writing for the stage Arnold Bennett, Glyn, and the prolific Edgar Wallace are examples. Mason recalled how his story "grew out of a picture" with a mise-en-scène of seventeenth-century costume, dueling, and the drama "of a girl walking in her sleep carrying her candle between the combatants." Mason's tales of action set in exotic locations proved attractive and Glyn's romances took place in, or were subversively relocated to, glamorous settings. For others it was the way the performative voice in private readings and recitals became public through radio from 1922 and talkies from 1932, which was the way in. Hugh Walpole, British author of the *Rogue Harries* series who adapted Dicken's *Great Expectations* for MGM in Hollywood introducing it on screen (Cukor 1935), was a regular speaker on arts topics on the early BBC Radio broadcasts. When he collaborated with Dorothy L. Sayers on a radio crime drama he insisted on reciting the story live and unscripted into the microphone. Walpole had the ability to tell and retell stories at different times and diversify them in the retelling using different media forms. It was the mark of a successful cross-media author of his time. Today the author has control of the characters and ideas and inventions, but the business can be considerably bigger and whole companies exploit the retelling.

In the interwar years a new relationship between movie and radio audiences and readerships emerged, and authors had to adapt their creative and business practices to a mass readership through segmentation. The "layers" of readers Albert Curtis Brown, the literary agent commented on, and Mary Hammond has written about, were separated by class and the price-structuring of books. However, with the advent of the cinema and radio these became segmented audiences defined still by class and price, but also by location, leisure pattern, and consumption. The 1930s saw a burgeoning of consumer brands and advertising as domestic appliances, groceries and travel became affordable. Merchandising became integral to the Hollywood system from Warner Brothers dog food link up for Rin Tin Tin to Shirley Temple dolls,[16] and role playing the character was aided by branded games and toys such as Dick Tracy's.[17] Literary agents and publishers recognized the opportunities for new revenue streams brought about by film, and subsequently by radio and television. In words reminiscent of the burgeoning of dotcom companies in the few years before the millennium, Henry Raymond bemoaned the low entry threshold for publishing that had led to increased competition, overproduction, and lower profit margins in 1938:

> There is no entrance fee and no examination, nor is any large capital outlay involved. As a result at least two dozen new publishing houses have started business since the War and publishing has become over-capitalised. . . . if full account is taken of all the capital already invested in publishing at the end of the War plus all that has been added since that date, I question whether the trade as a whole is earning even one per cent dividend.[18]

Publishing was more complicated in 1938 than twenty years previously, he observed; there was greater correspondence arising from the royalty system because the author had to be consulted on points that technically were the publishers' provenance. He claimed that publishers also had increased work from handling subsidiary rights for authors without an agent and that production and advertising were more complicated processes forcing companies to employ a larger staff to deal with the accounts. "[I]s there any general publisher who has not at least trebled his advertising expenditure during the last twenty years?" he asked.[19]

Yet as Frank Swinnerton said "the publisher lives by his list, and not by individual books in it" and so spread risk while the author had to build income from regular publication and learn to be proactive in rights management.[20] In this power shift in the media industry, the archives of publishers contain correspondence with authors struggling to understand the needs of movie studios' agents in the preparation of scenarios and with the studios representatives on the sale of film options on copyrights they owned. Literary agents following in their wake to protect individual author's interests took exception to the all-encompassing clauses some contracts contained and became increasingly adept at reserving subsidiary rights so that they could relicense the property as new recording technologies were developed. Authors set up companies to control and exploit their intellectual properties as rights proliferated, so that by 2011 companies like Chorion managed the estates of Agatha Christie, Georges Simenon, Margery Allingham, Raymond Chandler, and others. Then as now, the development of the technology challenged the limitations of copyright law, and judicious exploitation of the intellectual properties was a key to the success for media businesses.

TWENTY-FIRST CENTURY DIGITAL MEDIA CONVERGENCE

The invention of analog media required a new audiovisual grammar, as the invention of digital media required a new sign system. The restrictiveness of media specificity that "assumes that every medium is inherently 'good at' certain things and 'bad at' others" was prevalent in the 1920s and 1930s, although it was a limitation questioned by creative innovators. [21] The term *picturization* was used to describe the translation of a written story to the film medium. For Glyn in the days of silent cinema this was a *pantomime,* where gesture, facial expression, movement, setting, and the accompanying musical score created the dramatic narrative and the intertitles punctuated the visual action. Remediation is also often seen in these early films which frame the story through an opening "once upon a time" sequence of an animated book or reference the source book or magazine in the movie. The implication that his more modern media is a deriviation of the traditional gives the story a provenance. In her *Theory of Adaptation* (2012), Linda Hutcheon brings the media specificity discussion into the twenty-first century arguing that "some media and genres are used to *tell* stories (for example, novels, short stories); others *show* them (for instance, all performance media); and still others allow us to interact physically and kinesthetically with them (as in videogames or theme park rides)" and applies these to modes of engaging audiences. [22] As Samantha Pearce has argued, intense *readers* the audience enjoy challenge of testing their reading of the story against those of the adapting team. As *collaborators* the audience takes pleasure in a feeling of inclusion and ownership within the franchise and seeing their criticism of the novel rectified in the film adaptation. As *viewers,* the audience enjoys the pleasure of being surprised within the confines of a familiar story world in which they believe themselves to be experts. [23]

It has been claimed that twenty-first century digital media is distinct from its twentieth-century analog forebears by being user-led, participatory—often soliciting creative contributions—and in the way it engenders community. Looking back, it is clear that serendipity played a greater role in successful cross-media storytelling in the early twentieth century because release and publication dates, booking of exhibition venues, assignment of rights, and options were not planned with a view to synergy. Although in the twenty-first century according to Bowman and Willis (2003) "the audience has taken on the roles of publisher, broadcaster, editor, content creator (writer, photographer, videographer, cartoonist), commentator, documentarian, knowledge manager (librarian), journaler and advertiser (buyer and seller)." [24] [25] This audience is increasingly aware of the value of its attention and of the subversive politics of engagement and participation in brand adoption. In 2008 Henry Jenkins and Mark Deuze observed that convergence "must be understood as both a top-down corporate-driven process and a bottom-up consumer-driven process" as audiences offer both approval and resistance through for example fan writing, crowdsourcing cult films, and resistance to overt marketing in social media. Yet large content owning companies are seeking to exploit the intellectual property rights across multiple media and merchandising outlets, driving franchises, and promoting brand recognition of characters. The extent that this content is integrated into one story-line depends on the narrative and genre from citizen journalism to Marvel Comic's franchised superheroes. In some cases, multifaceted narratives and link across platforms in parasitic or synergistic ways.

Today new authors are creating readerships by part publication or e-book self-publishing before getting a book contract. To facilitate that we are witnessing the emergence of self-publishing departments within publishing houses and literary agencies. Mike Shatzkin predicted at Digital Book World January 2015 that there would be a new model of author agreements before long to include a you-hire-us self-publishing deal and already there are self-publishing parts of major publishers such as Atria within Simon Schuster. Once published such authors get feedback direct from fans online, often through official or moderated forums Duncan Pile's *Nature Sage* site. Authors can engage with readers and increasingly construct their own persona aided by guides to creating a social media presence.25 Those who have a public presence benefit from this as a public personality generates a level of interest and a potential market: one example is Alex Gerlis who moved into historical faction writing benefited from being a known journalist. In a crowded digital market, the focus is on discoverability.

Thus tracing the origins of the business practices of today's large and complex industry, with its combination of properties and rights, technologies, and expertise, to the early experiments with cross-media publication in the twentieth century brings into focus aspects that are key to the success of the published story. The observation that media convergence has led to a democratization in creativity cannot be simply applied to the publishing industry. Although processes such as word-of-mouth recommendation, audience-building, and author-reader engagement are more visible through social media, this does not mean they are new or more prevalent. We simply could not easily identify them previously. Similarly, we must nuance the notion of the participatory audience because spaces for audience/reader criticism and creative/subversive commentary are so obviously constructed by both the fan and professional, lending authority to one or the other in the retelling of and commentary on the story.

NOTES

This work is an outcome of the AHRC grant Cross-media co-operation in Britain in the 1920s and 1930s (AR112216).

1. See the Reading Experience Database at www.open.ac.uk/Arts/RED/, accessed 4 August 2015.

2. Particular thanks to my colleague Professor W. R. Owens whose research on John Bunyan's *Pilgrim's Progress* inspired this brief survey of 1912. This report on the

dedication of Bunyan window in Westminster Abbey is from the *Lichfield Mercury*, 2 February 1912, p. 3.

   3. *Luton Times and Advertiser*, 2 February 1912, p. 7.

   4. Barthes, *S/Z*, p. 4.

   5. Stevenson *Exposition of The Pilgrims' Progress*, Kelman's *The Road*, and a report on the Religious Tract Society publication of the translation of *The Pilgrims' Progress* in *Derby Daily Telegraph*, 4 July 1912, p. 2.

   6. *The Yorkshire Evening Post*, 8 March 1913, p. 4.

   7. Review of the film, *John Bunyan* in *Exeter and Plymouth Gazette*, 24 September 1912, p. 2, an item probably syndicated because it also appears in the *Hull Daily Mail* on 20 September 1912, p. 13. The mail had an advert on 20 December 1912, p. 6, advertising the showing of the film accompanied by Elsie Young (Contralto) and organ and piano "rendering descriptive musical items" by E. P. Graham. The film was produced by Societo Anonimo Ambrosio of Turin. The *Luton Times and Advertiser* described the three parts of the film in their columns on 27 September 1912, p. 7.

   8. *Hull Daily Mail*, 20 September 1912, p. 13.

   9. McFarlane, *Novel to Film*, pp. 26–27.

   10. *The Life of Bunyan* (Bradford: Riley Brothers, 1895), thirty-three slides and lecture texts such as Lectures for the magic lantern and pleasant readings for leisure hours (London: Millikin & Lawley, 1872), pp. 36–37 provided for such entertainments. See LUCERNA—*the Magic Lantern Web Resource* at http://www.slides.uni-trier.de/text/index.php?id=4004150, accessed 5 August 2015.

   11. Marshal MacLuhan, *The Gutenberg Galaxy : The Making of Typographic Man*. Toronto: University of Toronto Press, 1962.

   12. For example, Percy Terry on Baroness Orczy's *The Scarlet Pimpernel*.

   13. Mary Hammond, on The Manxman.

   14. Karen Randell and Alexis Weedon, "Reconfiguring Elinor Glyn: Ageing Female Experience and the Origins of the 'It Girl'." *Women, Celebrity and Cultures of Ageing*. Edited by Deborah Jermyn and Susan Holmes, Palgrave Macmillan, 2015, pp. 25–42.

   15. Elinor Glyn, *The Elinor Glyn System of Writing*. The Authors' Press. 1922, p. 356.

   16. Helen Powell, *Promotional Culture and Convergence: Markets, Methods, Media*. Routledge, 2013, p. 212.

   17. William Young and Nancy Young, *The 1930s*. Greenwood Press, 2005, p. 271.

   18. Raymond, *Publishing and Bookselling*, p. 11.

   19. Ibid., 12.

   20. Frank Swinnerton, *Authors and The Book Trade*. Gerald Howe Ltd. 1932, p. 78.

   21. Robert Stam, "Beyond Fidelity: The Dialogics of Adaptation." *Film Adaptation*, edited by J. Naremore, Athlone, 2000, p. 58.

   22. Linda Hutcheon and Siobhan O'Flynn, *A Theory of Adaptation*. 2nd, ed. Routledge, 2012.

   23. Samantha Pearce, "Adaptation as augmentation: Examining the ways in which Stephanie Meyer's *Twilight* is enhanced by its online fandom and how its film adaptation affects this enhancement," Masters by Research thesis, University of Bedfordshire, 2015.

   24. Shayne Bowman and Chris Willis, *We Media: How audiences are shaping the future of news and information* The Media Center at the American Press Institute, 2003. http://www.hypergene.net/wemedia/download/we_media.pdf, accessed 3 August 2015.

   25. Chris McCrudden, *Digital and Social Media for Authors: A 60-Minute Masterclass*, *guardianshorts*, http://guardianshorts.co.uk/digital-and-social-media-for-authors-chris-mccrudden-60-minute-masterclasses/#sthash.gXx4xFyJ.dpuf, accessed 3 August 2015.

SELECTED WORKS CITED

Barthes, Roland. *S/Z*. Hill and Wang, 1970.

Kelman, John. *The Road: A Study of John Bunyan's "Pilgrims' Progress."* Edinburgh: Oliphant, Andersen and Ferrier, 1912.
McFarlane, Brian. *Novel to Film: An Introduction to the Theory of Adaptation.* Oxford UP, 1996.
Raymond, Harold. *Publishing and Bookselling: A Survey of Post-War Developments and Present Day Problems.* J. M. Dent and Sons, 1938.
Stevenson, Rev. Robert. *Exposition of The Pilgrims' Progress.* A & C Black, 1912.

SEVEN

"And this also has been one of the dark places of the earth": Reading Levinasian Ethics and Literary Impressionism in Conrad's *Heart of Darkness*

Kenneth Womack

The impulse to moralize, to pontify, is a very strong one, and comes in many treacherous guises.
—Ford Madox Ford

All ambitions are lawful except those that climb upward on the miseries or credulities of mankind.
—Joseph Conrad

There is little doubt about the classic status of Joseph Conrad's *Heart of Darkness* (1899), a novella that exists at the cusp of early modernism. As the Victorian social aesthetic and fin-de-siècle decadence drifted into the ages, *Heart of Darkness* subverted its readers' ethical positions about empire and the cultural yen for colonization. Conrad's subversion epitomizes Irena R. Makaryk's idea that the concept involves "the articulation or 'becoming visible' of any repressed, forbidden, or oppositional interpretation of the social order" (636). Such articulation forces a series of uncomfortable ethical questions on the audience. What, indeed, was—*is*—the human cost of unchecked expansionism? How do we account for our roles in the desolation of one culture to elevate another's zeal for wealth, power, and privilege? Such questions share similarities with Paul Ricouer's hermenuetics of suspicion, "the double motivation" exemplified by "willingness to suspect, willingness to listen," and lead to the type of radical empathy needed to subvert complacency and hear the subaltern (27). With *Heart of Darkness,* Conrad merges the overarching Victorian desire for storytelling—for engaging in the act of storytelling or, perhaps more pointedly, for serving as the audience for other story-tellers—with the penchant for irony that characterizes modernism's necessarily complex and uncommitted attitude toward social critique.

We can usefully understand Conrad's compelling textual ethics by reflecting on his significant association with Ford Madox Ford, the novelist with whom he coined the phrase "literary impressionism" to account for the means via which each writer establishes an illuminating interrelationship with his readers. As one of proto-modernism's most visible and fruitful collaborations, Conrad and Ford's literary relationship resulted in the publication of three largely undistinguished novels, *The Inheritors* (1901), *Romance* (1903), and *The Nature of a Crime* (1909). More importantly, though, their decade-long collaboration completely altered the nature of each writer's aesthetic by providing Conrad and Ford with an explicit model for tapping into their readership's textual expectations and for establishing, particularly in Conrad's case, explicit ethical constructs in their fictions.[1] Their theories of the novel—most notably, their aspirations for honing a form of literary impressionism in their work—demonstrate their attempts to create a mechanism for eliciting an ethical response in their readers. Simply put, Conrad and Ford fashion a series of self-conscious appeals in their novels to what Hans Robert Jauss describes as the reader's "horizon of expectations," or the manner in which readers interact with and ultimately respond to literary works.[2] Conrad and Ford's literary impressionism, with its accent on the reader's experiences when encountering literary texts, attempts to subvert these horizons of expectation to produce new and eminently more complicated layers of ethical meaning in contrast with their literary precursors.

In his important essay, "On Impressionism," Ford relates their idea of Impressionism in terms of its capacity for impacting—and, indeed, ultimately shifting—readerly perspectives: "Always consider the impressions that you are making upon the mind of the reader," he writes, "and always consider that the first impression with which you present him will be so strong that it will be all that you can ever do to efface it, to alter it or even quite slightly to modify it" (39). In Ford's postulation, the Impressionist technique affords novelists with the ability to capture the nuances of genuine humanity that mark our lives and to ponder the occasional moments in which we reveal the nature of our inner selves: "I suppose that Impressionism exists to render those queer effects of real life that are like so many views seen through bright glass," Ford observes, "through glass so bright that whilst you perceive through it a landscape or a backyard, you are aware that, on its surface, it reflects a face of a person behind you. For the whole of life is really like that," Ford adds, and "we are almost always in one place with our minds somewhere quite other" (41). Ford's Impressionistic technique involves the careful construction of a series of layers of meaning that work in concert to evoke various images and emotions. As Max Saunders notes, Ford's fiction "does not work to subordinate everything to his voice. It re-creates the play of conflicting voices, volitions, attitudes, and viewpoints" (2: 211). Simply put, through their assembly of details and revelations in their novels concerning the lives and proclivities of their characters, Conrad and Ford attempt, in Ford's words, "to produce an illusion of reality" in the mind of their readers ("On Impressionism" 44).

This notion of an "illusion of reality" functions at the core of the writers' practice of literary impressionism in their novels. In his Preface to *The Nigger of the "Narcissus"* (1897)—written during the same period in which he and his collaborator formulated the ethical paradigm that would undergird their later novels—Conrad contends that literary impressionism ensures a given reader's response via its capacity for entreating the reader to tap into his or her auditory and visual senses:

> To snatch a moment of courage, from the remorseless rush of time, a passing phase of life, is only the beginning of the task. The task approached in tenderness and faith is to hold up unquestioningly, without choice and without fear, the rescued fragment before all eyes in the light of a sincere mood. It is to show its vibration, its colour, its form; and through its movement, its form, and its colour, reveal the substance of its truth—disclose its inspiring secret: the stress and passion within the core of each convincing moment. (*Prefaces* 52)

For Conrad, then, literary impressionism involves particular attention to the interaction between the writer's descriptive capabilities and the reader's capacity for registering sensory impressions.[3] The synergy between these two aspects of the reading experience accounts for literary impressionism's power as a narrative construct. Albert J. Guerard describes Conrad and Ford's literary impressionism as "a narrative method of deceptive emphasis and constantly shifting perspective, depending for much of its beauty on swift oscillations between the long view and the close, between the moralizing abstract and the highly visualized particular" (77).

In contrast with Ford—whose textual motives become eminently more diffuse with the publication of his post-Conrad fictions, especially *The Good Soldier: A Tale of Passion* (1915)—Conrad's overtly ethical imperatives remain fairly static throughout his career. Emmanuel Levinas's conception of alterity, contemporary moral philosophy's sine qua non for understanding the nature of our innate responsibilities to our human others, affords us with a useful methodology for interpreting the shape and nature of Conrad's textual ethics.[4] In "Is Ontology Fundamental?" Levinas discusses the ethical significance of other beings in relation to the needs and desires of ourselves. Our ethical obligations to others, Levinas reasons, find their origins in our inability to erase them via negation. Simply put, unless we succeed in negating others through violence, domination, or slavery, we must comprehend others as beings *par excellence* who become signified as "faces," the Levinasian term that refers to the moral consciousness and particularity inherent in others. This "primacy of ontology," in Levinas's words, demonstrates the nature of the collective interrelationships that human beings share with one another (10). In "The Trace of the Other," Levinas argues that "the relationship with the other puts me into question, empties me of myself" (350). More importantly for our purposes here, Levinas describes the concept of the face as "the concrete figure for alterity" (qtd. in Robbins 23). The notion of alterity itself—which Paul-Laurent Assoun characterizes as "the primal scene of ethics" (96)—refers to our inherent responsibilities and obligations to the irreducible face of the other. These aspects of our human condition find their origins in the recognition of sameness that we find in other beings. This similarity of identity and human empathy establishes the foundation for our alterity—in short, the possibility of being "altered"— and for the responsibilities and obligations that we afford to other beings.

In *Time and the Other* (1979), Levinas identifies the absolute exteriority of alterity, as opposed to the binary, dialectic, or reciprocal structure implied in the idea of the other. Hence, alterity implies a state of being apprehended, a state of infinite and absolute otherness. In "Philosophy and the Idea of Infinity," Levinas writes that "we can say that the alterity of the infinite is not canceled, is not extinguished in the thought that thinks it. In thinking infinity the I from the first *thinks more than it thinks*. Infinity does not enter into the *idea* of infinity, is not grasped; this idea is not a concept," he continues. "The infinite is radically, absolutely, other" (54). Alterity's boundless possibilities for registering otherness, for allowing us to comprehend the experiences of others, demonstrates its ethical forcefulness. Its exteriority subverts our self-absorption and challenges us to recognize an ethics of difference and of otherness. Such encounters with other beings oblige us, then, to incur the spheres of responsibility inherent in our alterity. When we perceive the face of the other, we can no longer, at least ethically, suspend responsibility for other beings. In such instances, Levinas writes in "Meaning and Sense," "the I loses its sovereign self-confidence, its identification, in which consciousness returns triumphantly to itself to rest on itself. Before the exigency of the Other (*Autrui*), the I is expelled from the rest and is not the already glorious consciousness of this exile. Any complacency," he adds, "would destroy the straightforwardness of the ethical movement" (54). In this way, the Levinasian concept of exteriority underscores the value of alterity as a means for engendering ethical knowledge.

We can perhaps most usefully comprehend Conrad's Levinasian ethics of alterity and otherness via the five levels of Jauss's reception theory.

Jauss's levels of readerly expectations assist us, moreover, in realizing literary impressionism's ethical imperatives. In *Aesthetic Experience and Literary Hermeneutics* (1982), Jauss creates a communicative model for understanding readerly expectations of literary works, as well as an interpretive framework for explaining the aesthetic pleasure that readers derive from literary texts. Jauss's reception theory includes five levels in which the reader achieves a sense of "aesthetically mediated identification" with the text.[5] During Jauss's first level, the associative level of interaction, the reader experiences the text by aligning himself or herself with the protagonist, often through games or other rites of competition. The second level involves the reader's unadulterated admiration for the protagonist, whereas the third level reflects the reader's sympathy for the text's central character, which the reader now recognizes as flawed and innately human. The fourth, cathartic level of interaction invites further reflection on the reading experience, particularly in terms of the reader's capacity for rendering moral judgment about the literary work. Finally, the fifth or ironic level of interaction involves the reader's sense of critical perception as he or she begins to formulate and refine a more sustained perspective of the literary work's larger meanings beyond the confines of the text (159).

Drawing on Levinas's critical matrix of alterity, a reading of Conrad's ethical aspirations in *Heart of Darkness* through Jauss's critical lens demonstrates the author's considerable humanistic agenda for altering (subverting) our ethical perspectives regarding the sociocultural dilemmas inherent in the colonial world, as well as in ourselves. In *Shadows of Ethics: Criticism and the Just Society* (1999), Geoffrey Galt Harpham observes that "ethics does not solve problems, it structures them" (37). In *Heart of Darkness*, Conrad structures his novella's ethical dimensions through his depiction of Marlow, the character who guides us on our journey to the ethical void. Conrad's Marlow finds his origins in *Lord Jim* (1900), which features a similarly named character who is forced to render moral judgments among difficult personal and psychological circumstances.[6] In dramatic contrast, though, the Marlow of *Heart of Darkness* functions as a more committed and forceful exemplar of humanity. Marlow intuitively understands his place in the world, as well as humanity's precarious role in an evolving society in which civilization can erode and ultimately topple at any moment. In terms of Levinasian philosophy, *Heart of Darkness* challenges Marlow to rethink his personal ethics as he travels deep into the Congo, where he witnesses the effects of European tyranny and greed upon native culture. The horror that he experiences as colonialism wrecks havoc on the Africans as well as the colonizers themselves fills him with a desire to recite his tale and, hence, to imbue his corrosive memories with ethical meaning.

As *Heart of Darkness* begins, Conrad establishes the reader's innate sense of identification with Marlow by highlighting the storyteller's credentials as the narrative's moral compass. Yet the novella is pointedly told from the perspective of an unnamed narrator who sits amid Marlow's audience while the old seafarer unfurls his tragic tale on a cruising yawl moored in the Thames Estuary. Seemingly a beacon of civilization and propriety, the sprawling expanse of London looms just beyond the *Nellie*, the vessel from which Marlow recites his tale. In so doing, Conrad underscores the power of Jauss's associative level of interaction in which readers align themselves with the narrator, who, like themselves, must receive Marlow's story via the virtually unmediated fashion in which he delivers it aboard the *Nellie*. The Buddha-like Marlow tells his story about a woe-begotten visit to the Congo to four rapt listeners; soon, though, we find ourselves, as with Conrad's narrator, equally transfixed by Marlow's vexing narrative. With "sunken cheeks, a yellow complexion, a straight back, an ascetic aspect, and, with his arms dropped, the palms of hands outwards, [he] resembled an idol" (18). After Conrad's nameless narrator genuflects verbally to London's yen for conquest and civilization-building—"What greatness had not floated on the ebb of that river in to the mystery of an unknown earth! . . . The dreams of men, the seed of commonwealths, the germs of empires"—Marlow interrupts with a flourish and explodes the narrator's sea of whitewashed praise: "'And this also,' said Marlow suddenly, 'has been one of the dark places of the earth'" (19). Can Marlow assist his audience in discovering the interpersonal rewards of alterity and otherness? Will the narrator be able to see beyond the unmitigated supremacy of Empire and subvert the dominant ideology?

Marlow's ostensible role as the novella's moral center allows Conrad's readers to identify with his protagonist. For this reason, Marlow pointedly inaugurates his story with a treatise on humankind's propensity for savagery, particularly when civilization's grasp begins to diminish. "The conquest of the earth," Marlow observes, "which mostly means the taking it away from those who have a different complexion or slightly fatter noses than ourselves, is not a pretty thing when you look into it too much" (21). In this manner, Marlow invites us, as judges of a sort, to enter into his story ourselves. In short, he asks us to consider—quite literally— the face of the other. Conrad purposefully represents Marlow in the act of putting forth concepts and offering illustrative scenes, yet the writer never allows his storyteller the opportunity to render any final judgments, which he cedes to the narrator and, ultimately, to the novella's readers. Marlow's journey begins, rather significantly, in Brussels, the picture of contemporary, civilized existence as revealed by Marlow's impressions of the city as "a whited sepulchre" in contrast with the Congo's evolutionary darkness. Marlow's aunt blissfully hopes that her nephew—as an "emissary of light, something like a lower sort of apostle" no less—will bring culture and the gleam of civilization to the Congo's ostensibly savage population. Her words reveal her culture's inability to register exteriority, to see beyond themselves and become truly altered. A pre-voyage visit to the company doctor seems even more ominous. Perfunctory at best, Marlow's physical examination occurs over drinks as the old doctor fumbles to check his patient's pulse. The physician admits that he never sees his patients again after their initial appointments with him. Besides, he adds, the "changes" that they experience "take place inside" the psyche. As Marlow prepares to embark on his voyage, the doctor soberly reminds him that "in the tropics one must before everything keep calm" (26).

As Marlow's expedition takes him ever deeper into the Congo, Conrad exploits the attributes of Jauss's second level of interaction in which readers further align themselves with the protagonist by sharing in his experiences. Hence, as civilization's reach recedes, Marlow finds himself confronted with successively greater moral challenges via which to impress his audience. As with his listeners—indeed, his readers—Marlow admits to being struck by the deafening clash between the untamed, colossal jungle and the vague fabric of civilization. His ship itself seems "incomprehensible" in relation to the jungle's vastness: "Nothing could happen," he notes. "There was a touch of insanity in the proceeding, a sense of lugubrious drollery in the sight" of the steamship as it navigates Africa's "formless" coast and its "uniform somberness" (28). Within the jungle itself, Marlow observes, nameless custom clerks with flagpoles and tin sheds attempt to exert the power of civilization upon an unflinching wilderness. At the mouth of the river, Marlow transfers to another vessel, and his journey into the heart of darkness begins in earnest. At the first company station, he encounters a "scene of inhabited devastation." At one point, he sees a deserted boiler in the grass—an obvious symbol of civilization's defeat at the hands of the jungle—before happening upon a chain gang of natives. Marlow grimly realizes that "I also was a part of the great cause of these high and just proceedings" (29–30). Reduced to mere black shapes by civilization's relentless onslaught, the natives "were dying slowly—it was very clear. They were not enemies, they were not criminals, they were nothing earthly now—nothing but black shadows of disease and starvation, lying confusedly in the greenish gloom" (31). For Conrad's readers, Marlow shines in comparison to what seem to be the jungle's deplorable and amoral ways. Yet how can Conrad assist his readership in subverting the dichotomous relationship that exists between "us and them" inherent in Empire's quest for sociocultural hegemony?

During Jauss's third level of interaction, the reader begins to feel sympathy for the protagonist's human qualities. Conrad accomplishes this end by characterizing Marlow in dramatic contrast with the various, largely unsavory figures whom he encounters during his journey. In one of the novella's most telling scenes regarding the strange contradiction that occurs in the wilderness between civilized propriety and the jungle's untrodden ways, Marlow describes his meeting with the company's chief accountant, "a white man, in such an unexpected elegance of get-up that in the first moment I took him for a sort of vision. I saw a high-starched collar, white cuffs, a light alpaca jacket, snowy trousers, a clean necktie, and varnished boots. No hat. Hair parted, brushed, oiled, under a green-lined parasol held in a big white hand. He was amazing, and had a pen-holder behind his ear" (32). The accountant—a "miracle" of modern civilization loosed upon the jungle—evinces an utter devotion to his books, via which he attempts to effect pristine order upon the wilderness. In addition to training a native woman to do his ironing, the chief accountant toils in a brutally humid office in which humongous, stabbing flies buzz overhead. In one instance, an agonizingly sick employee appears on a gurney. Amazingly, the accountant dares to complain that the man's groans "distract my attention. And without that it is extremely difficult to guard against clerical errors in this climate" (33). In this way, Marlow communicates to Conrad's audience the tragic fact that nothing, it seems, is worthy of interrupting society's amoralistic rage for order.

Jauss's third level of interaction is further revealed by Marlow's experiences with Mr. Kurtz, as well as other characters whom he encounters in the Congo. It is through the accountant that Marlow first learns about the storied Mr. Kurtz, a fabulously successful agent in the company's employ who trades in ivory in the jungle's interior. With a safari of sixty men in tow, Marlow begins his 200-mile journey to the Central Station. Along the way, Marlow encounters abandoned and pillaged villages, the devastating aftermath of slave traders. At this juncture, Marlow suffers another delay—his steamer will require nearly a month to undergo repairs—that will allow him to linger a bit and survey the jungle's psychologically overwhelming social and geographical landscape. The station manager, for example, suffers from the malaise engendered by life in the wilderness. "He was neither civil nor uncivil," Marlow observes. The jungle and his dreams of usurping Kurtz have reduced him to a "chattering idiot" (36, 37). Later, Marlow happens upon the company's nefarious brickmaker, who plumbs Marlow for information about the firm and its plans. The brickmaker's conniving, immoral behavior prompts Marlow to declare that "I hate, detest, and can't bear a lie, not because I am straighter than the rest of us, but simply because it appalls me. There is a taint of death, a flavor of mortality in lies—which is exactly what I hate and detest in the world—what I want to forget" (41). In this way, Conrad critiques Empire's blunt inhumanity—in short, the big lie that allows expansionism to continue unabated and without ethical reflection. For Marlow, colonialism's moral vacuousness can result in nothing more (or less) than spiritual death.

Heart of Darkness engages Jauss's fourth level of interaction—the level in which readers begin to reflect on their various interpretations of the novella and render moral judgments—almost entirely through Marlow's confused and often debilitating experiences as he nears and finally arrives at the Inner Station. Having heard Kurtz's name spoken of with a combination of reverence and fear, Marlow imagines the agent to be a man of moral determination and civilized demeanor—the antithesis of the Europeans whom he has encountered in the jungle thus far. In a supreme moment revealing Conrad and Ford's well-honed literary impressionism, Marlow describes the natives' surprise attack—a "tumultuous and mournful uproar"—on his steamer as the craft approaches the Inner Station. The death of his helmsman affects Marlow particularly deeply, and he is thunderstruck by the seemingly instantaneous calamity that the attack causes: "The rest of the world was nowhere, as far as our eyes and ears were concerned," Marlow remembers. "Just nowhere. Gone, disappeared; swept off without leaving a whisper or a shadow behind" (55). From Marlow's uninitiated purview, the sight of the steamship must have filled the natives with so much "extreme grief" that they had no other choice but to attack the vessel that was encroaching on the wilderness. Marlow feels even more dismay over the possibility of the natives having extinguished Kurtz as well: "I was cut to the quick at the idea of having lost the inestimable privilege of listening to the gifted Kurtz" (63).

By establishing Marlow as inherently flawed and capable of gross mistakes in judgment, Conrad prepares his readers for Jauss's fifth level of interaction in which they enjoy an ironic view of the novella itself and its larger moral implications. Marlow subsequently learns that Kurtz orchestrated the natives' attack on the steamer to continue his dominion over the natives and the Inner Station. To Marlow's great surprise and dismay, Kurtz, it seems, had been undone by the jungle's "solitude without a policeman" (64). In addition to encouraging and presiding over the natives' ritualistic self-sacrifices, Kurtz had been entrusted by the International Society for the Suppression of Savage Customs with the imperative of writing a report about the need to "Exterminate all the brutes!" (66). The increasingly jaded Marlow eventually reaches the Inner Station, where he finds Kurtz's headquarters in a putrid building surrounded by posts ornamented with human skulls. Kurtz's soul, Marlow reports, had been seduced by the jungle: "Being alone in the wilderness, it had looked within itself, and, by Heavens! I tell you, it had gone mad," says Marlow. "I saw the inconceivable mystery of a soul that knew no restraint, no faith, and no fear, yet struggling blindly with itself" (82). In short, the jungle's clash with civilization has left Kurtz hollow and soulless, virtually unable to draw on any innate sense of ethics or human decency. An empty shell of a man, he dies, thus leaving Marlow as the only witness to his terrible fate. As if entranced by the awful vision of his life in the wilderness, Kurtz mutters his notorious last words, "The horror! The horror!" (85). Moments later, the manager's boy dismisses the natives' oppressor with contempt and scorn: "Mistah Kurtz—he dead" (86).

Heart of Darkness completes its tour of Jauss's five levels of readerly expectation by returning Marlow to civilization, where he, as with the nameless narrator and with Conrad's readership, can finally recognize the extent of humanity's depravity, as well as the corrosive power of the colonial myth despite our paralyzing belief that it can sustain civilization's self-aggrandizing desires for moral elevation. And Marlow accomplishes this end by reciting the story of his own agonizing discovery of otherness and alterity. Hence, Marlow's experiences back in Europe—safe within the confines of Brussels, that sepulchral city—allow him to reflect on his own encounter with the void, "a vision of greyness without form filled with physical pain, and a careless contempt for the evanescence of all things" (86–87). He later presents a journalist with Kurtz's report on the "Suppression of Savage Customs," but only after having removed its most vile desideratum. Soon thereafter, Marlow visits the doomed agent's fiancée to return her correspondence and her portrait. When she demands to know Kurtz's last words, Marlow chooses to lie, despite his disgust for equivocation. "The last word he pronounced," Marlow tells her, "was—your name" (93). For Marlow, "it seemed to me that the house would collapse before I could escape, that the heavens would fall upon my head. But nothing happened" (94). Although his own ethical reification has altered his soul—and at a terribly painful cost, no less—Marlow simply cannot bring himself to destroy the cultural mythologies inherent in the mind-set of Kurtz's fiancée, as well as in much of Western culture during the colonial era.

As with Marlow's listeners on the *Nellie*, Conrad's readers are left only to ponder the vast heart of darkness that exists just beyond the reach of civilization's grasp. It is within that horribly empty place that ethics loses its hold and where human beings fill the ensuing void with disillusion and a potentiality for evil. Conrad's narrative, with its affecting literary impressionism, asks us to look within that void as well. Exploring the five levels of Jauss's communicative model underscores the ways in which Conrad's narrative establishes a vital interrelationship with his readers to challenge us into considering Levinas's ethics of otherness and becoming altered ourselves. In hindsight, Conrad's ethical imperatives must have seemed positively radical as one century of Western cultural dominion continued into yet another epoch characterized by civilization's unquenchable and often unscrutinized zeal for expansionism.[7] If nothing else, *Heart of Darkness*'s portraits of Kurtz and the post-Congo Marlow demonstrate precisely what happens when we become consumed with the needs of the self to the detriment of the larger communities in which we live. As the teachings of Levinasian ethics so often remind us, when we refuse to see the face of the other, we invariably cease to understand ourselves.

NOTES

1. Conrad and Ford's biographers continue to debate the exact nature of the writers' collaboration, as well as about the degree of its impact and influence on their future novels. Richard A. Cassell argues that, for Ford at least, "the collaboration with Conrad had permanently altered Ford's creative talents on writing and led to his years of intense literary activity" (9). Leo Gurko contends that the collaboration merely provided Conrad with the opportunity to work with a native English speaker who possessed considerable aesthetic sensibilities. "Conrad's motive was apparently linguistic and technical," Gurko writes (103). Norman Sherry reveals, moreover, that Ford often exaggerated his influence upon Conrad, especially regarding his role in the genesis of Conrad's *The Secret Agent* (1906). Yet many, if not all, of their biographers and critics agree that Conrad and Ford's conception of literary impressionism exerted a resounding impact on their individual novels. Carl D. Bennett, for example, describes their collaboration and its aesthetic rewards as "unquestionably symbiotic" (28).

2. We can more usefully understand Jauss's notion of an "horizon of expectations" by reviewing his postulation of the reading experience itself. Drawing on the insights of Aristotle and Montaigne, Jauss ascribes the reader's need for ethical catharsis to his or her desire to experience the "exemplary" aspects of the reading experience. Jauss defines the concept of the exemplary as the quality of reflection that the reader enjoys when contemplating the interaction between the aesthetic experience and the invariably shifting nature of the self. Perhaps even more importantly, Jauss's concept of the exemplary "can bridge the gap between aesthetic judgment and moral praxis and make clear the transition from aesthetic to moral identification" (111). In this way, readers achieve more expansive senses of identification with the literary work itself, as well as with the experiences of the characters in its pages. The textual experience affords readers with moments of aesthetic pleasure via their increasing transition into states of self-reflection and self-awareness.

3. In his essay memorializing Conrad's life and work, Ford writes that "we agreed that the general effect of a novel must be the general effect that life makes on mankind. A novel must therefore not be a narration, a report. . . . We in turn, if we wished to produce on you an effect of life," Ford adds, "must not narrate but render . . . impressions" (72–73).

4. The notion of a Levinasian critical matrix is itself a matter of considerable theoretical debate. In *Ethical Criticism: Reading after Levinas* (1998), Robert Eaglestone argues, rather unconvincingly, that "Levinas's thought cannot be turned into a methodology: it is not a philosophy that can be *applied*. . . . To ask for a Levinasian critical method is to ask for something that cannot and should not exist" (176; italics added). In fact, Eaglestone offers little evidence demonstrating the thrust of his contention beyond his observation that "there is obviously no one critical process which embodies Levinas's ideas, no one answer" (176). Yet Levinas's ethical philosophy quite obviously posits its own terminology—including such concepts as "adequation," "alterity," "the face," and "negation," among a host of others. Simply put, Levinasian philosophy, despite Eaglestone's misgivings, can easily be *applied* as an interpretive matrix in much the same interdisciplinary fashion as gender studies, psychology, history, and sociology—to name but a few of literary criticism's multitudinous allied disciplines, each of which possesses its own contingent of thinkers with their own critical vocabularies.

5. Jauss distinguishes his five levels of interaction from Northrop Frye's typology of the hero by noting that his own levels of reception exist "as a nexus of functions of the aesthetic experience," particularly as they "are derived from an examination of historically attested interaction patterns." In Jauss's estimation, Frye's five-pronged typology substitutes the generalities inherent in archetypal mythology for an understanding of the peculiar modalities of readerly reception that impinge upon the ways in which we encounter and ultimately ascribe meaning to literary texts (154).

6. Although *Lord Jim* was published a year later than *Heart of Darkness*, it was written for serialization before Conrad began working on the novella. Hence, the Marlow of *Heart of Darkness* represents a later, more mature incarnation of the character. See Bennett 75.

7. Our potential for unchecked hubris is perhaps best illustrated by the words of Ishmael Reed, who remarks that "in the twentieth century we've seen a lot of disasters happen because of people who thought they were right and everybody else was wrong" (338).

WORKS CITED

Assoun, Paul-Laurent. "The Subject and the Other in Levinas and Lacan." *Levinas and Lacan: The Missed Encounter*. Translated by Dianah Jackson and Denise Merkle, edited by Sarah Harasym. State U of New York P, 1998, pp. 79–101.

Bennett, Carl D. *Joseph Conrad*. Continuum, 1991.

Cassell, Richard A. *Ford Madox Ford: A Study of His Novels*. Johns Hopkins UP, 1962.

Conrad, Joseph. *Heart of Darkness*. Edited by Ross C. Murfin, St. Martin's, 1989.

———. *Prefaces to His Work*. Dent, 1937.

Eaglestone, Robert. *Ethical Criticism: Reading after Levinas*. Edinburgh UP, 1998.

Ford, Ford Madox. "On Impressionism." *Critical Writings of Ford Madox Ford*, edited by Frank MacShane, U of Nebraska P, 1964, pp. 33–55.

Guerard, Albert J. *Conrad the Novelist*. Harvard UP, 1962.

Gurko, Leo. *Joseph Conrad: Giant in Exile*. Macmillan, 1962.

Harpham, Geoffrey Galt. *Shadows of Ethics: Criticism and the Just Society*. Duke UP, 1999.

Jauss, Hans Robert. *Aesthetic Experience and Literary Hermeneutics*. Translated by Michael Shaw, U of Minnesota P, 1982.

Levinas, Emmanuel. *Emmanuel Levinas: Basic Philosophical Writings*. Edited by Adriaan T. Peperzak, Simon Critchley, and Robert Bernasconi, Indiana UP, 1996.

———. "Is Ontology Fundamental?" *Basic Philosophical Writings*, translated by Simon Critchley, Peter Atterton, and Graham Noctor, edited by Levinas, pp. 2–10.

———. "Meaning and Sense." *Basic Philosophical Writings*, translated by Alphonso Lingis, edited by Levinas, pp. 33–64.

———. "Philosophy and the Idea of Infinity." *Collected Philosophical Papers*, translated by Alphonso Lingis, Martinus Nijhoff, 1987, pp. 47–59.

———. *Time and the Other*. Translated by Richard Cohen, Duquesne UP, 1985.

———. "The Trace of the Other." *Deconstruction in Context: Literature and Philosophy*. Translated by Alphonso Lingis, edited by Mark C. Taylor, U of Chicago P, 1986, pp. 345–59.

Makaryk, Irena R. *Encyclopedia of Contemporary Literary Theory: Approaches, Scholars, Terms*. U of Toronto P, 1993.

Reed, Ishmael. "The Many Battles of Ishmael Reed." Interview with George Paul Csicsery. *Conversations with Ishmael Reed*, edited by Bruce Dick and Amritjit Singh, UP of Mississippi, 1995, pp. 314–338.

Ricouer, Paul. *Freud and Philosophy: An Essay on Interpretation*. Yale University Press, 1970.

Robbins, Jill. *Altered Reading: Levinas and Literature*. U of Chicago P, 1999.

Saunders, Max. *Ford Madox Ford: A Dual Life*. 2 vols. Oxford UP, 1996.

Sherry, Norman. *Conrad's Western World*. Cambridge UP, 1971.

Part III

Subversive Genres

EIGHT

"Count me in": Comedy in *Dracula*

Ira B. Nadel

1

> "Quick!" he said. "Bring the brandy."
> *Dracula*, Ch. X

Puzzlement, if not surprise, is one's likely response to the idea of *Dracula* as a comic novel. How, one might ask, can a story of vampirism and horror be humorous? Early stage adaptations, however, had no trouble in responding to its comic spirit. A 1927 West End production not only included numerous laugh lines—"I have lived too long in Italy to care for the smell of Garlic" exclaims the Count at one point—but also took liberties with the plot by modernizing the novel: Dracula arrives in England by plane not boat. Produced by the actor-manager Hamilton Deane, the show also employed a nurse to be on-call during performances to assist those overcome by the sensational action. One memorable performance required smelling salts for thirty-nine audience members. A souvenir of the 250th performance at the Prince of Wales Theatre in London included a special edition of Stoker's story "Dracula's Guest" with a hidden cardboard bat that flew out of the book as it was opened, propelled by a rubber band (Skal HG 75, 77).[1]

Filmmakers also reacted to the comedy in the novel. Roman Polanski's *Fearless Vampire Killers* (1969) with Sharon Tate, *Dracula Père et Fils* (1976) with Christopher Lee, *Love at First Bite* (1979) starring George Hamilton, and Mel Brooks' *Dracula: Dead and Loving It* with Leslie Nielsen (1995) are several examples among myriad remakes emphasizing the comic properties of the text. Christopher Lee, who played the Count in two adaptations and six sequels, remarked how silly it was to portray a vampire who stepped out of the shadows wearing a white tie, tails, patent leather shoes, and a cloak (Joslin 26). Every Dracula has been overdressed, although in the 1931 film version with Bela Lugosi, it seemed appropriate; the Count joins Dr. Seward's party at a London symphony to hear excerpts of Wagner's *Die Meistersinger* (Joslin 34).

The often campy presentation of Dracula's world in these works masks the horrific, while emphasizing the Gothic. The visually comedic is an antidote to fear, an alternate to the "world of dark and dreadful things" (D 398),[2] underscored by Lugosi's comic line to Renfield, "I never drink . . . wine," dialogue that does *not* appear in the novel. The source of the campy style, however, is the text itself, its essential comedy expressed in its theatrical language and action. *Dracula* is less a novel about horror and more a study in comic, if not melodramatic, extremes as in "His eyes. They burned into me, and my strength became like water" (D 321).

Melodrama, in fact, is the comic key to the work. Stock characters—the suffering hero, persecuting villain, figure of benevolence—plus conventional morality destined to eliminate evil characterize *Dracula.* The allure of the melodramatic dominates, the result of Bram Stoker's theatrical experience as a young drama critic in Dublin and his many years as Henry Irving's business manager in London's Lyceum Theatre. Stoker may have also understood that the success of his novel would be enhanced by grafting elements from melodrama, the most popular form of theatrical performance at this time, to his story. Stabbings, poisonings, shootings, and even bloodsucking were common obstacles to the onstage defeat of evil. Throughout *Dracula,* melodrama rules, although its comic representation undermines its overwrought manner, often associated with Irving's acting style. *Dracula*'s comedy critiques melodrama's believability. Irving was not the basis of *Dracula,* but his acting method may have inspired Stoker's criticism of the form.

Melodrama as a dramatic style was wearing thin in the late 1890s, but it provided a method for Stoker to present his story.[3] Stoker likely admired the genre's satisfying if unreal emotional vision and clear-cut morality of the genre. But the uncomplicated nature of melodrama, simplifying and idealizing experience, challenged Stoker who alternately took it seriously but chose to represent it comically in his novel. Comic relief, often through rapid change, is a vital feature of melodrama allowing release from desperate emotion and violence.

Stoker's encounter with melodrama began as a Dublin drama critic. From 1871 to 1876 he was an unpaid but productive theater reviewer for the *Dublin Evening Mail,* while continuing his career as an Irish Civil Servant. One of his biographers refers to him as "the most educated drama critic in Dublin" (Belford 51). What he saw was largely melodrama, the principal form of theatrical expression for the late nineteenth-century Irish theatergoer who "demanded spectacle" as Peter Kavanagh writes in his history of the Irish theatre (Kavanagh 396). Scenery, stage effects, and acting had to intrigue audiences and spectacular theater was a staple. Boucicault's move from the comedy of manners (*London Assurance*) to melodrama (*The Colleen Bawn*) represents the change. He previously, in 1852, adapted the libretto *La Dame de Pique*, a melodrama known as *The Vampire*. A production of *The Vampire*, a Gothic melodrama, played at the Theater Royal in Dublin as early as the spring of 1821 (Morash 80). T. W. Robertson's domestic dramas addressing social problems, as in *Caste*, were of note but not of great popular interest. The melodramas of Hubert O'Grady, however, triumphed, his play *The Famine* quickly becoming an Irish favorite.

Patriotic Irish melodramas were also a nineteenth-century dramatic tradition with titles like *Shoulder to Shoulder*, *The Nationalist*, or *The Spectre of the Past* common (Herr 6). Playwrights such as J. W. Whitbread and Patrick J. Bourke continued the genre (Herr 14–15). The 1877 revival of O'Grady's *The Shaughraun* was also immensely popular. O'Grady in 1885 would found the Irish National Company to produce his own political melodramas with titles like *Eviction*, *Emigration*, and *The Famine*, each title a clue to the action. Political melodramas continued through the early years of the twentieth century, Casimir Markievicz's *The Memory of The Dead: A Romantic Drama of '98* but one example. Melodrama, however, was a truant form, considered disrespectful of theatrical expression partly because of its sensational character. Queen Victoria was in fact criticized in the press for attending *The Corsican Brothers* at the Princess's Theatre. Boucicault's adaptation of Dumas's story was considered a great popular success (Rowell 83).

An important feature of melodramatic Irish political drama at this time, found in *Dracula*, was the bonding of the audience in "pleasurable hatred" against an enemy (Morash 112). A kind of communal condemnation emerged in works where the informer or villain was literally hissed by the audience. In *Dracula*, the creation of an army of four men plus Mina in hot pursuit of the Count makes it clear that virtue seeks, and will succeed, in rooting out evil. Readers are never confused about motive nor the identity of their moral heroes in the work. Condemnation builds up to be satisfied only in the spectacle of punishment, in Stoker's work the staking and beheading of the Un-Dead, and then the final killing of Dracula.

Another form of popular entertainment was the pantomime, which presented a transcendent world conceived in terms of space and magnitude mixing trick effects and spectacular exploits. In *Dracula*, this is Harker witnessing the Count's remarkable and silent descent down the castle's wall headfirst (D 65). Preceding this is a moment of reverse pantomime when Harker realizes the Count's image fails to appear in a mirror when he greets him one morning (D 56). The grotesque was often another feature, as well as satire and topical ideas (Booth 74). Panoramas, magicians, and even jugglers would also have a part.[4] Pantomimes became a staple of Irish theater from the early decades of the nineteenth century; *Aladdin* being one of the most popular with even a genie disappearing into a quart bottle (Morash 80, 82).

The Irish music hall was also a thriving form and it is possible that Stoker would have enjoyed its late nineteenth-century extension, vaudeville. This finds its way occasionally into *Dracula*, one comic example the almost slapstick action of John Seward when he comes to Lucy to express his love. Outwardly cool, he is inwardly nervous as Lucy narrates: "He had evidently been schooling himself as to all sorts of little things, and remembered them; but he almost managed to sit down on his silk hat, which men don't generally do when they are cool. . . ." (D 89).

A later example of unexpected if dark comedy occurs when Van Helsing hypnotizes Mina. Van Helsing then studies her teeth, warning Seward that "as long as they do not begin to sharpen there is no active danger of a change in her" (D 377).

Italian and later German operas were also popular entertainments among late nineteenth-century Dublin theatergoers. Christopher Morash in his history of Irish theater claims that Italian opera from the 1840s onward "completely overwhelmed the sound of the spoken work on Irish stages," which likely contributed to Stoker's conception of dramatic action in the novel (Morash 108). Works by Rossini, Bellini, Donizetti, and Verdi were among the favorites. By the 1880s, Wagner was equally admired, and at least one week a year, the Carl Rosa Company of Dublin presented *Tannhauser* or *Tristram und Isolde*. Between roughly 1850 and 1880, Dublin had visits from all the important European opera companies and singers, including Jenny Lind.

Gounod's *Faust*, for example, premiered in Dublin a month after its initial appearance in London in 1863; in Stoker's 1875 short story "The Primrose Path," the central character attends a dress rehearsal of Goethe's *Faust*, noting that the costumes were the same as those used in Gounod's opera. Irish opera, itself, was developing in the century, imitating on stage many of the exaggerated mannerisms of European productions; Michael Balfe's *The Bohemian Girl* (1843) and Charles Villiers Stanford's *Shamus O'Brien* (1896), first premiered in London, were two of the best known. The latter focused on the 1789 uprising.[5]

Stoker attended opera and actually knew Stanford because he provided some incidental music for Lyceum productions, including Tennyson's *Beckett*. In 1896, Stanford wrote to Henry Irving asking if he could engage Stoker to help with the theatrical side of mounting an opera. Little came of the invitation, however, although they shared a mutual love of music. Stanford had arranged for Stoker to get a pass for Wagner's *die Meistersinger* when it premiered in London in 1882 (Murray 95). Supplementing opera were the exaggerated gestures and elaborately acted songs of the Irish music hall, additional factors in Stoker's continued reliance on melodramatic presentation (Kavanagh 400).

In June 1878, Stoker arrived in London, the day before Irving's production of W. G. Wills's version of the Flying Dutchman legend, *Vanderdecken*, premiered. Wagner's *The Flying Dutchman* had first played in London in 1876 and H. L. Bateman, American impresario of the Lyceum, thought a play on the subject would be a draw and that Irving should star as the phantom sea captain condemned to eternal travel. Wills's *Vanderdecken* was the successful result. Stoker had assisted Irving in editing the text about a figure suspended between life and death, a work which had a lasting impression on his conception of *Dracula*.

In his personal reminiscence of Irving, Stoker records the impact of the melodramatic and sensational acting of Irving in *Vanderdecken*. He particularly notes how Irving gave "a wonderful impression of a dead man fictitiously alive." His first appearance "was the most striking and startling thing I ever saw on the stage" he writes. The scene was the landing place on the edge of the fiord. The recreation of nature with the sun and blue sky mesmerized the audience as a single mariner appeared in a cloak of brown and peacock blue with a touch of red. He wore a sable cap. He stood there silently "more like a vision made solid than a living man, realizing well the description of the phantom sailor" (PR I: 55–56).[6]

The description of the spirit the captain of the *Demeter* tries to kill in *Dracula* is similar, as is the Count's landing in England as a great hound in the storm at Whitby. Both echo this early image of Irving (D 119–20). The eyes of the captain shone "like cinders of glowing red from out the marble face," much like the eyes of Dracula who has eyes "like burning flames" (D 129). This quasi-Miltonic image parallels descriptions of Mephistopheles in Irving's *Faust* and earlier in *Vanderdecken*. In a comment on the scene, Stoker emphasizes the living/dead aspect of Irving's portrait that *Vanderdecken* outlines as the state "between the living and the dead!'" (PR I: 56). In a draft second chapter of the novel, Harker stops in Munich on his way to Transylvania to attend a performance of *The Flying Dutchman* (Belford 263).

Stoker's exposure and involvement with the plays and acting of Irving reaffirmed the importance and appeal of the melodramatic first presented to him in the Irish theater. For Stoker, from the moment he saw Irving act in Ireland through his years as manager of the Lyceum Theatre in London from 1878 until Irving's death, melodrama dominated. The influence of the Lyceum, however, has not been fully explored in studies of the novel (Auerbach 199). Yet it is inescapable. Adding to the on-stage melodrama and Irving's melodramatic acting style was Irving's mesmeric power over Stoker who idolized the commanding, self-absorbed figure off stage and on. Ellen Terry's biographer refers to Irving's "unholy charm" (Auerbach 199, 200).

As an actor, Irving was known for remounting the villain as a quasi-sympathetic figure, beginning with his 1871 success *The Bells*, a restaging of *Le Juif polonaise*. The play is about the guilt of Matthias caught in the grip of his early crime: murdering a Polish Jew who had been his guest at his inn and stealing his gold. Haunted by the image of his victim years later, he melodramatically relives the crime in a dream sequence on the eve of his daughter's wedding and in a second dream sequence is forced to confess through the use of hypnotism. At the conclusion, he staggers across the stage and falls dead. Throughout his long career, Irving specialized in such roles, a villain who combined evil with manners, qualities Stoker would develop in Count Dracula (Rahill 211). The Lyceum alternated elaborate productions of Shakespeare with such melodramas s *The Lyons Mail*, Charles Reade's adaptation of a French play, *Lady of Lyons* by Bulwer Lytton, and Watts Phillips's *The Dead Heart*.

Irving as an inspiration for Dracula, especially his power and presence, is uncertain but possible given his behavior and closeness to Stoker. An apocryphal story was that Stoker originally conceived the story as a play with Irving in the lead. Stoker's descriptions of Irving correspond closely with his portrait of the Count (as well as the reverse). Fear and animosity, as much as support and praise, defined Stoker's relation with the actor who in the late 1880s and early 1890s generated much friction with Stoker. During that period, Stoker faced a series of crises as manager, battling with members of Irving's company. He began to put his rivals in his early fiction. The Austin brothers, employees of Irving's whom Stoker despised, appear as bloodthirsty twins his tale "The Dualitists" (1887; Belford 178–9).

Irving's personal manner, as Max Beerbohm recorded, bordered on the horrific: "he had an incomparable power for eeriness—for stirring a dim sense of mystery; and not less masterly was he in evoking a sharp sense of horror." Stoker, himself, wrote that Irving was a "histrionic genius" (in Belford 71). Beerbohm later commented that Irving, who constantly observed others, "wished to be feared as well as loved"; he always sought control (in Belford 100). In 1876, he returned to Dublin to play a mesmerizing *Hamlet*, which Stoker praised in the *Evening Mail* leading that night to a meeting, a friendship, and subsequently a job. On their second meeting, Irving recited the melodramatic "The Dream of Eugene Aram" by Thomas Hood with such force that Stoker was spellbound (PR I: 28–29). Murder, a recovered corpse, and a hanging are central to the work that was so forceful in its presentation that Irving collapsed in a faint at the end before the stunned audience of twelve. A later reading at Trinity College, Dublin moved Stoker to write in the *Dublin Evening Mail* that Irving is "'a great melodramatic actor" and the "onlooker feels his blood turning cold to look at the actor's face and to listen to the broken tones of his voice'" (in Murray 73).

Irving's spectacular production of *Faust* (1885) is likely another source for *Dracula*. To establish authenticity, Irving and Stoker went to the Brocken Mountains in Germany where the climatic scenes were set. According to tradition, they are one of the meeting places of witches. The two then apparently went to Nuremberg for nearly two weeks, visiting among other sites, the town's torture tower which housed the Nuremberg Virgin, an instrument of torture employing iron spikes and later to be featured in Stoker's short story, "The Squaw" (1893; Murray 153). Irving was so taken with Nuremberg and the neighboring Rothenberg that he sent for his scene painter so that he could absorb the landscape later reproduced on stage and acquired antiques and other items to bring back to authenticate his production (although he altered Goethe's setting from Leipzig to Nuremberg because of the medieval setting). Stoker has Mina refer to Nuremberg at the opening of Chapter VI of *Dracula*. Critics have argued that Irving's interpretation of Mephistopheles—he had been playing the part five years when Stoker began to outline his novel, complete with flashing eyes and whirling scarlet cloak—is a source for Dracula's behavior. The rendering of Mephistopheles as recorded in the *Illustrated Sporting and Dramatic News* and on the cover of a musical score for the "Mephistopheles March" anticipate the image Stoker draws for Dracula (Booth figs. 19, 20).

Irving's production emphasized the supernatural, marked from his first entrance in mist as Mephistopheles. The first scene of Faust in his study, lit by moonlight and a single candle, also set the scene for how Stoker would show Dracula in his castle. Of particular note was the finale with a ladder of angels ingeniously arranged on a steel rail hung from the flies with iron arms on which the actors stood. Stoker describes the impact of the vision in his *Personal Reminiscences*. As Mephistopheles sweeps Faust away enveloped in his cloak, lightening flashes, music swells, angelic voices rise, and the back wall of the dungeon opens as rays of light illuminate the ascending angels singing of Margaret's ascent to Heaven. The play ended with this striking tableau, the music from the orchestra of more than thirty providing a crescendo. For some critics, the music transformed the production into opera. Sheet music from the production was readily available.

Faust was Irving's greatest hit, given 187 performances in its first season. It played periodically until 1902, including a major remounting of 76 performances in 1894 and 3 in 1895 during the period Stoker was working on the manuscript of *Dracula*. Irving played Mephistopheles 792 times between 1885 and 1902 (PR I: 175).[7] The *New York Times* review of the play in November 1887 noted that the work operated as a series of dissolving views, the entire drama moving panoramically while "stealthy and devilish figures flit in the shadows, and angelic faces burn out on the canvas" (in Booth 124). Many scenes were set at sunset, night, or the early dawn prefiguring the perilous state of vampire life. The result was mysterious and magical. And Irving, like Dracula, dominated: he appeared in all twelve scenes. He presented Mephistopheles as mix of a "debonair man-about town and the fiend" mixing sophistication with evil, habits not unlike those seen in Dracula (Booth 125). Critics questioned his mocking, flippant, pantomimic gestures, finding his comic gestures too emphatic, but it appears to have contributed to Stoker's conception of the Count. Irving's mannered acting style suited not only his interpretation of Mephistopheles but also Stoker's conception of Dracula.

Watching the rehearsal of the Brocken scene, Stoker was moved by the lighting, action, and "all the rush and whirl and triumphant cataclysm of unfettered demonical possession" (PR I: 146). A comment by Irving to Stoker at the time might have been another inspiration for detail in *Dracula*. Irving told him that his appearance in "flaming scarlet" would be intensified by a storm on the mountain and that Ellen Terry's white dress and "red scar across her throat will stand out in the midst of that turmoil of lightening" (PR I: 147). Here, melodrama, sexuality and drama unite to reappear in *Dracula*. At the ending, a vision of Margaret lying dead at the foot of the cross with a long line of descending angels, emphasizing the panoramic sweep of the stage, anticipates the broader, dramatic, and operatic scenes in *Dracula*, from the Count's stylized attack on Mina to the "posse's" encounter with the gypsies as they close in on the Count (D 322, 414–17).

Faust deeply affected Stoker's imagination. The opening on 19 December 1885, with the Prince of Wales in the audience, was impressive and exceeded in social terms only by the later visit of Emperor Frederick, then Crown Prince of Germany. One of the most dramatic scenes was the fight between Faust and Valentine with Mephistopheles, supposedly invisible, intervening. This was the first time electric flashes were used in a play. The ingenious transfer of electric charges that caused the crossed swords to flash on contact was new in the theater (PR I: 176; Booth 115–16). So, too, the fire that burst from Faust's table and from the ground on command of Mephistopheles. These effects find their way into the pictorial atmosphere of *Dracula*, which relies on repeated stage effects such as off stage sound: "there was a sort of scratching or flapping at the window, but I did not mind it" Lucy writes at one point in her diary (D 145).

Lighting in the novel is repeatedly theatrical whether the description of "sunset over London, with its lurid lights and inky shadows," or at Lucy's tomb where a "white streak" moves between "two dark yew-trees" against an overcast sky (D 152, 236). Throughout the novel, light combines theatricality with melodrama. Throughout the novel, remarks suggest its theatrical nature, providing its own sense of tragedy. At one point, Mina writes that all seems "like a horrible tragedy with fate pressing on relentlessly to some destined end" (D 296). Everything that one does, "no matter how right it might be" brings on its opposite (D 296).

Shakespeare was another source, especially in Irving's melodramatic productions that earned him great praise. His productions of *Hamlet*, *Macbeth*, and *Othello* visualized the dramatic presentation of danger and its consequences. When Irving enunciated Hamlet's cry, "Now could I drink hot blood," he implicitly links his action to vampires (III. iii. 398).

Extensive references to Shakespeare appear throughout the novel (see Miller, *Reflections*, Ch. 8; Hopkins 57–65). Stoker's early chapter outlines of the novel also read something like a theater program, drawing from stage vampires popular since the 1820 Parisian production of *Le Vampire* by Nodier and Jouffroy (Stoker, Notes, *passim*). Parts of this work in an English adaptation were performed at the Lyceum.

2

"I want to cut off her head and take out her heart."
Dracula, Ch. XIII

Melodrama permeates the novel. When the Count exerts control over Mina, he relies on excessive language, announcing at one point "a little refreshment to reward my exertions" before calling her "my bountiful wine-press" (D 327–28). Actions as well as language are melodramatic. When the Count enters a room in his London home with the waiting "hunting party," the action is violent: as they move to attack, Harker strikes out with his "great Kukri knife" of the Gurkhas (345). The count manages to leap back but "the blow was a powerful one. . . . a second less and the trenchant blade had shorne through his heart. As it was, the point just cut the cloth of his coat, making a wide gap whence a bundle of bank-notes and a stream of gold fell out" (D 346). The outpouring of gold is a melodramatic touch to the already dance-like action. Sensing, the threat of another blow, the Count dives under Harker's arm, scoops up several sovereigns and crashes through the window only to recover and curse the "posse" before disappearing (D 347). Earlier, when the wafer sears Mina's forehead, insurance for her protection from the Count, she sinks "on her knees on the floor in an agony of abasement" (D 336). Agony reappears on the page when Harker, listening to the distraught narrative of Mina's encounter with the Count, writes that he threw himself "beside her in an agony of helpless grief," the exaggerated action extending the melodramatic mode (D 336). Harker's early attempt to find the key to release himself from his room in the Count's castle, ending with his attempt to smash the Count while he lies, smirkingly, in his coffin, mixes the melodramatic with the horrific: "the last glimpse I had was of the bloated face, blood-stained and fixed with a grim of malice which would have held its own in the nethermost hell" (D 83–84).

Melodrama's control over the action of *Dracula*, even when most violent, finds expression in various individual remarks. "There was something diabolically sweet in her tones" Seward recounts when Lucy, under the Count's power, tempts Arthur to come to her is one example (D 250). Only Van Helsing's intervention prevents Arthur's seduction by the new vampire. But melodrama rules, often through language: when Van Helsing tells Seward what must be done to eliminate the Un-Dead status of

Lucy, he blurts out that "I want to cut off her head and take out her heart" (D 202). The unexpectedness and violence of the statement is almost comic in its suddenness and intent. Francis Ford Coppola's 1992 *Bram Stoker's Dracula* emphasized this in the deadpan manner with which Anthony Hopkins, as Van Helsing, delivered the line. Other moments, mixing the melodramatic and comic, include Harker's remark as they arrive in Varna: "Thank God! this is the country where bribery can do anything, and we are well supplied with money" (D 375).

Similar melodramatic moments include the bursting in to the Harkers' bedroom by Van Helsing, Seward, and Quincey Morris. The conversation is more comic than urgent. The Texan Quincey pauses, asking if they should disturb the married couple. "We must" is Van Helsing's terse reply. Quincey still hesitates but the professor replies, "You are always right; but this is life and death. All chambers are alike to the doctor; and even were they not[,] they are all as one to me tonight." The door, however, does not open, so the men throw themselves against it, tumbling in with the professor falling on the floor. But the comedy comes up sharp; they discover Jonathan Harker sleeping in a trance and the Count standing next to Mina in the bright moonlight holding her arms with one hand and forcing her head down to his bosom with the other (D 322). At this operatic and erotic moment, Stoker reverts to a comic, or at least misplaced, image: that of a "child forcing a kitten's nose into a saucer of milk to compel it to drink" (D 322).

In describing the hellish look of the Count at this moment, melodrama again rules: "his eyes flamed red with devilish passion; the great nostrils of the quite aquiline nose opened wide and quivered at the edge; and the white sharp teeth behind the full lips of the blood-dripping mouth, champed together" (D 322). Although this parallels moments in J. R. Planché's 1820 melodrama, *The Vampire; or, The Bride of the Isles* (cf. pp. 36 and 41), it also sacrifices fear to excess. Only the Sacred Wafer held up by the professor stops the Count from jumping on them. With crucifixes raised, the party then forms a sacred chorus line, advancing in unison toward the Count as he retreats and then transforms himself into a black cloud that sails out into the moonlight (D 322). A later moment echoes the melodrama of the scene when we learn that fire has destroyed the manuscript Mina had been typing. "Thank God there is the other copy in the safe!" is the welcomed if slightly laughable reply (D 325).

Earlier melodramatic moments in *Dracula* include Lucy's sleepwalking, the Count's perilous journey to England by ship recounted by the Captain who lashed himself to the wheel, and the final boat trip by the Count to Russia, pursued by our heroes. In all the scenes, exaggerated action joins sensational presentation to deconstruct the horrific. The original ending of the novel was to emphasize this feature: it was to consist of a volcanic eruption and the explosion of the castle creating a melodramatic cataclysm. Equaling the verbal extremes is the excessive physical and emotional behavior in the novel. In the melodramatic imagination, nothing is left unsaid. The unspeakable is given voice so that even the shocking statement of Van Helsing wanting to cut off Lucy's head can be uttered with conviction (D 202). As well as being expressive, the melodramatic language of the novel heightens and polarizes reader reaction.

The meaning of melodrama, according to Peter Brooks, is "to locate and articulate the moral occult" (Brooks 5). This is the hidden world of attraction and repulsion of Dracula and the Un-Dead, isolated in Transylvania but then unleashed in England. It is Harker fearing for his life at the hands—or rather mouth—of the three female vampires but saying, as the lips and teeth of one graze his neck, "I closed my eyes in languorous ecstasy and waited—waited with beating heart" (D 70). The novel uncovers the spiritual and sexual innuendoes of this world normally masked by convention. Melodrama is the repository of myth, framing the story of vampires and their eradication as outlined by Van Helsing to Seward and Harker. It parallels the unconscious mind where base desires rule, allowing for the expression of emotion in the form of dreams, which are important for the novel.

The melodramatic imagination of the novel is necessary to allow the acting out of impulses both sexual and psychological. Dracula's actions release the unrepressed. The conflict, as the novel makes so clear, is between Manichaean forces of light and darkness, strong emotionalism, and moral division edged by acute situations and actions. But as in the pattern of all melodrama, virtue triumphs: the Count dies and Mina recovers. The innocent man (Harker) and the defenseless woman (Mina) survive. Laughter derives from the incompatibility of melodramatic action and expression with the psychological and urban, if not modern, setting (at least in England) of the novel. Melodrama is displaced by the subconscious and archetypal worlds of the novel. But its presence is legitimate if out of step; it is a device to ensure the popularity of the work, while acting to mediate the horror of vampires and their bloodletting. Presented melodramatically, the violence has the potential for being, at least momentarily, laughable, although not diminishing its erotic and psychological importance.

The sexuality and action of the scenes between the Count and Lucy or Mina render the positive value of melodrama, which becomes the means to convey the dreaded (or feared) while at the same time distancing itself from it. The choreography of the vampire scenes mirrors melodrama on stage. "Acting to music, with regular and accurate divisions of time, making for definite and patterned gestures in movement as well as speech, was one of its theatrical features (Rahill 211). Gordon Craig said of an Irving performance, for example, that it was "'a song and dance . . . his movements were all measured. He was forever counting'" (in Rahill 212). In his study of Irving, Craig further detailed the actor's intensity expressed by vivid and ambitious gestures (Craig 56–58). Irving imposed

himself on audiences. Pattern and purpose define melodramatic movement, something transferred to the action in *Dracula*. Scenes presented as
stage sets characterize the novel as when Mina describes Lucy at East
Cliff at midnight with a shadowy figure "whether man or beast" hover-
ing behind her with light dramatically illuminating and then obscuring
the scene (D 124–25).

Craig's reference to counting suggests something of the treatment of
numbers in *Dracula*. They play a critical role and expand, if comically, the
thrice repeated phrase "Count me in" (D 135, 189, 277). In fact, the number three is the first number we encounter in the novel, repeated twice in
the first line of Harker's journal, which opens the volume. It is also the
last number in the novel, as Harker again refers to his new life seven
years after the events with himself, Mina and their young son. The cross,
which held before Dracula halts his actions, is of course another embodiment of three in the novel, its obverse the three female vampires who try
to seduce the Harker at Dracula's castle early in the book. Lucy of course
has three suitors who become the principal pursuers of the Count led by
Van Helsing. The Count himself inserts himself into the couples to create
an unholy set of three (as in Mina, Harker, and the Count). Only three
notebooks contain any authentic account of the adventures according to
Harker on the last page of the novel (419). Characters measure their
health and progress by numbers: "*17 September*—Four days and nights of
peace" writes Lucy at one point (D 171).

Mathematics even has a moral dimension. Midway in the novel just
after Quincey tells Van Helsing, "Count me in," and Lord Godalming
joins the rescue group, Van Helsing explains that numbers have power,
even against evil. "We have on our side power of combination—a power
denied to the vampire kind" (D 277). The resources of science are upheld
and the freedom to "to act and think; and the hours of the day and the
night are ours equally," which, of course, is not true for the Count who
only flourishes after sunset (D 277). After a summary of vampiric behavior, Van Helsing emphasizes that the Count is not really free: he cannot
go easily about. He must obey the laws of nature: "he may not enter
anywhere at the first" unless invited, numbers again defining his limitations and power. He can change himself only at noon or "at exact sunrise
or sunset" (D 279). Time—numbers—control his being with numbers
even inhabiting the superstitions of Transylvania where the devil claims
the tenth scholar as his due at the unusual school (the *Scholomance*) in the
mountains where the secrets of nature are taught (D 280, 441–42).

Ironically, reliance on the numerical throughout the book is another
element of the comic: alluding to the scientific aspect of the story, numbers actually highlight the unreliability rather than certainty of the math-
ematical world. Numbers in *Dracula* are unstable or unknown and in
their effort to impose order, actually disrupt it. Trains are late, schedules
change, and time fluctuates. Dates of letters, diary entries, and journal

records are numbered, as are the documents kept by Mina, but they are not always trustworthy. But numbers provide the clue to the discovery of Dracula in London. Tracing the fifty boxes that Dracula has delivered to Carfax—some of them removed, others perhaps still at the villa—is a trying but ultimately successful quest (D 280–81). The pursuit of the boxes is the pursuit of numbers.

The death of Dracula is numerical as recounted by Mina Harker in her journal. Observing the gypsies who are carrying the coffin of the Count, racing to his castle before sunset so he can revive, she writes "*one* and all were quite unaware of our presence" (D 16; my italics throughout). *Two* voices shout "halt!" to the gypsies and "*one* was my Jonathan's, raised in a high key of passion." Suddenly, the *four* pursuers (Jonathan, Arthur Godalming, Dr. Seward, and Mr. Morris), witnessed by Mina and Van Helsing, confront the gypsies carrying the somnolent Count in his coffin. They challenge the gypsies with their Winchesters. The gypsy leader points "*first* to the sun," close to setting, but before he can act "all *four* men of our party threw themselves from their horses and dashed towards the cart" (D 416). A battle ensues with Jonathan "on *one* side of the ring of men," Quincey on the other. The *two* battle to the coffin, pry off the lid, and with Jonathan's Kukri knife slicing through his throat and Morris' Bowie knife plunging in the heart, the Count expires. The *two* doctors soon attend to the wounded and dying Morris. "With *one* impulse the men sank on their knees" out of respect and admiration for his heroism (D 418).

But numbers in the novel remain essentially ironic in that they contradict their objective of ordering time and nature. They are neither reliable nor dependable. They, like language and the Count, are in flux and metamorphosize. Although they form a chorus to the action, they distort and are uncertain. They form part of the comic properties of the novel, undercutting the attempt of science to combat the Count. Only religion (and garlic) seem to do the trick.

Comedy and horror are also often united in the novel often masked by the melodramatic. When the zookeeper narrates the escape and then terrorizing behavior of a wolf from a London zoo, the emphasis is first on fear. But after describing the wolf's unusual behavior, the animal surprisingly returns, the reporter in the *Pall Mall Gazette* writing, "the whole scene was an unutterable mixture of comedy and pathos. The wicked wolf that for half a day had paralysed London . . . was there in a sort of penitent mood" and greeted as a "sort of vulpine prodigal son" (D 177). After Renfield suddenly attacks Dr. Seward with a knife and cuts his wrist, he immediately changes into a playful dog who licks the blood that has dripped to the floor (D 177–78). Seward then comically remarks "I cannot afford to lose blood just at present," having been transfused for Lucy's sake. And when Dracula makes his visit to Lucy, we first hear flapping at her window before it is broken the head of a giant wolf (D

179–80). To overcome the fear of the maids who eventually come to her rescue (and remove her dead mother lying across her body in a melodramatic pose), she orders them to dining room for a restorative glass of wine, a moment of comic generosity (D 180). This backfires: the half-empty sherry decanter had been doctored with laudanum and the servants become drugged (D 181).

Stoker's short stories preceding *Dracula* indicate his fascination with the spectral, melodramatic, and the unconsciously comic. "Death in the Wings" (1888) combines these elements as he recounts the story of an actor killed on stage by a vengeful props manager. His death is as surprising as it is melodramatic when a counterweight fails to open a trap for him (MT 66–67).[8] "The Man from Shorrox'" is another prelude to *Dracula*, published in 1894 in the *Pall Mall Magazine.* Told in an Irish dialect, it narrates how a corpse can seem to come alive through a comic mix up in a hotel room (MT 117–18). The final scene mixes the macabre and the comic, anticipating moments in *Dracula.* Melodrama was Stoker's method, the origin of the elements that would shape the presentation of scene and action in his novel providing its comic underpinning. Stoker may in fact have seen the comic properties of melodrama and begun to question them during the writing of his novel. *Dracula's* origins are theatrical.[9]

This may be true in a literal as well as literary sense. In addition to the productions Irving mounted, it was at the Lyceum's famous Beefsteak Room, the private dining room at the rear of the theater, which could seat thirty-six and had its own private chef and wine cellar, where Stoker met Professor Arminius Vambery from the University of Budapest on 30 April 1890. Stoker may have been intrigued by the Hungarian scholar, although it is only speculation, as Elizabeth Miller has pointed out, that he derived any notion of vampires or Transylvania from him. Stoker devotes the last chapter of his *Personal Reminiscence of Henry Irving* to Vambery, although he does not mention his knowledge of vampires (I: 371–72).[10]

The source of Dracula himself is, of course, less clear, although another theatrical source might be the Greek actor-husband of Sarah Bernhardt, Jacques Damala who regularly dined with Irving and Stoker when his wife performed in London. In his *Personal Reminiscences*, Stoker commented that Damala "looked like a dead man . . . his eyes staring out of his white waxen face, seemed hardly the eyes of the living" (MT 7) Supplementing these encounters were the hundreds of melodramatic scripts Stoker read for Irving, scripts sent for consideration, including one by Arthur Conan Doyle titled "Waterloo."

3

"The scene . . . was becoming too comically grave."
Dracula, Ch. XVIII

The pun in the preceding quote comically conveys the comedic tensions in the novel, which duplicate the more notable contrasts beyond the disconnect between melodrama and actual fear: medieval versus modern, religion versus science, hypnosis versus action, belief versus Satanism, and England versus Transylvania. These contraries establish an ongoing set of opposites that provide a struggle within the text relieved only by comic action. The context for the quote is Renfield's cogent argument to be let out of the sanatorium, although he cannot explain why. "I am not my own master in the matter. I can only ask you to trust me" he implores. Dr. Seward then peremptorily decides to end the interview because it was "becoming too comically grave."

Such "comically grave" scenes or situations are replete throughout the novel. Garlic is one cause. Used repeatedly to ward off vampires, it quickly becomes a comic device as Mina Harker reports in Chapter XXVII. The peasants who host the rescue party in their pursuit of the Count as they journey to Transylvania are superstitious and go to the trouble "of putting an extra amount of garlic into our food." Mina confesses, however, that she can't stand it (D 402).

Mina's actions are themselves suitably parodic when she learns of the terrible story of Lucy's death: "I lay back in my chair powerless. Fortunately, I am not of a fainting disposition" (D 262). Her response to Lucy's grim death is to take off the cover of her typewriter and write out a narrative for Dr. Van Helsing when he arrives in London. She then begins to "typewrite," transposing material from an early form of recording machine to make three copies of the diary. Optimism tempers fear, expressing the contradictory themes of *Dracula*: "the world seems full of good men—even if there are monsters in it" (D 263). Mina, however, also realizes the irony underlying action in the novel "Everything that one does seems, no matter how right it may be, to bring on the very thing which is most to be deplored" (D 296).

Understatement is another form of comic expression in the book. At one point, Dr. Seward casually observes that "a strong man with homicidal and religious mania at once might be dangerous." "Might" is the comic fulcrum of the sentence. "The combination is a dreadful one" he adds in a deadpan manner (D 135). Throwaway lines also abound: "it is wonderful . . . what intellectual recuperative power lunatics have" (D 152); "I want to operate but not as you think" (D 202). Comedy comes to control so many of the events that serious acts are misunderstood as comic. Lucy tells the professor that "I believe you are only putting up a joke on me. Why, these flowers are only common garlic." "No trifling with me. I never jest!" Van Helsing sharply replies (D 166).

Other comic figures in the novel begin with Mr. Swales, the elderly guide to the dead in Whitby. When he meets Mina and Lucy in Chapter VI, he offers his black comedy at the cliffside graveyard pointing out that all the tombstones lie. In his comic dialect, he tells them that all the loving and sentimental statements are no more than "air-blebs!" invented by parsons from the pulpit and then printed on paper and cut into tombstones. Comically, he tells them that the tombstones tumble over because of the "weight o'the lies wrote on them" (D 97, 98). George Canon, listed as dying from a fall on the rocks, actually committed suicide so that his "hell-cat" of a mother would not collect the insurances she put on his life (D 99–100). His irreverent attitude toward death, he later explains, is actually his way of confronting mortality and repressing his fear of it. He looks light on it as a way to "cheer yup my own heart a bit" (D 107). He senses that the wind might in fact be blowing in death; ironically, we learn in Chapter VIII, after the shipwreck of the *Demeter* and the arrival of Dracula in the form of a giant dog, that Swales is found dead at Mina's and Lucy's favorite lookout, "his neck being broken" (D 121). The comic and the tragic intermingle.

Other comic figures in the novel include the brash Texan, Quincey Morris, Lord Godalming, and Renfield, Dr. Seward's patient whose bipolar behavior alternates between sanity and insanity. The presence of the Texan seems the oddest addition to the book but may represent Stoker's homage to William Cody (Buffalo Bill) and his Wild West show. Stoker corresponded with Cody in the 1880s and 1890s, providing tickets for the Lyceum and receiving tickets for Cody's show in return (Murray 207). In 1887, Stoker and Irving hosted Cody in his first visit to London where his show dazzled the country. Queen Victoria made one of her rare public appearances when she attended a performance that included Indian warriors, cowboys, women sharpshooters, and Mexican vaqueros. The show soon became the best-known representation of America and Cody perhaps the world's most famous American.[11] Cowboys were especially appealing to Stoker; not only is Quincey a Texan in semi-western dress but the Slovaks Harker meets in Chapter 1 also wore "big cowboy hats," "heavy leather belts" with studs and "high boots with their trousers tucked in." In true Western style, they also had "heavy black moustaches" (D 33).

By making Morris a Texan, Stoker may also be offering a satiric dig at Irving whose promotion and association with Cody was so strong in 1887 that comics suggested he would soon become a "Texan cow-boy" to attract Queen Victorian to see one of his performances as she had been lured to attend one of Cody's shows. Irving, as a Texan, seemed appropriately ludicrous.[12] One source of Quincey's humor is his idiom and bravado: responding to Lucy's rebuff of his love with "don't cry, my dear. If it's for me, I'm a hard nut to crack; and I take it standing up. If that other fellow doesn't know his happiness, well, he'd better look for it soon, or he'll have to deal with me" (D 92).

America in the novel, however, has an ambiguous role, Seward chauvinistically praising the country Stoker had visited several times and admired. Appreciating Morris's resolve in the face of Lucy's death, Stoker writes "if America can go on breeding men like that, she will be a power in the world indeed" (D 211). This is the land where the Winchester rifle, featured in Buffalo Bill's 1887 Wild West London show, reigns, four of them used to stop the Gypsies at the end of the novel. Supplementing them was another symbol of Western force, Quincey's "great bowie knife" (D 416, 417). Harker's knife may cut the throat of the Count, but it is Quincey's Bowie knife, a weapon that saved the American West, that plunges into the Count's heart and destroys him. The idealized West defeats the corrupt East, although at the cost of Quincey's life (D 418). In a postscript, Harker ironically acknowledges that the date of his son's birth is the day Quincey died, forgetting it is also the day Dracula was killed.

Stoker visited America for the first time in 1883–1884 in the company of Ellen Terry and Henry Irving, repeating the visit in 1884–1885 and then, on his return, delivering a lecture, "A Glimpse of America," at the London Institution. In 1888 he spoke on Lincoln, partly derived from his growing library of American books, speeches, and lectures he began to acquire on his trips to the states. He also visited America in the 1890s as well as in 1903 and in 1909 published an essay, "Americans as Actors." In the novel, Renfield gives a positive speech about the United States.

All of Stoker's characters offer unconsciously comic explanations of events. Renfield, alternately distracted and incisive, argues for his own release in a display of probity and self-understanding. That he should be a Gentleman and a member of Windham Club intensifies the contrast with his mental state, noting that he supported Lord Godalming's father in his application to the Windham and that he was "the inventor of a burnt rum punch much patronized on Derby night" (D 283). His exhibition of rational thinking, identifying and contextualizing each of his quartet of visitors (Van Helsing, Seward, Morris, and Lord Godalming), seemingly undermines his insanity and control by the Count. Seward cuts off the conversation fearing Renfield will make too much sense (D 285).

Early in the novel, Harker writes "let me be prosaic, so far as facts can be" (D 56). In this way, he hopes to reign in the imagination and deflate the danger he discovers in Transylvania but his approach fails. Comedy then becomes more prevalent to offset the grimness of the story. The phonetic spelling of Sam Bloxam in Chapter XX is an example of turning to language again. Tracking the movements of Count Dracula and his escape from England, Harker reports receipt of a letter but he is misled by spelling errors and distortions of language, beginning with the name of the lodging house which was Corcoran, not Korkran as in the note (D 302). Imitating the often phonetically distorted speech of minor characters in Dickens, the speech of Bloxam contains mispronounced words and misspellings, the distortions of language equalizing the distortions of moral order in England and beyond.

Dialect, which Stoker had used in several of his short stories, becomes another source of comedy. Captain Donelson, who transported Dracula from London to the Black Sea, recounts his harrowing adventure with unusual speech: "'Man! . . . but it made us afeard, for we expeckit that we should have to pay for it wi'some rare piece o'ill luck, so as to keep up the average.'" On the behavior of his partly Roumanian crew and their fear of the evil eye, he says "the sueprsteetion of foreigners is pairfectly rideeculous!" (D 388, 389). Even the idea of Mina Harker *typing* her account of their pursuit of the Count seems comic. "I should feel quite astray doing the work if I had to write with a pen" she remarks when praising the usefulness of "the 'Traveller's' typewriter" (D 391). But when exhaustion prevents Mina from typing, Van Helsing takes over the narrative in comically ungrammatical English: "as madam Mina write not in her stenography, I must, in my cumbrous old fashion, that so each day of us may not go unrecorded" (D 404).

To Van Helsing, nature is a "carnival," although Mina, who now sleeps almost continuously, does not witness it because "she is with that Vampire baptism" (D 406). In the tomb at the Count's castle and distracted by the voluptuous bodies of the three vampires, only "the soul-wail of my dear Madam Mina" keeps Van Helsing from falling under their spell. He then proceeds to grimly restore the women to their dead selves from the condition of the Un-Dead, beginning with the severing of their heads from their bodies (D 412). This is not redemptive but, in his quasi-comic language, "butcher work" (D 412).

As various characters at various moments question the seriousness of individual acts, comedy repeatedly disrupts the moment. When the professor asks Arthur Lord Godalming to accompany him to the churchyard where Lucy is buried and to enter the tomb, he replies, "are you in earnest or is it some monstrous joke?'" (D 243). The comic allows and even encourages expressions of disbelief. Faced with extreme and grotesque action, the immediate response is to explain the act as a trick. Seeking to deflate the horror—the Count is no more than "one of those big bats that they call vampires" (D 188)—humor is the means, nowhere more comically then when Morris, responding to Seward and Van Helsing's need for help to confront the danger of the Count, punningly cries "Count me in" (D 189), an echo of Renfield's previous statement to the attendant: "'I don't want to talk to you; you don't count now; the Master is at hand" (D 135). A further pun occurs when Van Helsing rhetorically asks Harker, "is there not more at stake for us than for him?" (D 344), referring to the Count, and echoed by Mina when she tells the party in pursuit of the

Count that her blood is poisoned and that "my soul is at stake." (D 371). The reference is grimly comic given the need to stake the hearts of the Un-Dead to ensure their destruction.

Nationalities come in for their satire as well, first suggested in "Dracula's Guest," thought by many to be an excised early chapter from the novel. There, a telegram from the Count about Harker, who has unexpectedly entered a tomb and encountered an alluring woman on Walpurgis-Nacht, reads "He is English and therefore adventurous" (D 432). Throughout the novel, the Irishman Stoker satirizes English habits beginning with a report that when an agitated Harker arrived by train from Klausenburg, "he rushed into the station shouting for a ticket for home. Seeing from his violent demeanor that he was English, they gave him a ticket for the furthest station on the way thither that the train reached" (D 134).

English habits even seep into the Count who soon masters British train schedules through his leisurely reading of Bradshaw's railway guide in his library (D 53). He also owns copies of the London Directory, the Army and Navy lists, and guides to the nobility (D 50). And he soon takes comic offense at Harker's unfriendly habit of writing in shorthand in his journal, "an outrage upon friendship and hospitality!" (D 74). Titles also come in for their satiric treatment. The Count alternates between claiming his hereditary power and denying it, at once telling Harker of his long line at the same time he acts as doorman, carrying his bags. Yet Arthur, Lord Godalming, advances his title as protection: when the group plans their break-in at the Count's London home, he claims that "my title will make it all right with the locksmith, and with any policeman that may come along" (D 339).

The leading comic theorist in the novel, however, is Dutch. Dismayed by Lucy's death, Van Helsing senses her "capture" by Dracula and realizes what dramatic steps must be taken to eliminate her from the Un-Dead. Suspense surrounds his activities which he shares with Seward, although he strangely gives way to hysterics in the coach after Lord Godalming and Quincey depart following Lucy's burial. But they were not hysterics Van Helsing insists, "only his sense of humour asserting itself under very terrible conditions. He laughed till he cried. . . then he cried till he laughed again" (D 211). Challenged by Seward over this behavior, he explained that laughter was necessary to balance his grief.

Laughter, he begins, is a king who enters and leaves at will. He suffers over Lucy but laughs at her grave (D 211, 212). The world is dark and troubled but when "King Laugh" comes, sunshine arrives. Van Helsing here outlines the psychological power of laughter, Stoker's explanation for its presence the psychological response to the story's grimmest moments. "Men and women are like ropes drawn tight with strain" causing tears says Van Helsing and at times the strain "become too great, and we break. But King Laugh he come like the sunshine, and he ease off the strain again; and we bear to go on without labour, what it may be" (D 212). Laughter provides a kind of luminous sanity.

Seward challenges Van Helsing's theory: "I don't see where the joke comes in" (D 213). The professor then explains that he knows Lucy is under the spell of Dracula but before he can elaborate, Seward's diary entry ends and a report from the *Westminster Gazette* appears. The headline reads, "A Hampstead Mystery": "'a bloofer lady'" has been accosting young children in the evening, the phrase itself thought to be "supremely funny" by a correspondent to the paper. The writer then remarks that some of "our caricaturists might . . . take a lesson in the irony of grotesque by comparing the reality and the picture" (D 214). A kind of in-joke then occurs when Stoker adds that the writer "naively says that even Ellen Terry could not be so winningly attractive" as some of these children "pretend and—even imagine themselves—to be" (D 214). Terry, of course, played opposite Henry Irving at the Lyceum Theatre. It quickly becomes apparent that the small throat wounds on these young children is the result of the "bloofer lady," recognized by the reader as Lucy, now an Un-Dead vampire. Van Helsing confirms this to Seward who, in melodramatic style, "threw himself with a despairing gesture into a chair, and placed his elbows on the table, covering his face with his hands as he spoke:—'They were made by Miss Lucy!'" (D 231).

The form of laughter Van Helsing describes parallels views expressed by Henri Bergson that laughter "is a sane type of madness" (Bergson 180). Explaining what seems to be macabre action as necessary, Van Helsing tells Seward that "I can laugh at her [Lucy's] very grave—laugh when the clay from the spade of the sexton drop upon her coffin" (D 212). Laughter and sadness have the same source: "No more think that I am all sorry when I cry, for the laugh he come just the same" (D 212). Here, the ambiguous but therapeutic nature of laughter is clear as is its reverse: "I have cried even when the laugh did choke me" (D 211). In Bergson's essay, published three years after *Dracula*, he outlines the properties of laughter and its restorative nature Stoker anticipated.

Preceding Bergson, however, was George Meredith whose "Essay on Comedy" appeared in 1877. In this work, Meredith defines the importance of the comic spirit as an antidote to the mechanical and deadening nature of life. He also acknowledges that laughter gives "tone to the feelings" but Bergson is more direct, beginning his essay with the question, "What does laughter mean?" (Meredith 44; Bergson 61). What Bergson notes is that laughter allows one a disinterested view of experience, necessary to assess it. The comic demands, in his phrase, "a momentary anesthesia of the heart" (Bergson 64). In a word, *detachment*. This allows Van Helsing and others in *Dracula* to gain distance on the horrific. The utility of laugher, Bergson stresses, is social, functioning this way for the reader as much as for the characters of *Dracula*. Readers can confront and escape the admittedly grotesque stakings and deaths through the comic, an element integral rather than extraneous to the novel.

A sentence late in Bergson's essay links the scientist and the humorist and offers a further explanation of the function of comedy in *Dracula*. It is an expression of morality, reinforcing the code of England in contrast to that of Transylvania. Bergson writes "A humorist is a moralist disguised as a scientist, something like an anatomist who practises dissection with the sole object of filling us with disgust; so that humour . . . is really a transposition from the moral to the scientific." (Bergson 143). This reads as if Bergson had himself met Van Helsing and had him in mind.

4

"Last night he banqueted heavily"
Dracula, Ch. XXII

In-jokes run throughout *Dracula* from references to Le Fanu's *Carmilla* to allusions to the life of Angela Burdette-Coutts, one of England's wealthi-est women. Among other positions, she was chief shareholder of Coutts and Company, the bank where Dracula has his accounts. Stoker bor-rowed the name Harker from Joseph Harker, chief scene painter at the Lyceum. Dracula's London address at 137 Piccadilly was only yards away from where Stoker's younger brother, Dr. George Stoker, practiced. The superintendent of the Hampstead hospital in the novel where the children are taken after they have been bitten by the "bloofer lady" was his cousin, Ernest Stoker (Davies 124).

Characters even play jokes on each other. When Van Helsing visits Mina Harker in Exeter and is offered Mina's journal recording her im-pressions of Lucy's behavior and sleepwalking at Whitby, he is per-plexed. It is written in shorthand and he cannot decipher it. "By this time my little joke was over," Mina injects, she exchanges it for her transcribed, typed copy (D 220). Van Helsing earlier observed "the grim irony of it all" referring to Lucy's death in which she looked so beautiful, yet the burial service seemed so comic and irrelevant (D 212–13). "I can laugh at her grave" he remarks, expressing both sorrow and surprise at her demise (D 212). King Laugh occurs at unexpected moments through language that mixes the risible and the sensible. "That sentence is a pud-dle" he remarks of his own humorous efforts to be understood (D 354).

Ironically, at the very moment of greatest danger in *Dracula*, comedy appears. Mina recounts the Count's words when she awakens to find him in her room. First, a threat: if you make a sound, I shall dash your hus-band's brains out before your eyes. And then "with a mocking smile," he grasped her shoulder and bared her throat, announcing in a melodramat-ic tone as if to an unseen theatre audience, "First, a little refreshment to reward my exertions" (D 327). The remark seems unexpectedly comic, matched by her own erotic-melodrama: "strangely enough, I did not want to hinder him" as he placed his "reeking lips upon my throat'" (D 327).

One-liners appear throughout the text. In Chapter XXV, for example, Mina Harker tells Dr. Seward and her husband, after she has been infected by the Count, that "my soul is at stake" unaware of her pun and its implications (D 371). An earlier, punning reference to stakes appears on page 344. Hypnotism is another source of comedy, at first disbelieved, then useful and then less powerful in providing details about the Count's movements. And characters begin to make fun of themselves. Mina after hearing of Lucy's "terrible" death, "I lay back in my chair powerless. Fortunately I am not of a fainting disposition" (D 262).

But always in the midst of danger, there is humor. Arriving in Veresti, Mina notes the lovely country and that if things were different, she and Jonathan would amble through the countryside "to stop and see people, and learn something of their life." To fill their minds with "all the colour and picturesqueness of the whole wild, beautiful country and the quaint people" would be a joy, "but alas!" they have a dangerous mission to fulfill (D 401). This idyll parallels the opening when Harker makes his first visit to the count. Unwilling to admit or recognize the impending danger signs, he prefers to comment on the world of natural beauty or the cuisine, praising the paprika chicken—"get recipe for Mina" he writes (D 31–32).

Dracula is ultimately not a comic novel, but comedy exists throughout as a means to deflect or assimilate the horror and intensity of the events. The 1927 stage version and 1931 film version exploited this when Van Helsing reappeared in the middle of the end-titles leaning against a stage to deliver this epilogue from the stage play:

> Just a moment, Ladies and Gentlemen! Just a word before you go. We hope the memories of Dracula and Renfield won't give you bad dreams, so just a word of reassurance. When you go home tonight and the lights have been turned out and you are afraid to look behind the curtains and you dread to see a face appear at the window—why, just pull yourself together and remember that after all *there are such things.* (in Skal HG 139)

The epilogue was meant as a joke but it was cut from the film after its initial release for fear that it might be taken literally by church groups as an endorsement of vampire beliefs.[13] Some jokes, even in *Dracula,* can have too much bite.

NOTES

1. Skal, *Hollywood Gothic.* Hereafter HG.
2. Stoker, *Dracula.* Hereafter D

3. For a brief account of melodrama see Michael Booth, "Introduction." *Hiss the Villain, Six English and American Melodramas*. Edited by Michael Booth, Benjamin Blom, 1964, pp. 9–40. For a critique of the Irving influenced readings of *Dracula*, see Miller, *Dracula, Sense & Nonsense*, pp. 76–81.

4. Interestingly, the tradition continues with the Royal Winnipeg Ballet's *Dracula*, first produced in 1998, incorporating a pantomime at the opening of the Act II. The pantomime provides a condensed and comic summary of Stoker's novel.

5. There are few studies of opera in nineteenth-century Ireland but among the best are John Allen, "Italian Opera in Dublin." *Music in Ireland 1848–1998*, edited by Richard Pine. Mercier, 1998; Joseph J. Ryan, "Opera in Ireland before 1925." *Irish Musical Studies 7; Irish Music in the Twentieth Century*. Edited by Gareth Cox and Axel Klein, Four Courts Press, 2003, pp. 39–55; and Axel Klein, "Stage-Irish, or the National in Irish Opera, 1780–1925." *Opera Quarterly*, 21, 2005, pp. 27–67.

6. Stoker, *Personal Reminiscences of Henry Irving*. Hereafter PR.

7. For the most detailed description of the production and its performance history, see Booth, *Victorian Spectacular*, pp. 93–126.

8. Stoker, *Midnight Tales*. Hereafter MT.

9. Demonstrating the impact of melodrama on Stoker was the one-time-only copyright reading of a stage version of *Dracula* presented at the Lyceum on 18 May 1897, several days prior to the publication of the novel, done for copyright reasons and possibly to interest Irving in a stage production. Stoker wrote an opening speech for the event that is a near parody of Victorian melodramatic expression. At the door of Dracula's castle, Harker asks, "I wondered why the people in the Hotel at Bistritz were so frightened and why the old lady hung the Crucifix round my neck and why the people on the coach made signs against the evil eye! By Jove, if any of them had this kind of experience, no wonder at anything they did—or thought. This is becoming more than a joke." (in Skal "His Hour" 374). I disagree with Lisa Hopkin's statement in her recent biography of Stoker that Irving's influence has been "over-estimated" (Hopkins, 60).

10. See Miller, *Dracula, Sense & Nonsense*, pp. 30–31. In Chapter XXXIV of Vol. I of *Personal Reminiscences of*, Stoker devotes twelve pages to listing the major guests to the Beefsteak Room. They included The Prince of Wales, Dion Boucicault, Paderewski, J. M. Barrie, Arthur Conan Doyle, Samuel Clemens, P. T. Barnum, Whistler and Sarah Bernhardt, as well as U.S. Senators, university presidents, generals, ambassadors, publishers, painters, and politicians such as Asquith, Balfour, Churchill, and Gladstone. When the room was too small, the invitees gathered on the stage, 350 guests seated on the stage on 14 February 1880 to celebrate the one hundredth night of *The Merchant of Venice*.

11. Louis S. Warren makes this point in his important article, "Buffalo Bill Meets Dracula: William F. Cody, Bram Stoker and the Frontiers of Racial Decay." *American Historical Review* 107, October 2002, pp. 1124–57. Warren also suggest that Cody and the frontier myth provide a complex alternative to Dracula and his decadence in terms of racial encounter. *Dracula*, he argues, is a crucial frontier tale. The article also contains some insightful remarks on the inept American, Quincey Morris.

12. "Texan cow-boy." *Illustrated Bits*, no. 113, 26 March 1887, p. 7. Stoker saved a clipping from *Punch* saying that Cody would soon take over the role of Mephistopheles in Irving's *Faust*. See "Waiting Verification." *Punch*, 7 May 1887.

13. Quoted in Miller, *Reflections on Dracula*, p. 130.

WORKS CITED

Auerbach, Nina. *Ellen Terry, Player in Her Time*. W. W. Norton & Company, 1987.
Belford, Barbara. *Bram Stoker, A Biography of the author of Dracula*. Knopf, 1996.
Bergson, Henri. "Laughter." *Comedy, An Essay on Comedy by George Meredith. Laughter by Henri Bergson*. Johns Hopkins UP, 1984, pp. 61–190.

Booth, Michael R. *Victorian Spectacular Theatre 1850–1910*. Routledge, 1981.

Brooks, Peter. *The Melodramatic Imagination, Balzac, Henry James Melodrama, and the Mode of Excess*. Yale UP 1976.

Craig, Edward Gordon. *Henry Irving*. Longmans, 1930.

Davies, Bernard. "Inspirations, Imitations and In-Jokes in Stoker's *Dracula*." *Dracula: The Shade and the Shadow*, edited by Elizabeth Miller, Desert Island Books, 1998, pp. 131–37.

Haining, Peter. "Introduction." *Bram Stoker, Midnight Tales*, edited by Peter Haining, Peter Owen, 1990, pp. 9–16.

Herr, Cheryl, Ed. *For the Land They Loved, Irish Political Melodramas, 1890–1925*. Syracuse UP, 1991.

Hopkins, Lisa. *Bram Stoker, A Literary Life*. Palgrave Macmillan, 2007.

Joslin, Lyndon W. *Count Dracula Goes to the Movies, Stoker's Novel Adapted 1922–2003*, 2nd ed. McFarland and Co. 2006.

Kavanagh, Peter. *The Irish Theatre*. Kerryman Limited, 1946.

Meredith, George. "An Essay on Comedy." *Comedy, An Essay on Comedy by George Meredith. Laughter by Henri Bergson*. Johns Hopkins UP, 1984, pp. 3–57.

Miller, Elizabeth. *Dracula, Sense and Nonsense*. Desert Island Books, 2000.

———. *Reflections on Dracula. Ten Essays*. Transylvania Press, 1997.

Morash, Christopher. *A History of Irish Theatre, 1600–2000*. Cambridge UP, 2002.

Murray, Paul. *From the Shadow of Dracula, A Life of Bram Stoker*. Jonathan Cape, 2004.

Planché, J. R. *The Vampire; or the Bride of the Isles, A Romantic Melo-Drama* in *The Hour of One, Six Gothic Melodramas*. Edited by Stephen Wischhusen, Gordon Fraser, 1975, pp. 85–102.

Rahill, Thomas. *The World of Melodrama*. Penn State UP, 1967.

Rowell, George. *The Victorian Theatre 1792–1914, A Survey*. Cambridge UP, 1978.

Skal, David J. "'His Hour Upon the Stage:' Theatrical Adaptations of *Dracula*." Bram Stoker, *Dracula*, edited by Nina Auerbach and David J. Skal, Norton, 1997, pp. 371–81.

———. *Hollywood Gothic, The Tangled Web of Dracula from Novel to Stage to Screen*. Norton, 1990.

Stoker, Bram. *Dracula*. Edited by Glennis Byron, Broadview Press, 2000.

———. *Midnight Tales*. Edited by Peter Haining, Peter Owen, 1990.

———. *Notes for Dracula. A Facsimile Edition*. Annotated and Transcribed by Robert Eighteen-Bisang and Elizabeth Miller, McFarland & Col, 2008.

———. *Personal Reminiscences of Henry Irving*. 2 vols. W. Heinemann, 1906.

NINE

"The seasoned spirit of the cunning reader": The Textual Subversions of *The Turn of the Screw*

Ruth Robbins

The title for this chapter comes from Henry James' Preface to *The Altar of the Dead and Other Tales*, in the New York Edition of his collected works (1909). Its force comes from its context, the Preface to a collection of ghost stories in which James claims that his ghost tales are designed for his own writerly pleasure ("He has revelled in the creation of suspense and surprise and alarm and relief" [James 103], he writes of himself in the third person); and he has practiced these serial acts of climax and anti-climax to pit himself against the credulous naïve reader and, preferably, also against the sophisticated "cunning" one. And cunning readers, of course, have spent more than a century unravelling the puzzles of his most famous ghost story, *The Turn of the Screw* (1898). The question this chapter pursues above all is the question of genre, which at its simplest is the set of clues that direct (or misdirect) readers how to read. I am concerned with the readers inside the text, particularly the governess, and Douglas who reads her story aloud to an internal audience gathered for a Christmas party; but I am also interested in the implied reader who is a proxy for the real readers, ourselves. Genre is at once guide and red herring. It gives a direction of travel for interpretation, but it also jolts us out of the tracks of such a reading. The effects are deeply unsettling, and leave us, as Virginia Woolf suggested, "afraid of the dark" (Woolf in Esch and Warren 160). James's text subverts and mixes the genres to which it apparently belongs, undermining any sense that readers might have that time might tell. This observation is about the novella's tangled relationship to the genre to which it apparently belongs—the ghost story; it is also about several other genres to which it makes reference (the romance, the gothic novel, the fairy story); and above all, it is about reading and misreading and the misleading conclusions that too strict an adherence to ideas about genre might bring us.

The key question that most of a century of criticism has raised is that of whether or not this is "really" a ghost story: do the ghosts exist in the fictional world of Bly, or are they hallucinations proceeding from the troubled mind of the governess? It is, as Peter Beidler has observed, a binary approach, an either–or set of interpretations.

> Are the ghosts real? Is the governess mad? These two choices had long been considered mutually exclusive: if the ghosts are real, then governess is sane; if she is mad, then the ghosts are mere figments of her imagination. (Beidler 134)

Since the 1970s, though, he goes on to suggest, there has been another habit of reading: "Instead of 'X *or* Y', contemporary scholars tend to say 'X *and* Y'" (134–35). She is both mad and haunted, which means that the ghosts are real to her, and also potentially, if not actually, real for others. Whether or not they are real, of course, they certainly have "real" effects in the world of the story, where two children are horribly frightened, and one is scared quite literally to death. The choice any reader makes is a choice about genre—ghost story and/or psychological case history. The clues about which is the "right" interpretation, though, come at least as much from the preferences of the reader, real or implied, as they do from the text itself. The *and/both* version of the story, where two apparently exclusive views are simultaneously held, undoes any certainties that even the most cunning of readers might have.

At the level of its mise-en-scène *The Turn of the Screw* adheres extremely closely to some of the traditions of the ghost narrative of the Victorian period, traditions that were in fact so well-worn as to be clichés by the turn of the century when it was published. It begins in a well-heeled social setting at a country-house party at Christmas, where a group of guests regale each other with tales of the creepy and the unexpected. This kind of setting where tales are told in good fellowship as a marker of the joys of the festive season is an extremely common opening for ghost stories. Elizabeth Gaskell's "The Old Nurse's Story" (1852), for instance, opens by signaling this situation on a domestic scale: "You know, my dears, that your mother was an orphan and an only child; and I daresay that you have heard that your grandfather was a clergyman . . ." (Gaskell in Cox and Gilbert 2). The title tells us that the nurse is a faithful family retainer; her mode of address to the family ("my dears") signals her affection for them and her expectation that it is returned. Her story is a kind of hearsay or gossip, safe and domestic (though the story itself does not quite live up to the gentle promise of its opening lines). Allusion is made to a similar situation in J. S. Le Fanu's "An Account of Some Strange Disturbances in Aungier Street" (1853):

> It is not worth telling, this story of mine—at least not worth writing. Told, indeed, as I have sometimes been called upon to tell it, to a circle of intelligent and eager faces, lighted up by a good after-dinner fire on a winter's evening, with a cold wind rising and wailing outside . . . it has gone off. . . . Indifferent well. But . . . Pen, ink, and paper are cold vehicles for the marvellous, and a "reader" decidedly a more critical animal than a "listener". (Le Fanu in Cox and Gilbert 19)

Le Fanu's opening with it allusion to oral narrative traditions and its unwilling retelling as text is actually very close to the situation that James establishes in his "preface" or framing of his story. And in this case, the pen, paper and ink are all faded, and the original narrator is herself ghostly because she is dead.

In James's narrative, ghost stories have also been told around the fireside; one guest announces that he has a ghost story to relate that will top the tale of a haunted child by doubling the horror to two turns of the screw: *two* children demonically possessed. The story, despite this setting however, is both oral and highly literary. It is a written account written in "old faded ink and in the most beautiful hand" (James 2). It will be read aloud to the assembled audience when its recipient, Douglas, is quite ready (he creates the suspense of delay almost as if he is deliberately constructing his audience's excitement for the story's half-revelations). Douglas primes his fellow guests and his external audience also with details of the governess's back story. "The youngest of several daughters of a poor country parson" (4), the governess, who is nameless throughout is conjured as a stock-character ingénue. Needing to earn her own living, and having only the skills of a nursery governess, she answers an advertisement to an address in well-heeled Harley Street, where she meets the bachelor guardian of her prospective charges:

> this prospective patron proved a gentleman, a bachelor in the prime of life, such a figure had never risen, *save in a dream or an old novel*, before a fluttered anxious girl out of a Hampshire vicarage. One could easily fix his type. . . . He was handsome and bold and pleasant, off-hand and gay and kind. He struck her, inevitably, as gallant and splendid. (4, my emphasis)

Some of the earliest clues about misreadings and misidentification of genre are located in this passage. The bachelor-uncle is, for the girl, a fantasy figure from "a dream or an old novel." Her reading is not to be trusted because she is a fluttered anxious girl from a background that has rendered her utterly naïve. She reads him as the "type" of the romantic hero, and perhaps, more fool her. The internal audience to this information reads it as evidence of her sweetness and simplicity, not as evidence of her stupidity, and they also believe that they are assisting at the reincarnation of a romance, which they figure as Douglas's unrequited love for the woman the governess later becomes. Douglas gives them some ammunition for this view. "She was a most charming person, but she was ten years older than I," [Douglas] quietly said. "She was the most charming woman I've ever known in her position" (2). If the governess was charming, then the young Douglas was charmed, the audience surmises. But there is a devastating sting in the tail in his comment on her social position, which clearly implies that she is unthinkable as a love object for him: too silly, too old, too socially low.

These various contexts—the country-house party at Christmas, an audience of ghost-story connoisseurs, a delay to the apparently unwilling telling of the narrative, and the prefatory remarks with which Douglas introduces the governess's narrative—all manipulate the two audiences, internal and external to the text, and prime them (us) for a ghost story. The story's genre is overdetermined by the set-up which frames the governess (it is a partial frame narrative), and which perhaps also frames its readers in the sense that it misleads them (us) into a too easy acceptance of the ingénue's words.

Her words are highly problematic for any reader to understand with certainty for her syntax is labyrinthine and her revelations are only ever partial. This is in part a function of history itself. The social histories of the periods in which the story is set, and the period in which it was written, militate against clarity in describing the things that we might fear most. The phrase *pas devant les enfants* ("Not in front of the children") stood in Victorian England for series of habits of reticence, which included the lower orders, the servants, as well as the children. Servants and children were those who had to be protected from forms of knowledge that might damage them. But the fact that they appear to require protection implies that they are vulnerable beings who are easily led astray. *Pas devant . . .* stands for a convention of *not speaking* about certain topics: not articulating scandal, sexuality, death, or other adult matters like politics and religion in front of those deemed either innocently vulnerable or socially inferior. The habit of mind that leads to social silences, euphemism and elegant periphrases, where one never calls a spade a spade, structures the narrative of *The Turn of the Screw*. Repeatedly what is happening is not put clearly—the language in which it is written, even the reported speeches of its protagonists, is elliptical, distorted, digressive, and periphrastic, not clear nor straightforward. Much of the story takes place in the gaps and silences of the governess's descriptions, in the things that she refuses to say out loud. Her first encounter with what she interprets in hindsight as Peter Quint's ghost is a fascinating case in point:

> It was plump one afternoon, in the middle of my very hour [of freedom
> from caring for the children]: the children were tucked away and I had

> come out for my stroll. One of the thoughts that, as I don't in the least
> shrink now from noting, used to be with me in these wanderings was
> that it would be *charming as a charming story* suddenly to meet some
> one. Some one would appear there at the turn of the path and would
> stand before and smile and approve. I didn't ask more than that—I
> only asked that he should *know*; and the only way to be sure he knew
> would be to see it, and the kind light of it in his handsome face. That
> was exactly present—by which I mean the face was—when, on the first
> of these occasions. . . . I stopped short on emerging from one of the
> plantations, and coming into the view of the house. What arrested me
> on the spot—and with a shock much greater than any vision had al-
> lowed for—was the sense that my imagination had, in a flash, turned
> real. He did stand there!—but high up, beyond the lawn and at the
> very top of the tower. (15, first emphasis mine)

This is not the setting for a traditional encounter with a ghost. It is broad day light in the middle of June. But it is a setting for romantic day dreams. The governess does not name the object of her fantasy. He is simply a "some one" who might appear and might approve of her actions. She veils her inappropriate desires for a man outside her experience and social station in a vague designation, and sees it only as a "charming story" she is telling herself. The charm is belied, however, by the sentence structures. After the initial scene setting sentence, all the sentences meander to their point, taking circuitous routes which deceive the writer into thinking her thoughts are appropriate, and which set out to deceive the reader into the same view. But the grammar cannot undo the horror. The daydream turns sour possibly because there is indeed a ghost instead of the master standing at the top of the tower, or just possibly because the governess cannot entirely disguise her own erotic imaginings from herself. What she claims to desire is recognition of a job well done because her position precludes any possibility of a respectable relationship with the master. She may be mistress, nominally in charge at Bly, but she remains her master's servant, and the risk she runs in her daydreaming is that she might lay herself open to an entirely different kind of mistressing. She cannot speak this desire aloud because it is improper. And because her desire is forbidden, it is repressed, and the fantasy lover—handsome, bold and charming—is distorted into the monstrous figure of Peter Quint.

This is a plausible psychoanalytical reading. There might, however, be other explanations, one of which is this is a text about how readers are misled by their own generic expectations. Lying behind the governess's interpretations of her situation is a course of English literature reading that includes explicit references to the Gothic fictions of Ann Radcliffe and to the breezy sentimentalism of Henry Fielding, whose *Amelia* (1752) our heroine has just begun to read before the quoted passage. If *Amelia* is not exactly a gothic novel, it is a text very much concerned with feminine virtue outraged and threatened and with a rakish irresponsible masculinity that might equally refer to the "some one" of the governess's fantasy. It also contains a number of more veiled references to the well-known stories that most attach to the governess's own situation: Samuel Richardson's *Pamela* (1740–41) and Charlotte Brontë's *Jane Eyre* (1847), both of which place vulnerable young women in quasi-gothic settings and then threaten them with the improper attentions of the "master." That course of reading, in other words, might just be the objective correlative for the governess's misreading of the genre in which she is actually placed — gothic rather than realistic, because the former gives her a chance to be heroic at least by her own lights, rather than mundane as perhaps she actually is. The various fictional intertexts predispose her to think herself a threatened heroine and tempt some external readers to think the same. The misunderstanding of fictional models is, as a trope, pretty much as old as the novel itself. Don Quixote tilts at windmills because he has mistaken the fictional world of chivalric romance for the one he actually lives in; Frankenstein's monster learns all he thinks he needs to know about being a human being from a course of reading that informs him about man's relationship with is creator (Milton's *Paradise Lost*), about man's relationship with the forces of history (Plutarch's *Lives of the Roman Emperors*), and about man's relationship with woman (Goethe's novel of sentiment, *The Sorrows of the Young Werther*). He does not understand that there are motives that fiction does not deal with. Pamela in Richardson's eponymous novel imagines herself as a protestant martyr based on her readings of Foxe's *Lives of the Saints*. Catherine Morland in *Northanger Abbey* believes herself to be a gothic heroine is a story that is really very horrid. All of these fictional readers are wrong. The implied reader is invited to judge differently; the cunning reader is meant, up to a point, to know better.

The setting at Bly is also misleading. The house shares some of the key features of the gothic mansion being both isolated and crenellated. The isolation may be real. The crenellations are fake: "architectural absurdities, redeemed in a measure indeed by not being wholly disengaged nor of a height too pretentious, dating, in their gingerbread antiquity, from a romantic revival that was already a respectable past," the governess informs us (15). She is shown the house by the younger of her two charges, Flora, and despite her first view of it being largely prosaic ("Wasn't it just a story-book over which I had fallen a-doze and a-dream? No; it was a big ugly antique but convenient house, embodying a few features of a building still older" [9]), she continues to see it as an enchanting, enchanted fairy-tale place. Like the prose in which the description is written, the house is a labyrinth, filled with "empty chambers and dull corridors [and] crooked staircases" (9). It appears to be the classic locus of the female gothic. But it is seen in high summer, with more light than shade, belying the genre to which the governess apparently refers us. Like the story itself, there is an either–or version here: this is either the site of horrific doings or it is just a house, larger than normal, a bit grander than the governess is used to, a bit more isolated than is common, but "really" just a building in which ordinary events can take place. As such it partakes *avant la lettre* of the Freudian uncanny, being at once domestic, familiar and comfortable and weird, unfamiliar and strange, a location that speaks of the governess's dislocation from her homely home into the *unhemilich*, and which also implies that the reader has no firm ground to stand on either in interpreting the setting.

If the governess is misled by (and misleads us about) the story's setting, it would also appear that she is not terribly good at reading people either. This is particularly the case with her readings of the children. Sheltered and naïve as she may be, she has come from a home in which there are other children. But perhaps because she has mistaken her genre and placed herself in a fiction in which moral certainties are absolute—characters are either wholly good *or* wholly evil in a binary economy which admits of no shades of grey—she does not see Miles and Flora clearly; or rather she sees them clearly but misinterprets what she sees. In her various misreadings of the children she embodies the contradictions of the two periods of the story, the 1820s when it is set and the 1890s when it was written. As James Kincaid has amply demonstrated in *Child-Loving: The Erotic Child and Victorian Culture*, the figure of the child accumulated a highly conflicted set of discourses around it. On the one hand, there was a residual notion of children as the site of original sin which had to be trained, beaten, or managed out of them. On the other, the child was the locus of nostalgic ideals of innocence and perfection. The Victorians lived out these contradictory perceptions of childhood. The children of the poor, whose childhoods were generally curtailed by the economic necessity of work, were little adults before their time. The upper- and middle-class child, in contrast, enjoyed or endured a prolongation of dependency, with a long-lasting education and forms of nurture that were meant to keep them both young and innocent. Kincaid suggests that much anxiety was expressed on the question of a child's precocity, in which early development, whether physical (early puberty), emotional, intellectual, or (im)moral was generally deemed to be a marker of lower-class status. As he puts it, quoting from a 1904 essay collection of *Studies of Boy Life in Our Cities*:

> children of the urban lower class, children of the street, are so commonly [deemed] precocious [in Victorian culture] that it is foolish to speak of their innocence: "it is part of a street-bred child's precocity that he acquires a too early acquaintance with matters which, as a child," he ought not to know about. (Kincaid 123–24)

At the same time, the rigorous protection of the upper-class child's innocence was a central trope of the period. As Claudia Nelson has suggested, though, the will to protect the innocent was much more about adult needs than about the child itself: "A major function of childhood was to serve . . . as . . . a dose of innocence and purity" for the grown-ups (80)

When she first meets her charges in *The Turn of the Screw*, the governess reads them in the light of the preferred Victorian story of childhood innocence. Miles and Flora are angelic. They had, we are told "a gentleness . . . that kept them . . . almost impersonal and certainly unpunishable. They were like those cherubs of the anecdote who had . . . nothing to whack" (19). They appear to be consistently affectionate and obedient, well-mannered, caring, loving, everything that could be seen as desirable in a small human being. But as the governess becomes more haunted, their nature appears to change, so that their innocence is in fact hypocrisy, their affection a performance, their lovingness a trick to lull the governess's vigilance. The shift from angel to devil is most apparent in the climactic final scene between the governess and Flora, by the side of the lake when the governess insists that the ghostly Miss Jessel is present, and Flora vehemently insists that she is not:

> Flora continued to fix me with her small mask of disaffection, and even at that minute I prayed God to forgive me for seeming to see that, as she stood there . . . her incomparable childish beauty had suddenly failed, had quite vanished. I've said it already—she was literally, she was hideously hard; she had turned common and almost ugly: "I don't know what you mean. I see nobody. I see nothing. I never *have*. I think you're cruel. I don't like you!" Then, after this deliverance, which might have been that of a vulgarly pert little girl in the street, she hugged Mrs Grose more closely and buried in her skirts the dreadful little face. In this position she launched an almost furious wail. "Take me away, take me away—oh take me away from *her*!" (70)

When the child ceases to be angelic (marker of her upper-class status), she becomes the emanation of a devilish and lower-class street child. Her face is mask and her beauty becomes ugliness; she becomes "common," like a "vulgarly pert little girl in the street," cheeky, rude, furious—none of which are behaviors permitted to the well-ordered upper-class angel child. The governess reads this scene as the child's final lie, as evidence that she has seen the ghost, and that she has sided with it. There is of course, though, another explanation. This is an ordinary child throwing an ordinary tantrum because she has been misunderstood. In a fiction world, a psychomachea makes sense: the struggle for the child by the forces of good and the forces of evil. But if this is not a story world, if it is not the world of fantasy, daydream and make-believe that the governess has constructed, then child is just being a child.

Children are, perhaps, always a bit uncanny. They are homely because they belong in the familiar world of the family. But, like several of Freud's examples of the uncanny, they provoke a hesitation of uncertainty. Are they miniature people (subjects with minds and wills of their own) or are they doll-like, objects to dress, and play with, and dispose of as the adult world chooses? And just maybe *they are both*, just as they are also both angels and demons in the same outer covering. The governess, in her fantasy world, cannot perform the intellectual sleight of hand that is needed to entertain the contradiction. Hers is an either–or world, not one of and/both. Readers who cope with the fiction and the realities they reflect, though, have to be cunning enough to believe at least these two impossible things before breakfast—that Flora is a lovely child who is behaving badly indeed.

Children and servants in a grand household share some important things. Both are "lesser beings" whose comfort is sacrificed to that of the adults who own the place. Both are meant to be docile and obedient, seen very little and heard hardly at all. Both are in some sense already "ghostly," though in James's story this is disguised by the fact that the children are so central to the plot. Apart from Mrs. Grose and the two ghosts, the servants at Bly are scarcely seen at all. The footman Luke provides Miles with some male companionship when the governess's charms pall. Apart from that, the servants do not appear to "count much," as Miles puts it towards the end of the story (79). The Victorian middle-class homes— even relatively poor ones—employed domestic servants because the management of a house (carrying water and coal, cleaning up after coal and water) was hefty work. The shape of a family among the reading classes was almost always inclusive of people who were employees not relations. These people counted enormously in the domestic comfort of the home, but did not count as individuals, and their labor was meant to be unseen. In grander homes, of which we must assume that Bly is one, separate entrances corridors and stair cases carried the laborers to their tasks. As Simon Hay has recently suggested, the ideal of Victorian domesticity was to render the labor that made it pleasant as invisible as possible, which the corollary that therefore ghosts and servants had a great deal in common (110).

If I were seeking simple explanatory frames to dismiss the ghosts in *The Turn of the Screw*, I could do worse than follow Bruce Robbins and posit that the ghosts are not dead servants, but living ones: "it is intriguing how much the ghosts have in common, looked at from above, with servants who are *not* ghosts, who are very much alive," he writes (286). The establishment at Bly is described, in reported speech, by Douglas as modest, considering the size of the house. There is a housekeeper, Mrs. Grose, "and there were, further, a cook, a housemaid, a dairywoman, an old pony, an old groom and an old gardener, all likewise thoroughly respectable" (5). As Robbins has suggested, the fact that the servants don't count much is made in that list by the inclusion of the pony: "Cooks, ponies, and gardeners are equal, levelled out as items on a list of Bly's possessions; none of these servants counts more than an animal.

Servants, like ghosts, are something less than human beings" (286–87). Governesses are also servants of course; but they are servants occupying an anomalous position in relation to the household they serve and the servants who generally are required to serve them. In the world of upstairs/downstairs relations, governesses presumably occupy a space around half way up (or down) the flight. The ambiguity of their social situation is one of the reasons that there was an enormous vogue for governess fiction in the mid-century and beyond—of which *Jane Eyre* is merely the most famous example—because their social mobility and uncertainty is one of the few ways in which a female protagonist can be set into motion in a plot that might question her respectability but that does not destroy it for the purposes of the propriety of fiction.

In fact, the ghosts probably cannot be so easily dismissed as unknown servants. The small staff at Bly means that the governess would surely recognize all the people with whom she comes into daily contact, even if she saw them in unusual circumstances. Trespassers or prowlers might be an explanation. But the story does not invite us to explain them away. Something is rotten in this Eden, and it might well be that the governess is inhabiting the wrong story. Imagining herself the heroine of a romance, a gothic fiction, or a fairy tale, she views herself as heroic, which leads her to obey the unreasonable, ridiculous injunction not to "bother" the master with any of her domestic troubles because obedience to unreasonable prohibitions is precisely what happens in fairy stories. In her fictional dream world heroism requires a might battle. The ghosts are her pretext—her pretext in already written script from another genre—for her to play out the role of ingénue princess in the hope that, as with Pamela, her virtue will be rewarded. But the generic frame does not fit; in fact, it is broken. The story's opening, with the frame narrative of ghost stories told at Christmas in a country house does not recur and there is no return to "normality." The internal audience does not respond. Only we—real as well as implied readers—are left to (mis)read and (mis)interpret. Genre has overspilled its boundaries. This isn't a safe "irresponsible little fiction," as James called it (123); it rebounds on its cunning and on its naïve readers.

James's namesake though he was not a relation, M. R. James, wrote of his own practice as a ghost story writer:

> [The setting should be] fairly familiar and the majority of the characters and their talk such as you may meet or hear any day. A ghost story of which the scene is laid in the twelfth or thirteenth century may succeed in being romantic or poetical: it will never put the reader into the position of saying to himself, 'If I'm not careful, something of this kind might happen to me!' (qtd. in Briggs 124)

In *The Turn of the Screw*, it just did. For whether we are cunning or not, we are all readers, and one way or another, we have all been fooled.

WORKS CITED

Beidler, Peter G. *Henry James: The Turn of the Screw*. Bedford Books, 1995.

Briggs, Julia. *Night Visitors: The Rise and Fall of the English Ghost Story*. Faber and Faber, 1977.

Freud, Sigmund. "The Uncanny," [1919] in *Art and Literature: Penguin Freud Library*, vol. 14. Penguin, 1990, pp. 339–76.

Hay, Simon. *A History of the Modern British Ghost Story*. Palgrave, 2014.

Kincaid, James C. *Child Loving: The Erotic Life of the Victorian Child*. Routledge, 1994.

Nelson, Claudia. "Growing up: Childhood." *A Companion to Victorian Literature and Culture*, edited by Herbert V. Tucker, Blackwell, 1999, pp. 69–81.

Robbins, Bruce. "They don't count much do they?" The Unfinished History of *The Turn of the Screw*, in Beidler, pp. 283–96.

TEN

"Fallen" Clergymen: The Wages of Sin in Hawthorne's *The Scarlet Letter*, Charles Reade's *The Cloister and the Hearth*, and Henry Arthur Jones's *Michael and His Lost Angel*

Jeanette Shumaker

Think, confessor, how easily pure love, which has only souls in view, can be soiled by the mire of earth, and how often a stream perfectly clear at its source changes into a murky and destructive torrent. —Canon A. Guerra, 1901

Ghostly, guilty ministers and priests abound in Victorian literature on both sides of the Atlantic. Contrast these ascetics with the portly clergymen in eighteenth-century novels who live long hedonistic lives, untroubled by illicit attractions. Except in Anthony Trollope and George Eliot, clergymen in Victorian literature tend to either be overly proud and authoritarian like Charlotte Brontë's St. John Rivers, or emasculated by guilt like Dimmesdale.[1] Even Eliot's Rufus Lyon in *Felix Holt* castigates himself for breaking his vow of celibacy when he marries a widow who would probably have died without his impassioned help; maybe her daughter, who becomes *Felix Holt*'s heroine, would have died as well. Through such fruitful passions as Rufus's, Victorian literature involving a "fallen" minister questions the era's gender stereotypes such as the supposed bestial masculinity of desire and the equation of chastity with virtue. Not only Victorian heroines but also ministers commit adultery because of love, not lust. Love leads clergymen to adultery in Henry

Arthur Jones's little-known play, *Michael and His Lost Angel* (1895), and in Nathaniel Hawthorne's historical novel of Puritan America, *The Scarlet Letter* (1850); it creates adulterous fantasies for a priest in Charles Reade's historical novel of the Middle Ages, *The Cloister and the Hearth* (1861). Neither are clerics' desires bestial nor are these writers sure that they should be repressed, particularly in Jones's late-century play.

The emasculation of ministers who renounce erotic love suggests that decline, not development of the self or of the community, results from repression. Such repression is a part of the feminizing of virtue as self-denial that occurs in Victorian culture (Sussman 10). Virtue becomes a resistance to temptation that would be associated with femininity for many Victorians, rather than the heroic action stereotypically associated with masculinity. A passive notion of virtue became popular because the greed of the industrial marketplace made the activity associated with men suspect.[2] Norman Vance explains that the Oxford Movement made clergymen question their traditional masculine pursuit of hunting: "This new clericalism, which frowned not only on clerical sportsmen but on any kind of clerical worldliness, appalled that manly clergyman Charles Kingsley" (16). The celibate male—the figure of the monk or priest— became, according to Herbert Sussman, a key symbol "through which to register male anxieties" (2). One of these anxieties was whether the intellectual labor of clergymen and scholars was effeminate, according to James Eli Adams (2). Another question was whether clergymen should marry: Kingsley struggled with his future wife's reluctance to wed for that reason (Vance 36). Kingsley sees the idealization of clergymen's celibacy as resting on an "abhorrence of women, which Kingsley works into the opening chapter of [his novel] *Hypatia*" (Vance 38). Vance adds, "Devotees of this kind of [celibate] religious life were easily recognized as emaciated and effeminate young curates" (39).

In the 1850s Kingsley's "muscular Christianity" supplanted the previous ideal of male asceticism fostered by both early Evangelicals and the Oxford Movement in Britain (Adams 108; Vance 31). Concern over health and sanitation, along with challenges to the British Empire's power, fed the popularity of Kingsley's movement (Adams 109). So did the "the restoration of the Roman Catholic hierarchy in England" in 1850, which stimulated xenophobic anxieties that recalled those around the Spanish Armada centuries before (Vance 40). Kingsley described "a healthy and manful Christianity, one which does not exalt the feminine virtues to the exclusion of the masculine" (qtd. in Miller 36). Vance observes that in both England and America, chivalry gained popularity as part of the neo-medievialist movement, helping to shape Kingsley's ideas of Christian manliness (17). Kingsley's movement applied not only to Evangelicals, but also to High Anglicans, according to Lori M. Miller: "High Anglicanism and displays of conventional norms of masculinity (including muscular Christianity) were not mutually exclusive" (40). Muscular Christianity was an ideal of manliness as self-control that helped to stitch "together England's sutured hegemony of capitalist and landed classes in opposition to radical working-class movements within England/Britain and anti-Imperialist forces overseas," explains David Alderson (169).[3]

The ambivalence toward masculine asceticism seen in the novels of Reade and Hawthorne plays off of the ideological shift toward muscular Christianity in the mid-century. Like other American intellectuals of his century, Hawthorne was influenced by British ideological debates such as the one about manliness. His novel set in Puritan America caustically mirrors Victorian New England (Baym 179), which, as a postcolonial society, both imitates and rebels against its motherland, England. Susan L. Roberson argues that in the late 1820s Ralph Waldo Emerson preached a form of masculinity that serves as an ancestor of Kingsley's notions in some ways (150–51); this is another sign of the convergence of clergymen's thinking about gender in both England and America.

Late in the century aestheticism's notions about androgyny challenged muscular Christianity (Alderson 119). Writing at the close of the century, Jones struggles with aesthetics' celebration of artistic and sensual freedom, as well as with the contradictory, Christian ideal that masculinity entails self-control. Sue Morgan explains that fin de siècle British clergymen had weathered "a steady erosion of professional esteem in the face of unyielding secularization compounded [by a] crisis of gender" entailed by the women's movement and early stirrings of homosexual culture (180). As a result, clergymen began a movement to foster male chastity through such organizations as the Church of England Purity Society (Morgan 179–80). "In the Church's quest for greater cultural authority the discourses of spiritual and sexual self-mastery combined to buttress religion against the twin crises of masculinity and secularization," Morgan explains (191). She adds, "Man was no mere animal," so the dissolute—whether by promiscuity, adultery, or masturbation— found themselves "alienat[ed] from the kingdom of God" (Morgan 182). The purity movement also built on "fears over racial degeneracy" to motivate men to change (Morgan 180). Morgan contends that, "Sexual purity provided the clerical elite with a particularly effective vehicle of proselytization enabling them to tap into public fears of social instability and moral vacuousness" (188).

Reade, Hawthorne, and Jones examine the dilemmas of adulterous priests and ministers who emulate Christ from the feminized angle of resistance to temptation rather than from mere masculine self-mastery. "Over the course of the century . . . commentators increasingly distinguished between a masculine self-discipline, which they represent as an ongoing regimen of aggressive self-mastery, and a feminine self-denial, which they represent as a spontaneous and essentially static surrender of the will to existential authority" (Adams 8–9). Hawthorne, Reade, and especially Jones expose the crises of identity that result for men who try to fulfill the ideal of "aggressive self-mastery," but end up adopting a feminized notion of virtue instead.[4]

Repression does not prevent effeminacy in so-called fallen clergymen even though it prevents the venereal disease that was supposed to cause it.[5] As ministers turn inward they turn deathward.[6] Nietzsche writes that "there is something unhealthy in such priestly aristocracies and in the habits ruling in them which turn them away from action and alternate between brooding and emotional explosions, habits which seem to have as their almost invariable consequence that intestinal morbidity and neurasthenia which has afflicted priests at all times" (32). It is interesting that Nietzsche noticed this problem in 1887, during an age when virtue was feminized, particularly for ministers.[7]

Because of the Victorian double standard, a man's so-called "fall" can hardly be caused by seduction unless he is a minister.[8] Like a woman, a minister belongs to the (spiritual) family he nurtures. Supported by his parish, he is its property and as such is not free. A related reason for the Victorian stress on clerical chastity is that theologians such as St. Augustine consider sex to be man's main distraction from God (Smith 218). Widely read during the nineteenth century, Milton's *Paradise Lost* portrays Adam as sinning because his love for Eve exceeds his love for God, who would have provided him with a new wife. Adam blames Eve's beauty for his fall even though love, not lust, seems to have been the cause—but a love between bodies not between man and God. Like St. John Rivers in *Jane Eyre*, the priests in *Michael* and *The Cloister* focus on lust—with its disgust-producing discourse of taints and stains—to prevent themselves from recognizing that their loyalties to God and a woman are irreconcilable.

Fear of disgrace leads clergymen into hypocrisy that is treated as a worse sin than lack of chastity in both *Michael* and *The Scarlet Letter*. Unlike the conventional so-called fallen mother whose child prevents her from being self-absorbed and hypocritical, a minister has no intimate to keep him honest. Surprisingly, hypocrisy enhances Dimmesdale's preaching, much as Lancelot's greatness grows from adultery in Tennyson's *Idylls of the King*.[9] As one of the community of sinners, Dimmesdale can move his audience: "The complaint of a human heart, sorrow-laden, perchance guilty, telling its secret . . . never in vain! It was this profound and continual undertone that gave the clergyman his most appropriate power" (242). That Hawthorne says that Dimmesdale's eloquence is "appropriate" supports the minister's view that he should preach, though at the cost of hypocrisy. In calling Dimmesdale a "subtle, but remorseful hypocrite" (143), however, Hawthorne seems to agree with Dimmesdale that he cannot save souls while deceiving them. But Dimmesdale apparently does redeem souls with his eloquence though imperiling his own through lies.

On the other hand, the virtuous ministers in Hawthorne's novel are much less effective preachers than Dimmesdale.[10] The unrealistic demands for perfection placed on both Victorian and Puritan ministers underly Dimmesdale's dilemma. Thomas Balguy, Archdeacon of Winchester during the late eighteenth and early nineteenth century, stressed to his clergy that they must "produce" the "fruits of piety and virtue" through "their godly exhortations and blameless examples" (16). Hawthorne suggests that if ministers do reach these ideals they may rise too far above their congregation to be able to touch them through their "exhortations"—a double bind.

The power of preachers such as Dimmesdale—and Reade's Gerard—rests in their expressiveness and vulnerability that may have been seen by nineteenth-century readers as stereotypically feminine. Pamela J. Walker observes the feminization of religion in Great Britain in the Victorian era: "Mid nineteenth-century Christianity was more often associated with a feminine piety and emotionalism than with any masculine virtue" (92). For example, when working-class Englishmen joined the Salvation Army that was founded in London in 1865 to attract men to Christianity, "Workmates and neighbours ridiculed and taunted the faithful and called them effeminate" (Walker 92).

In *The Feminization of American Culture*, Ann Douglas explains that the nineteenth-century American clergyman's mastery over logic, theology, and an educated male audience declined as a result of the church disestablishment; the clergy then turned to women through appealing to their emotions. Though Dimmesdale is a Puritan, Hawthorne's characterization of him is affected by such a feminizing trend. Studying biographies of Puritan ministers, Roberta Weldon explains that these ministers often resemble Dimmesdale in being sickly, frail, and sensitive: "In fact, in the ministerial biography sickness is frequently a sign of saintedness" (Weldon 15). Such qualities as ill health and sensitivity are usually seen as feminine in the 1800s. Dimmesdale uses sentiment but is also learned—a throwback to the kind of scholarly yet emotional preacher whom Hawthorne seems to prefer. Dimmesdale's self-flagellation does not sentimentalize him but, instead, makes the reader take his guilt seriously. His hypocrisy is partially excused by the death sentence he would probably have faced for adultery; in 1641, a Puritan minister was cast out for lust alone, so Dimmesdale's fear makes sense (Newberry 185). That Hawthorne creates a minister who sins then lies about it is in keeping with the decline in the clergy's status in his own day, which Douglas and Walker explore. Dimmesdale's hypocrisy recalls that of renowned nineteenth-century American minister Henry Ward Beecher, who denied that he had seduced a married woman, leaving her to face disgrace alone (Douglas 241–43).[11]

Along with the so-called fallen women in British and American literature who slowly destroy and redeem themselves through ascetic penances, Dimmesdale enacts a myth of self-transformation that is troubling because it results in his death and his sacrifice of his tie to Hester and Pearl. Roberta Weldon argues that Hawthorne critiques Victorian Christianity's belief that death is more important than life, and male immortality more important than familial or romantic love, through Dimmesdale's story. "While Dimmesdale thought it a fair bargain to sacrifice Hester for God and male immortality, Hawthorne seems more inclined to sacrifice the transcendental for the natural" (31). The lure of a holy death seems to have meant much to Victorians because it appears often in their literature. In reading about the consequences of adultery in the Puritan era in *The Scarlet Letter*, Victorians could reflect on their own struggles with illicit desires at a safe distance. Or perhaps Victorians liked to project the heroic scale of sin onto their mundane lives. Some of them did live their lives as matters of salvation or damnation in the manner of Dimmesdale, if we can believe Samuel Butler.

Because Dimmesdale's penance allows him to prolong his hypocrisy, it is hardly consistent with the feminized virtue of sacrifice that he seeks to affirm.[12] Hester's penitential asceticism parallels yet contrasts with Dimmesdale's, as hers is free of hypocrisy. Like his, however, hers questions the value of self-denial. She even rejects the pleasure of sewing, "like all other joys," as "sin" (Hawthorne 83). Embroidery, which Hawthorne tells us is the only available art form for a Puritan woman, allows Hester to express her "taste for the gorgeously beautiful . . . expressing, and therefore soothing, the passion of her life" (83). Her passionate nature leads her to become an artist as well as leading her to an illicit affair. Hester gradually turns away from both her art and her passion because they defy Puritan plainness, instead becoming known as "Able" for nursing at sickbeds. Her community redefines her scarlet letter as positively as she had hoped they would if she were "worthy" (168). Although Hester's moral growth is admirable, she must do violence to herself to accomplish it. She becomes "this dreary woman, gliding silently through the town" (85). Like Dimmesdale, she welcomes killing loneliness as a penance. As Roberta Weldon comments, "*The Scarlet Letter* has been described as a love story, but, in fact, it is a story that explains the reasons that men deny women, do violence to and punish them, and keep themselves apart from them" (18).

During a scene that contrasts with Dimmesdale's lonely vigil in front of a looking glass, a mirror in the governor's palace distorts Hester's image. All that the characters can see is her scarlet letter. Pearl says, "See you here. Look! Look!" (105). The most obvious meaning is that Hester's sin defines her. That is what the magistrates intend for her punishment and her community's benefit. She is to be a daily reminder, the very body of sin. Even her grave memorializes only her sin, not her virtue. Yet Pearl is too young to know that the scarlet letter is supposed to be a sign of adultery alone. For Pearl, it is a sign of her mother's condition: a sign of her sadness, her discipline, her kindness, and her isolation. The difficulty of pinning down the scarlet letter's meaning comes from the ambiguity of the lovers' sin, which, according to Hester, had its own "consecration" (194). An ironic twist occurs regarding their love during the forest scene. Dimmesdale's vitality is restored at the same time he finds out for certain that he committed adultery; Hester's husband is alive, she tells him. Is Dimmesdale's sin the source of his health? Is adultery always a sin? The complexity of the scarlet letter springs from the difficulty of labeling the multiple, changeable self as bad or good.[13] In recognition of this ambiguity, Hester does not explain her situation to Pearl. Harvey Gable contends, "Hester is unable to admit her guilt to Peal because Pearl is an image of Hester's own self in flight from regulation" (82). Yet when Hester ends her flight, she embarks on a death-in-life that resonates with Dimmesdale's actual death. Hawthorne's other novels similarly concern the insoluble conflict between passion and repression (Baym 176). Hawthorne's ambivalence about Hester's rebelliousness, Dimmesdale's asceticism, and the lovers' adultery questions the feminized self-denial that his age espoused.

When Dimmesdale plans to escape his sin by leaving Salem with Hester and Pearl, the "strong animal nature" that Chillingworth notes (Hawthorne 129) revives the minister's failing health. Dimmesdale struggles against blasphemous impulses that would ruin his saintly reputation. Hawthorne links Dimmesdale's health and energy to his sinfulness—and the minister's death to his resistance of temptation. To triumph over conflict as Dimmesdale does, however briefly, one must kill or at least control the so-called sinful self. However, only a rigid self dead to passion can exist without conflict. The turmoil beneath a virtuous image like Dimmesdale's shows its falsity. His ability to sin persists though it lies as dormant as Hester's beauty that briefly reappears when she and Dimmesdale plan to escape. Yet "deadly pallor" replaces Hester's vivid "blush" as soon as Pearl forces her to don the scarlet letter, symbol of her inescapable punishment (209).

That the couple cannot escape because Pearl, Chillingworth, and their own consciences stand in the way shows that Hester's plan to flee the consequences of sin is unrealistic. Dimmesdale's plan is no better, however: his avoidance of humiliation through asceticism and hypocrisy drives him to madness and illness. Hester exhorts Dimmesdale to "Exchange this false life of thine for a true one. . . . Preach! Write! Act! Do anything, save to lie down and die. Give up this name . . . and make thyself another . . . such as thou canst wear without fear or shame" (197). Inventing a name suggests that the self that the name represents is changed as easily as donning different clothes. When Dimmesdale fears "his tongue should wag itself," he puts on a new, reckless self that he later rejects as evil (215). Hawthorne's narrator writes that "No man . . . can wear one face to himself, and another to the multitude, without finally getting bewildered as to which may be the true" (215). In his sermons Dimmesdale publicizes the one face of sinner that is his most authentic one even while he avoids telling the secret that would prove he has fallen. His confession at his death suggests that past selves cannot be shed.

When Hester sees that Dimmesdale's struggle will kill him, she prescribes a stereotypically masculine cure of action—escape. On the other hand, his wish is to lie "passive for evermore" (187) like a woman. His is "a spirit so shattered and subdued, that it could hardly hold itself erect" (195). Effeminate in his weakness, he begs Hester to "Resolve for me!" (195). She takes a directive role that is stereotypically masculine.[14] Yet when she pulls him "enfeebled" to her breast she shows a mother's tenderness (194). He does act like a child until his confession on the scaffold: he does not help Hester to raise Pearl and does not share their shame. He forfeits his traditional role of head of the family to Hester, whose strength enables her to bear it well.

Despite his childish ineffectuality, Dimmesdale carries shame internally. Pearl correctly reads his mannerism of keeping his hand over his heart as the counterpart of her mother's scarlet letter. The novel contrasts the public punishment of Hester with the scorching, private one of Dimmesdale. It argues for appearing as one truly is, despite the difficulty of determining identity when besieged by contradictory impulses. Hester learns to tell the truth through the searing discipline of curious stares at her bosom, the embarrassingly fitting location for her sign of adultery. Such looks are cruel invasions of Hester's privacy.[15]

These public stares are, however, less hostile than those Dimmesdale receives from Chillingworth.[16] Dimmesdale can only escape Chillingworth's plan to damn him eternally for his hypocrisy by admitting his sin on the scaffold. At one point in the writing process, Hawthorne had planned to have Dimmesdale confess to a Catholic priest; however, in the Puritan context, public confession is needed for Dimmesdale's expiation (Newberry 186). Public confession is the only way to get free of both his hypocrisy and of the "tempter" who wishes him to prolong it (Hawthorne 250). D. H. Lawrence describes Chillingworth and Dimmesdale as "the black, vengeful soul of the crippled, masterful male, still dark in his authority: and the white ghastliness of the fallen saint! The two halves of manhood mutually destroying one another" (qtd. in Rountree 81). What Lawrence sees as a divorce of body and spirit, I call dangerously estranged Victorian stereotypes of masculinity as sin (action, desire) and femininity as virtue (denial, repression). Confession defines the minister as a sinner, a partial truth that lets Dimmesdale briefly assert the so-called "masculine" confidence he had lost to effeminacy during his attempt to reform himself through asceticism. Yet the restoration of the traditional gender polarities of male strength and female submissiveness cannot last; Dimmesdale dies serving feminized virtue. As these gender polarities dissolve, so does the power of feminized virtue. The variety of

Hester's endurance, activity and contemplation becomes the most promising notion of virtue, surpassing gender stereotypes. [17]

Though *The Scarlet Letter* continues to be widely read, *The Cloister and The Hearth*, one of the most popular English novels of the 1800s in England and America, and a bestseller in England up through 1921, has fallen out of fashion (Spencer 70; Vitanza 86). Henry James and W. D. Howells considered Reade to be a novelist of the first rank, according to Dianna Vitanza (71). Richard Fantina likewise attests to Reade's reputation in his lifetime "as a controversial author of the first rank" (1). Mark B. Spencer speculates that the decline of Reade's popularity, like Walter Scott's, in the 1920s may have occurred as a result of the development of history as a professional field of study in western nations beyond Germany, resulting in a new historical consciousness in England and America that found Reade and Scott to be reductionists in their historical romances (83).

As in *The Scarlet Letter*, Reade's women in *The Cloister* are more resilient than the men who become self-sacrificing examples of feminized virtue. Richard Fantina argues that, "Reade's female characters stand at the forefront of the most vibrant women in Victorian literature and anticipate the novels of other male authors sympathetic to the 'woman question,' such as Thomas Hardy and George Gissing" (163). Reversing gender stereotypes, Reade's *The Cloister and the Hearth* involves the decline of a medieval priest into weakness and the strengthening of his wife through raising their son, who will become the great intellectual, Erasmus.

Reade's Gerard is a young painter who leaves Holland to make his fortune in Rome. He tries to kill himself when two of his brothers deceive him into thinking that his beloved wife is dead; he does not know that Margaret lives and has borne him a son. Comforted in his grief by priests, he decides to become one rather than reconstruct a life of new affections. As a priest he is renamed Clement. Reade's novel focuses on Gerard's/Clement's struggle to reconcile his love for his wife with duty to God after he finds out that his wife is alive.

Because Gerard fears that he will violate his priestly vows of celibacy, he retreats to a cave, becoming a self-castigating hermit. In isolation he learns that "I must needs own I have been worse tempted here with evil imaginations than in the world" (698). He finally agrees with Margaret that he should return to preaching, so becomes a parson to his hometown parish. Insulted that Gerard had not trusted her to help him stay celibate, Margaret convinces him that they can raise their son Gerard together as friends; they do avoid adultery despite their continued mutual attraction. Ten years later Margaret dies of the plague. Destroyed by her death, Gerard retires to a monastery to mourn her and dies soon afterwards. When monks lay him out, they find a lock of her hair under his hairshirt.

Although Gerard never violates his vows of chastity, he becomes obsessed with sexual fantasies about Margaret while he is a hermit. Like Jimmy Carter, Gerard sins in his heart by desiring Margaret, who is now forbidden; because of that desire, he labels himself a fallen priest. He tells Margaret that all the saints, including Jerome and Anthony, went through similar struggles to deny sexual desire (698). Gerard attributes his own hallucinations about sex to the Devil; he thinks the Devil masks himself with Margaret's shape. Gerard's fear of Margaret as a temptress recalls the dread of Spenser's Duessa in *The Faerie Queene* and of Coleridge's Geraldine in "Christabel"—beauties who appear to be manifestations of the Devil. They will entrap a man into deserting God's ways, as Eve—from a misogynistic point of view—did Adam. However, Margaret shows the preposterousness of Gerard's suspicion that she is a temptress when she helps him to resist temptation. She says that although they were married once, now they will merely be each other's most trusted friends.[18] Because a tabooed relationship can only continue without guilt if it becomes platonic, her belief that her feelings have cooled is a necessary self-deception that succeeds in controlling her behavior, if not desire, while allowing her to continue to see her beloved. Margaret's advice to Gerard to return to his pastoral duties fits that of Archdeacon Balguy to his clergy that "a studious and solitary life exposes us more than anything to the delusions of Fancy" (158). Solitude tortures both Gerard and Dimmesdale, increasing their illicit desires and their guilt about them.

Margaret convinces Gerard to trust her through a ritual of mutual absolution in which she acts primarily as his confessor because he, more than she, has felt improper desires. In acting as his confessor, she, ironically, fulfills the priestly role of moral authority that he, like Dimmesdale, has failed to fulfill. By contrast, in most Victorian novels about so-called fallen women, men act as confessors. In forgiving Gerard for misjudging her as a temptress, Margaret shows the unconditional motherly love that had allowed Hester to forgive Dimmesdale for abandoning her. Yet in directing Gerard to leave his self-centered life as a hermit, Margaret acts like an authoritarian father. Unlike Hester, Margaret gives righteous advice; ironically, Gerard is never restored to family leadership the way Dimmesdale is before his death. To avoid offending Gerard while she tells him what to do, Margaret humbly reiterates that "I am but a woman" to make him feel as though he is the stronger of the two (703). But really she is the stronger, more dynamic of the two throughout their trials. Spencer states that Margaret reminds Gerard "that it is spiritual selfishness and egotism for a priest to take care only for his own soul, since so many other worse sinners need his attention" (80). She resourcefully supports herself and her son during the years when Gerard is gone, never losing faith that he is alive despite rumors of his death. On the other hand, he believed that she had died because of a mere letter from his brothers. She combines chastity with resourcefulness and determination. In her strength she resembles Hester Prynne. However, instead of Hester's freedom of thought Margaret holds standard moral views.

Like Dimmesdale, Gerard is weaker than the woman he loves. Instead of being able, like Margaret, to resist desire through immersion in child-raising, Gerard gets stuck in a sterile conflict that only Margaret's determined interference can halt. In consonance with their contrasting psychological states, Margaret looks as blooming as ever when they meet while Gerard looks ailing and tormented. His decline without her reveals his dependence on her, a dependence that exceeds hers on him—another parallel with *The Scarlet Letter*. Margaret's ability to repress love for Gerard and, by cherishing that love, make herself flourish exceeds his.[19]

Gerard's weakness in contrast to Margaret's resilience may come as a shock to the reader because his depression is the opposite of his previous optimism; tried by grief, he adopts the paralysis that is a negative stereotypical trait of femininity, losing the confidence to act that is a positive stereotype of masculinity. His suicidal reaction to Margaret's supposed death may also seem feminine in a negative way as the epitome of his depressed inability to continue life without her. Marguerite Higgonnet observes that committing suicide because of lost love was stereotyped as feminine by nineteenth-century novelists (73). Gerard's suicide attempt is the clearest expression of his effeminate, self-disintegrating personality that emerges under the stress of grief. Feminine self-annihilation hides underneath Gerard's facade of confidence, ready to take over when aggressiveness fails. Gerard has a dual nature, alternating between extremes of masculinity and femininity. His feminine self-destructiveness resurfaces after Margaret has died. Gerard's emasculation after he adopts feminized virtue shows the danger of it for men, much as Dimmesdale's decline does.

In going to Rome to earn a fortune as a painter and returning to Holland humbled, having forsaken his worldly goals, Gerard conforms to the conventional Victorian pattern of an ambitious man's quest, failure, and transformation through guilt that likewise appears in Hawthorne's *The Blithedale Romance*, Dickens's *Dombey and Son*, and Henry James's *The Wings of the Dove*. But Gerard is not portrayed as overly ambitious like the heroes of those novels; instead, he is the victim of his brothers' envy and greed, which lead them to lie to prevent Gerard from claiming his inheritance.[20] Reade's portrayal of grasping brothers confirms the Victorian distrust of masculine ambition that led to the age's preference for virtue as resistance to temptation rather than as the active, creative virtue that the young, confident Gerard exhibits before he becomes a priest. Yet Gerard's (and Dimmesdale's) physical deterioration after embracing feminized virtue shows that it is no panacea for masculine ambition. Margaret masculinizes the hearth as the seat of action in the world as well as of feminine love; domesticity no longer means passivity. Opposed to Margaret's hearth is the feminized cloister of priests who fear the body, sublimating their sexual desires into service for God, as Dimmesdale does in his pseudo-monasterial home with Chillingsworth.[21] Margaret's strength, like Hester's, offers only a partial solution to the conflict between duty and desire that the protagonists face. Both women praise self-denial even while it kills much of their joy in living.

Gerard at last becomes content after he throws himself into charity. Margaret, too, feels happier after she immerses herself in philanthropy; once her son is too old to need all of her attention, she wants to bear another child but must either give up that desire or her faithfulness to Gerard. The charity of Gerard and Margaret doesn't jeopardize their repression of illicit passion. Rather, charity is a pastime that elevates them in the Victorian readers' hierarchy of merit based on the ability to repress that is explored by John Kucich (120). Hester, too, becomes a heroine through sublimating her passion for Dimmesdale into charity. That Gerard drops his charitable activities after Margaret dies shows that they were a socially acceptable way of being with her, rather than satisfying for their own sake. Charity elevates the couple in a Victorian hierarchy of sacrifice that depends on an eroticizing of self-destruction.

In a culture in which E. P Thompson notes that Methodist hymns encourage workers to channel their eroticism into sacrifice for Christ, such a pattern as that found in *The Cloister* and *The Scarlet Letter* is not surprising. The popularity of *The Cloister* may have come from the Victorian fascination with medievalism, priests, and antique religiosity, the latter two of which stem from Newman and the Oxford movement. Fascination with Catholicism often led, paradoxically, to virulent prejudice against Catholics that was consistent with Britain's ancient desire for dominance as an imperial power over competing Catholic powers. As the muscular Christians of Protestantism often saw themselves in a positive light as masculine Imperialists, they also degraded Catholics as effeminate. Having such a predisposition against Catholicism, Protestants reading Darwin may have wondered whether celibacy was natural for priests. *The Great Red Dragon*, a book of anti-Catholic propaganda published supposedly by an ex-priest in 1856, argues that forbidding marriage for priests pushes them into seducing their female confessants. Though Reade avoids such ludicrous and crude charges, *The Cloister* does contend that celibacy creates unnecessary misery. Margaret and Gerard's dilemma also allowed Reade to investigate gender roles and Calvinistic views of the body in a way that may have seemed non-threatening to Protestant readers because it made such issues seem peculiarly Catholic. Yet such issues were perplexing to non-Catholic Victorians even across the water, as *The Scarlet Letter* demonstrates.

Reade was inspired to write *The Cloister* by Erasmus's tale about his parents' impossible love in his *Compendium vitae* (1524) (Spencer 71). Erasmus's parents struggled to renounce their sexual love for each other because priests must be celibate, a rule that Reade criticizes from his

Protestant viewpoint.[22] Mark B. Spencer observes that Erasmus was a key pre-Reformation figure: "The distaste of Erasmus for monasticism was notorious" (78). Spencer believes that although many in England and America embraced the medieval revival of the 1800s, Reade's novel bolstered Protestant criticism of medieval Catholicism (79). "Reade was both a social reformer and a committed Evangelical in the vein of Kingsley's 'muscular Christianity'" (Spencer 80).

A renunciation of sexual love that intensifies it likewise appears in *Michael and His Lost Angel.* Like Reade, Jones is a once respected but now neglected author. Despite the fact that George Bernard Shaw viewed Jones as the best playwright of his generation (Wallis 21), Jones's plays are little known today.[23] Typical of the skepticism of the fin de siècle, *Michael* criticizes self-denial without making it seem heroic, unlike the somewhat sentimental *Cloister* and the possibly devout *Scarlet Letter* of the more optimistic mid-century. Jones also differs from Hawthorne and Reade in being somewhat misogynistic in his portrayal of the fallen woman. As Penny Griffin argues, "Jones's attitude to women, though typical of a certain type of Victorianism, is, a century later, largely unacceptable" (31). Yet Jones was influenced by the non-misogynistic Hawthorne. Bruce Wallis asserts Hawthorne's influence on Jones in his highlighting of scenes of confession that dramatize a clergyman's fall (24). Jones also echoes Hester's plea near the end of *The Scarlet Letter* that she will unite with Dimmesdale after death in his heroine and hero's similar plea at the end of his play.

The plot of *Michael and His Lost Angel* may be quickly summarized. When an unhappy society woman who pretends that she is single seduces her self-righteous minister, the two fall in love. Later, Michael Feversham finds out that Audrie Lesden paid her husband to desert her, yet they are still married; as a result, Michael and Audrie cannot marry. Michael renounces Audrie for the benefit of their souls, but he cannot stop longing for her even as he prepares to become a priest in the manner of Cardinal Newman and some other Anglicans who belonged to the Oxford Movement. Michael finally meets with Audrie when she is dying. Michael wants only to rejoin her in death, yet he believes the quickest, surest path to heaven is through the priesthood.

This play resembles *The Cloister* in having its hero choose the priesthood because of having lost his beloved; that choice is seen as self-destructive by both Reade and Jones. Similarly, Catholic M. Paul chose celibacy and a life of futile sacrifice after the beloved girl of his youth died, as described in in Charlotte Brontë's *Villette*. Resembling Michael Feversham, Lancelot in Tennyson's *Idylls of the King* enters the cloister out of guilt over committing adultery. Puritan Dimmesdale likewise fits into this tradition of guilt-ridden, self-destructive clergymen. Frederick Newberry contends that Dimmesdale's self-flagellation and unwillingness to marry code him as a Catholic priest in spirit if not in fact (184). All of these works share a subtle anti-Catholicism that allows a largely Protestant readership to distance itself from the heroes' dilemmas rather than seeing them as typical of the feminization of Victorian culture that Douglas describes in its American form. That *The Scarlet Letter*, *The Idylls*, and *The Cloister* are set in bygone eras serves a similar function of letting readers pretend that they do not involve Victorian issues.

Because of his guilt, the supposedly fallen minister turns from thwarted love to self-disintegrating religion. The so-called fallen woman is a more blatant outcast who allows readers to distance themselves from both the double standard and female martyrdom—consider, for example, Elizabeth Gaskell's Ruth in the novel of that name, Dickens's Little Em'ly in *David Copperfield*, Wilkie Collins's Mercy Merrick in *The New Magdalen*, and George Eliot's almost fallen Maggie Tulliver in *The Mill on the Floss*. When the fallen woman becomes a redemptive figure, as is the case with Hester, she spiritually rescues her lover but is not allowed to enjoy a normal life. Her self-denying virtue continues to act negatively on herself, if positively for others.[24] Fallen women and ministers' channeling of eroticism into self-denial comes from their defining virtue as resistance to temptation, not as active heroism. In *The Idylls*, Lancelot renounces his martial heroics as inextricably woven with his sexual transgressions. After he falls, Michael Feversham ceases to care about the restoration of his church, his ambitious project to improve the world. All of his passion goes into resisting his love for Audrie, so he no longer works for the good of his parish. Whereas guilt makes Dimmesdale a better, more empathetic preacher, it absorbs Michael to the point of making him ineffective.

Not only is Michael's love for Audrie adulterous, but it may also seem to insult God; like Adam's love for Eve in *Paradise Lost*, Michael's love for Audrie exceeds his love for God. As Lancelot betrays King Arthur, his god on earth, Michael is disloyal to his God because of a woman. Whereas Dimmesdale deeply regrets his disloyalty to God, Michael remains so wrapped up in Audrie that he forgets God. Perhaps that is the reason why Dimmesdale is effective at moving his parishioners as a fallen preacher, whereas Michael does not even try.

Such disloyalty as Michael's causes the breaking of laws that Victorian men, as authority figures, were supposed to uphold and which, ultimately, a male God represents. Tony Tanner posits that nineteenth-century novels of adultery question the righteousness of laws through questioning the rectitude of authoritative men. The conventional, ambiguously portrayed temptress thus reveals the hollowness of male integrity as well as the injustice of laws created by men. Through the ambiguous yet sympathetic portrayals of hypocrites such as Lancelot, Dimmesdale, and Michael, the pride with which Victorian men justify their authoritarianism is lost. Male humiliation allows women like Hester and Margaret to grow far beyond stereotypical dependence on their former mates, subverting the gender expectations of their creators' era. A consequence of the culture's cherishing of feminized virtue is the strong women and weak men seen in *The Cloister*, *The Scarlet Letter*, and *Michael*.[25]

Through its melodrama, Jones's play suggests that the law that makes divorce difficult to obtain is unfair.[26] *The Scarlet Letter* can also be seen as complaining about the indissolubility of marriage bonds. Tanner argues that nineteenth-century novels about adultery criticize binding social contracts, especially marriage, showing the need for divorce. The permanence of marriage is based on the medieval notion that a woman's body belongs first to her father and then to her husband. According to this view, sexual transgressions pollute both a woman's honor and her family's because her chaste body symbolizes family integrity (Pitt-Rivers 52). Michael holds this view when he says, "I will keep you [Audrie] white and stainless from me" (91). But Jones questions Michael's belief in the correctness or even possibility of renunciation. Michael wastes away into half-insanity because he cannot forget Audrie. Paradoxically, he chooses to become a priest to earn the right to love her after death. His prioritizing of the afterlife over this life develops into a longing for death that is not a longing for God.

The irony is that Michael values the afterlife only because he hopes to be reunited with his co-adulterer. That Michael has a selfish motive for entering the priesthood is evident when he exclaims that he will do anything to become a priest if only he can see Audrie after death. He is willing to trade his will for a chance to see her in Heaven—a bargain with God that is as dubious as Audrie's bargain with the Devil that he can have her if she can have Michael. That both characters prostitute themselves to immortal beings blurs God with the Devil. Breaking away from the underlying Christian faith of previous works such as *The Scarlet Letter* and *The Cloister*, *Michael* portrays faith as destroying the couple's chance for earthly happiness as much as physical desire does. The protagonists' motives for faith are as pathetically earthbound as they are in Graham Greene's *The End of the Affair*.

Dying, Audrie says, "I haven't the strength to feel sorry," with a hideous laugh that mocks their renunciation (Jones 105). Michael casts her as his good angel, "the holiest thing on earth to me" (91). She, however, calls herself his "creature" and "daughter," resembling the conventional fallen heroine in prostrating herself before a superior male for whom she reforms.[27] The male confessor is usually not the fellow adulterer, though; Michael's superiority is clearly an illusion, consistent with late-Victorian doubting of clergymen. The wisdom of Audrie's dependence on his strength—that of the minister, patriarch, God—is put into doubt by the futility and loneliness of their sacrifice.

Michael's renunciation of Audrie is futile in that it does not eradicate his love for her but increases it, as Freud's theory of repression might predict. Like Gerard and Dimmesdale, Michael can no longer focus on God because repression and guilt consume all his energy. His conflict weakens Michael—who earlier was an active, popular minister—so that he becomes a living skeleton. Michael says, "I have no present, no future. I've only the past when she was with me" (99). Michael survives on memories of Audrie. Dead to the living world, he resembles hermits like Reade's Gerard, who become ineffective priests. Michael overly feminizes virtue as resistance not action. His is the same conflict between self-absorption and interest in others that Gerard resolves in favor of charity after Margaret criticizes him for being a hermit. Repressive natures like Gerard and Michael's ultimately embrace isolation and inaction, however. Their conflicts make them desire a "peace" which can only come with death (Jones 99). Bruce Wallis also remarks upon Jones's "association of righteousness with death" (24), which he sees as a cause of Michael's paralysis (23). This deathward orientation detracts from the potential usefulness of self-denial, making it a diversion from social ills, not their cure. Instead of adhering to the Victorian penchant for usefulness, Jones's fin de siècle play aestheticizes death as erotic self-annihilation. Such an ending questions the sexual freedom aesthetics espoused. In a world that values self-control in men, particularly ministers, sexual freedom can only come at a terrible price, as it has for fallen heroines throughout the centuries.

The name Feversham suggests the two Romantic-era flaws in Michael that lead to his self-destruction—conceit and passion. At the beginning of the play, he forces Rose, his aide's daughter, to admit her adultery to the congregation. Later, though, in his sham phase he hides his adultery, echoing Dimmesdale. Even when Michael eventually confesses his sin to his congregation, he refuses to reveal Audrie's name. Before his fall, Michael's excessive confidence in his own goodness resembles that of Hawthorne's Hollingsworth in *The Blithedale Romance*. As with that reformer, Michael's humiliation causes a new excess—self-castigation that makes him a useless, pitifully emasculated figure. In his self-loathing he resembles Dimmesdale, who also launches into self-destruction as a result of his guilt over and wish to continue adultery. Michael never conquers his desire as well as Dimmesdale does through his firmer faith, but both are destroyed by the conflict.

Although Michael, like Dimmesdale, confesses his adultery to his parishioners, confession does not redeem him as it did the Puritan minister. Under Jones's late-century treatment—which is as skeptical as Hardy's in *Tess of the D'Urbervilles*—confession is no longer a powerful, transforming ritual. That Dimmesdale dies after confessing conveniently saves him from further temptations, whereas Michael lives on, broken. But unlike Hester Prynne, who faces life without her beloved with active heroism as well as "feminine" resistance to temptation, Michael retreats into his memories of Audrie. His weakness contrasts with the strength that some so-called fallen women such as Hester and Margaret use to compensate for their partners' ineptitude. Nor does Michael achieve the status of martyr to an unjust society that Gaskell's Ruth, Eliot's Maggie Tulliver, and Hardy's Tess earn. Instead, his sterile conflict bespeaks the futility of repression of which Freud warns.

The decline of Dimmesdale, Gerard, and Michael reveals that Victorian morality's denial of physical desire fostered a feminized form of virtue that involved a longing for death. Initially too stereotypically masculine in his overconfidence, self-righteousness, and ungoverned sexual passion, Michael compensates by becoming stereotypically feminine in a negative sense by eroticizing self-denial to the point of self-destructiveness. His shift into madness completes his identification with troubling feminine stereotypes. That identification suggests how difficult it is for men to feminize virtue. Renunciation of passion is as annihilating not only of the body but also of the spirit as fulfillment would have been. Motivated by guilt, clergymen like Michael, Gerard, and Dimmesdale substitute masochistic religious passion for earthly desire, in the tradition of female medieval mystics like Julian of Norwich. In Jones's play, the cleric's religious passion takes on an aestheticized cast that questions the fin de siècle's approval of pure extremes above all else. Because their guilt, Michael, Gerard, and Dimmesdale move toward the contemplative feminine, which robs them of the vitality stereotypically associated with the masculine. Self-absorption prevents Michael, Dimmesdale, and Gerard from carrying out the social activism of priests like those in South America during the latter half of the twentieth century. Thus, the feminized virtue of self-sacrifice and the related cult of domesticity preserve the status quo of Victorian capitalism rather than transforming it through charity.[28] The good works of God's appointed servants—at least of the fallen ones—are merely sidetracks from their primary focus: contemplation of the inescapability of sin and death.

Ben Wilson's historical study of the formation of Victorian values through 1837 suggests that Hawthorne and Jones, in their emphasis on confessing adultery, might be responding to fears that the strictness of the new morality encourages insincerity—or "cant" (Wilson 20–21). Wilson argues that Victorian values arose as a reaction against "a world seemingly menaced by perpetual war, anarchy, famine and disease" (375). Survivors of that world "felt that the hard truths of revivalist religion and political science held out the promise of certainty and, above everything else, reassurance" (375). Though Hawthorne is an American writing about America, a similar tightening of morality in the face of rising Evangelicalism occurred in eastern America in the mid nineteenth-century, creating American Victorianism. "It was as if the pious had a monopoly on morality," remarks Wilson about Great Britain in the 1830s (373); some critics of this new morality "saw the repression of instincts and the desire to control others as a movement toward puritanism," according to Wilson (21). Jones, Hawthorne—and Reade—appear to be in this camp that "feared that refinement, progress and the tyranny of public opinion would make everything artificial and bogus" (Wilson 388). Their texts show the deathly consequences of such self-policing.

NOTES

1. Ministers are satirically shown in Austen's *Pride and Prejudice* and somewhat sentimentally in Eliot's *Scenes from Clerical Life*, though not in *Middlemarch*.

2. See Carol Christ's essay about feminized heroes in Ruskin and Dickens in Martha Vicinus's *Suffer and Be Still*. See Mario Praz's and Ann Douglas's studies of the feminization of Victorian literature and culture on each side of the Atlantic.

3. Like Alderson, John Tosh examines British masculinity late in the 1800s as it relates to Imperialism. Tosh remarks on "the unprecedented scrutiny of the fitness of both sexes which has strongly imperial overtones: women as mothers of the race, men as the active, assertive element. . . . The defence of the empire required more men and better men" (195).

4. According to Adams, Kingsley's heroes "experience an unusually violent oscillation of desire and restraint," which suggests "a powerfully masochistic impulse in Kingsley's novels" (110). Like the writers discussed in this essay, Kingsley attempts to masculinize self-denial but finally feminizes it as erotic self-destruction.

5. Much of the purity and medical literature recommends continence for men as well as women; frequent sex could cause insanity in both genders, effeminacy in men, and masculinity in women (Marcus 19; Haller 112; Gay 332). The symptoms of some venereal diseases explain why these views were held.

6. Of course some actual Victorians who were repressive centered their lives around public projects; they were not self-absorbed, at least not in the same way as the fictional fallen ministers I discuss.

7. See Ann Douglas for a discussion of ministers' adoption of sentimentality.

8. Studies of nineteenth-century sexuality report that young men, even young married men, were expected to have affairs (Haller 237); they apparently did, if the large, but perhaps exaggerated, count of prostitutes in London is taken as evidence (Gay 357).

9. Baym notes that sin makes Dimmesdale into an artist, but because he feels himself a hypocrite, he loathes his success at preaching (188).

10. Dawn Coleman argues that Dimmesdale's model is an eminent Unitarian minister who died young, John Emery Abbot. "Hawthorne continued and intensified his resistance to Unitarianism by rewriting the saintly Abbot as the miserable sinner Dimmesdale. . . . Hawthorne critiqued . . . the hero-worship that surrounded ministers across denominations" (Coleman 2).

11. Evelyn A Kirkley describes American clergymen's early twentieth-century movement to rescue what they saw as a dangerously feminine church: "God needed manly men to rescue an effeminate church" (83).

12. Kenneth D. Pimple also dwells on Dimmesdale's hypocrisy. "[H]e values both his social face and his immortal soul, but he cannot save one without losing the other. His inner torment springs from this dilemma, and his effort to serve two masters leads him into continual doubletalk and makes his life an ongoing deception" (270).

13. Critics such as Yvor Winters and F. O. Mathiessen note the ambiguity of Hawthorne's symbols throughout his novels and that he presents multiple interpretations of characters' behavior without resolving them (Rountree 63, 83). Tadd Ruetenik's original, provocative view of the scarlet letter is that its function is "the disclosure of the scapegoat mechanism. The innocent Dimmesdale, setting himself up for sacrifice, is the truth at the heart of it" (83). Ruetenik argues that Dimmesdale did not commit adultery with Hester, but rather, takes on her sin in the way Christ might.

14. Marilyn Mueller Wilton argues that Dimmesdale is the paramour and Hester is the hero of the novel, which centers on Hester's knightly quest for a Holy Grail of unrequited love (220, 222).

15. Elizabeth Aycock Hoffman argues that Hawthorne's "presenting the self-denying woman as exemplary points up his own complicity in the political program that effects the subjection of the individual" (218).

16. That Chillingworth conceals his identity from Dimmesdale much more successfully than Dimmesdale does from Chillingworth suggests that the physician's duplicity exceeds the minister's, though the minister's sin caused it.

17. In *Dombey and Son*, Dickens has Dombey's confession to Florence lead him to regain a little confidence. As a result, Dombey launches a more longlasting reformation than Dimmesdale's.

18. In her mistaken belief that a consummated love relationship can be transformed into a platonic one, Margaret resembles the heroine of Rousseau's *Julie*; similarly, Maggie, in *The Mill on the Floss* (1864), deludes herself that she and Stephen can safely see each other alone after they have confessed their forbidden love.

19. In Victorian novels that center on confession and renunciation, the denial of romantic love is often a source of moral strength: see James's *The Wings of the Dove*, Ellen Wood's *East Lynne*, Eliot's *Daniel Deronda, Tess*, Gissing's *The Unclassed*, and Collins's *The New Magdalen*.

20. Gerard's brothers betray him just as Joseph's brothers do in the Bible; Gerard forgives as freely as does Joseph.

21. St. John Rivers is another such clergyman.

22. Reade's anti-Catholic tone resembles Brontë's in *Villette*. Charles Kingsley's attacks on priestly celibacy are more explicit than Reade's yet both cater to the tastes of a Protestant public that was irritated by Catholic Emancipation and the Oxford Movement, according to Dianna Vitanza. Both Mark B. Spencer (72) and Vitanza argue that Reade's resentment over the celibacy required for his fellowship at Magdalen College, Oxford colors his treatment of priestly celibacy. Discussing several forgotten Victorian works of historical fiction other than Reade's, Miriam E. Burstein makes a similar argument to Vitanza and Spencer's about the novels' anti-Catholic content: "Written in response to a perceived tide of pro-Catholic sentiment, such novels sought to make the Victorians remember a past they might otherwise be doomed to repeat" (Burstein 163).

23. Bruce Wallis explains the reason for Jones's eclipse: "our own historical position in the sexual rebellion" makes us see Jones' plays about adultery as "trite . . . and thus prevents us from taking seriously a dramatist who can be read quite richly" (25).

24. An exception to this pattern is Elizabeth Barrett Browning's Marian Erle in *Aurora Leigh*. However, Marian is a victim of rape, not of seduction; since she never acceded to corruption, she does not have to live the death-in-life of the typical passionate fallen woman.

25. Gilbert and Gubar consider the pattern of strong women and weak men to be a criticism of patriarchy's expectations for each gender.

26. So do Grant Allen's *The Woman Who Did* and Hardy's *Jude the Obscure*, also written during the nineties.

27. Such a pattern is seen in Eliot's *Daniel Deronda*, Collins's *The New Magdalen*, and Gissing's *The Unclassed*.

28. See Susan Morgan's *Sisters in Time*, Nancy Paxton's *George Eliot and Herbert Spencer*, and Nancy Armstrong's *Desire and Domestic Fiction* for other arguments about feminine values in Victorian literature.

WORKS CITED

Adams, James Eli. *Dandies and Desert Saints: Styles of Victorian Masculinity*. Cornell UP, 1995.

Alderson, David. *Mansex Fine: Religion, Manliness, and Imperialism in Nineteenth-Century British Culture*. Manchester UP, 1998.

Armstrong, Nancy. *Desire and Domestic Fiction*. Oxford UP, 1987.

Balguy, Thomas, D. D. *Discourses on Various Subjects and Charges Delivered to the Clergy of the Archdeacon of Winchester*, 2 vols. Edited by James Drake, Smith, 1822.

Baym, Nina. "Passion and Authority in *The Scarlet Letter*." *New England Quarterly*, vol. 43, 1970, pp. 209–30.

Burstein, Miriam Elizabeth. "Counter-Medievalism." *Beyond Arthurian Romances*, edited by Jennifer Palmgren et al., Palgrave Macmillian, 2005, pp. 147–68.

Coleman, Dawn. "Critiquing Perfection: Hawthorne's Revision of Salem's Unitarian Saint." *Nathaniel Hawthorne Review*, vol. 37, no. 1, 2011, pp. 1–19.

Douglas, Ann. *The Feminization of American Culture*. Knopf, 1977.

Fantina, Richard. *Victorian Sensational Fiction: The Daring Work of Charles Reade*. Palgrave, 2010.

Freud, Sigmund. *New Introductory Lectures on Psychoanalysis*. Norton, 1933.

Gable, Harvey L., Jr. *Liquid Fire: Transcendental Mysticism in the Romances of Nathaniel Hawthorne*. Peter Lang, 1998.

Gavin, Anthony. *The Great Red Dragon or the Master-Key to Popery*. Jones, 1856.

Gay, Peter. *The Tender Passion*. Vol. II of *The Bourgeois Experience: Victoria to Freud*. Oxford UP, 1986.

Gilbert, Sandra M. and Susan Gubar. *Sexchanges*. Vol. 2 of *No Man's Land: The Place of the Woman Writer in the Twentieth Century*. Yale UP, 1989.

Griffin, Penny. *Arthur Wing Pinero and Henry Arthur Jones*. St. Martin's, 1991.

Guerra, Canon A. *The Confessor After the Heart of Jesus: Considerations Proposed to Priests*. Translated by C. Van der Donckt, B. Herder, 1901.

Haller, John S., Jr. and Robin M. *The Physician and Sexuality in Victorian America*. U of Illinois, 1974.

Hawthorne, Nathaniel. *The Scarlet Letter*. Edited by Harry Levin, Houghton, 1960.

Higgonnet, Margaret. "Speaking Silences: Woman's Suicide." *The Female Body in Western Culture*, edited by Susan Rubin Suleiman, Harvard UP, 1985, pp. 68–83.

Hoffman, Elizabeth A. "Political Power in *The Scarlet Letter*." *American Transcendental Quarterly*, NS4, March 1990, pp. 13–29.

Jones, Henry Arthur. *Michael and His Lost Angel*. Macmillan, 1905.

Kirkley, Evelyn A. "Is it Manly to Be Christian? The Debate in Victorian and Modern America." *Redeeming Men*, edited by Stephen B. Boyd et al., John Knox, 1996, pp. 80–88.

Kucich, John. *Repression in Victorian Fiction: Charlotte Brontë, George Eliot, and Charles Dickens*. U of California P, 1987.

Marcus, Steven. *The Other Victorians: A Study of Sexuality and Pornography in Mid-Nineteenth-Century England*. Basic, 1964.

Miller, Lori M. "The (Re)Gendering of High Anglicanism." *Masculinity and Spirituality in Victorian Culture*, edited by Andrew Bradstock et al., St. Martin's, 2000, pp. 27–43.

Morgan, Sue. "'Writing the Male Body': Sexual Purity and Masculinity." *Masculinity and Spirituality in Victorian Culture*, edited by Andrew Bradstock et al., St. Martin's, 2000, pp. 179–93.

Morgan, Susan. *Sisters in Time*. Oxford UP, 1989.

Newberry, Frederick. *Hawthorne's Divided Loyalties*. Fairleigh Dickinson UP, 1987.

Pimple, Kenneth D. "'Subtle, but remorseful hypocrite': Dimmesdale's Moral Character." *Studies in the Novel*, vol. 25, no. 3, 1993, pp. 257–71.

Pitt-Rivers, Julian. "Honour and Social Status." *Honour and Shame: The Values of Mediterranean Society*, edited by J. Peristiany, U of Chicago P, 1966, pp. 19–78.

Praz, Mario. *The Hero in Eclipse in Victorian Fiction*. Translated by Angus Davidson, Oxford UP, 1969.

Reade, Charles. *The Cloister and the Hearth*. Heritage, 1932.

Roberson, Susan. "'Degenerate effeminacy' and the making of a masculine spirituality in the sermons of Ralph Waldo Emerson." *Muscular Christianity: Embodying the Victorian Age*, edited by Donald D. Hall, Cambridge UP, 1994, pp. 151–72.

Rountree, Thomas J. *Critics on Hawthorne*. U of Miami P, 1972.

Ruetenik, Tadd. "Another View of Arthur Dimmesdale: Scapegoating and Revelation in *The Scarlet Letter*." *Contagion*, vol. 19, 2012, pp. 69–86.

Smith, Eric. *Some Versions of the Fall: The Myth of the Fall of Men in English Literature*. U of Pittsburgh P, 1973.

Spencer, Mark B. "Romancing the Pre-Reformation: Charles Reade's *The Cloister in the Hearth*." *Corporate Medievalism II*, edited by Karl Fugelso, D. S. Brewer, 2013, pp. 69–84.

Sussman, Herbert. *Victorian Masculinities*. Cambridge UP, 1995.

Tanner, Tony. *Adultery in the Novel*. Johns Hopkins UP, 1979.

Thompson, E. P. *The Making of the English Working Class*. Pantheon, 1963.

Tosh, John. *Manliness and Masculinities in Nineteenth-Century Britain*. Pearson, 2005.

Vance, Norman. *The Sinews of the Spirit: The ideal of Christian manliness in Victorian literature and Religious Thought*. Cambridge UP, 1985.

Vicinus, Martha. ed. *Suffer and Be Still: Women in the Victorian Age*. Indiana UP, 1972.

Vitanza, Dianna. "*The Cloister and the Hearth*: A Popular Response to the Oxford Movement." *Religion and Literature*, vol. 18, no. 3, 1986, pp. 71–88.

Walker, Pamela J. "'I live but not yet Christ liveth in me': Men and Masculinity in the Salvation Army, 1865–90." *Manful Assertions: Masculinities in Britain Since 1800*, edited by Michael Roper and John Tosh, Routledge, 1991, pp. 92–112.

Wallis, Bruce. "*Michael and His Lost Angel*: Archetypal Conflict and Victorian Life." *Victorian Newsletter*, vol. 56, 1979, pp. 20–26.

Weldon, Roberta. *Hawthorne, Gender, and Death: Christianity and Its Discontents*. Palgrave, 2008.

Wilson, Ben. *The Making of Victorian Values*. Penguin, 2007.

Wilton, Marilyn Mueller. "Paradigm and Paramour: Role Reversal in *The Scarlet Letter*." *The Critical Response to Nathaniel Hawthorne's "The Scarlet Letter,"* edited by Gary Scharnhorst, Greenwood, 1992, pp. 220–32.

ELEVEN

Sherlock Holmes: The Criminal in the Detective

Joseph Wiesenfarth

To kill Sherlock Holmes is a hard job of work. Professor James Moriarty tried and failed; Colonel Sebastian Moran tried and failed. Even Arthur Conan Doyle tried and failed. And Holmes himself took a shot at it in "The Dying Detective" and "The Final Problem," only to live to tell Dr. Watson the story.

When Conan Doyle tried to free himself of Holmes, it was a case of premeditated murder. He, however, had a different sense of it: "I hold that it was not murder, but justifiable homicide in self defence, since, if I had not killed him, he would certainly have killed me."[1] By August 1893 when he vacationed in Switzerland where he met Silas K. Hocking, he was tired of having to breathe life into Holmes in adventure after adventure. Speaking to Hocking of Holmes, Conan Doyle said, "I intend to make an end of him. If I don't he'll make and end of me." Hocking then suggested that Conan Doyle bring Holmes "out to Switzerland and drop him down a crevasse." "Not a bad idea," Conan Doyle replied with a laugh.[2] Indeed, it was so good an idea that for ten years the public thought that Holmes went to his death with Moriarty in his grasp at the Reichenbach Falls. But "The Final Problem" did not prove final. Holmes's disappearance simply gave Conan Doyle a breather. Then Holmes returned to carry on in the name of justice, if not always in the name of the law, in "The Empty House." He was, after all, just like his creator: brilliant at solving crimes because he was brilliant at conceiving crimes. As Conan Doyle acknowledged: "the psychologists tell us that we really are very multiplex people. . . . There may be represented in my being some strands of Sherlock. If so all the villains I have created may be also represented by strands in my personality."[3] By simultaneously upholding and subverting the moral order, Holmes could be no different than his creator. Thus Christopher Rodern thinks of Holmes and Moriarty "as two halves of a whole"; consequently, "there is a certain inevitability in both men plunging to their death in the Reichenbach Falls together."[4]

But Moriarty could not kill Holmes precisely because he could not surprise Holmes. When Watson questions Holmes in "The Final Problem" about Moriarty's plans, asking "What will he do?" Holmes replies that Moriarty would do "What I should do." (*Memoirs* 260) Likewise when Colonel Sebastian Moran attempts to shoot Holmes with his airgun and hits the mannequin Holmes has prepared for the event, Holmes chides the still famous, now infamous, big-game hunter, using the Hindu term for such a sportsman:

> I wonder that my very simple stratagem could deceive so old a shikari, said Holmes. "It must be very familiar to you. Have you not tethered a young kid under a tree, lain above it with your rifle, and waited for the bait to bring your tiger? This empty house is my tree, and you are my tiger. You have possibly had other guns in reserve in case there should be several tigers, or in the unlikely supposition of your own aim failing you. These," he pointed around, "are my other guns. The parallel is exact."
>
> Colonel Moran sprang forward with a snarl of rage, but the constables dragged him back. ("The Empty House," *Return* 20)

Holmes's "other guns" are, of course, these constables. They and everything else Holmes says to Moran suggest that the criminal mind is working efficiently in the detective.

The mannequin is just one form of disguise that Sherlock Holmes employs in Conan Doyle's many stories. Indeed, in the last of the them, "His Last Bow," Holmes grows a goatee and masquerades as Altamont, an Irish-American spy for Germany, for two years to outwit a German spy-master named Von Bork: "Mr Von Bork: you are a sportsman, and you will bear me no ill will when you realize that you, who have outwitted so many other people have at last been outwitted yourself" (*His Last Bow* 170). Not only has Holmes outwitted Von Bork, he has also stolen his papers. And all this he has done as a private individual. Consequently, Von Bork complains loudly:

"The whole proceeding is absolutely illegal and outrageous."

"Absolutely," said Holmes.

"Kidnapping a German subject."

"And stealing his private papers."

"Well, you realize our position, you and your accomplice here. If I were to shout for help as we pass through the village—"

"My dear sir, if you did anything so foolish you would probably enlarge the too-limited titles of our village inns by giving us "The Dangling Prussian" as a sign post." (*His Last Bow* 171).

Holmes can suggest that Von Bork would be hanged by the villagers should his indignation lead him to attempt to arouse their compassion because his story was published in September 1917, toward the end of the First World War, even though it is set on 2 August 1914, just two days before the war began. Conan Doyle is depending on English hatred of German aggression to smooth over any possibility of an anachronism here. And when Von Bork threatens Holmes with revenge by saying, "If it takes me all my life I shall get level with you!" Holmes replies, "The old sweet song,' said Holmes. 'How often have I heard it in days gone by! It was a favourite ditty of the late lamented Professor Moriarty. Colonel Sebastian Moran has also been known to warble it. And yet I live and keep bees upon the South Downs" (169). For Sherlock Holmes it is worth breaking the law to bring Von Bork to justice just as it is worth being Altamont for two years to outwit the outwitter. But in the end, Holmes lets Von Bork know where he lives if he wishes to follow the path of Moriarty and Moran. Then he goes off with Watson to cash the check for £500 that Von Bork paid him for his work as a spy.

Stories like "The Last Problem" (1893), "The Empty House" (1903), and "His Last Bow" (1917) employ characteristics of Sherlock Holmes that we see Conan Doyle developing at length in previous stories like "A Scandal in Bohemia" (1891), "The Speckled Band" (1892), and "The Man with the Twisted Lip" (1891), all from *The Adventures of Sherlock Holmes* (1892). "The Man with the Twisted Lip" is the story of Neville St. Clair, who finds that he can make more money by begging than by being a newspaper reporter; so he gives up the latter occupation for the former and lives happily doing nothing respectable until his wife makes a surprise visit to the city and notices him at the window of an opium den, which turns out to be the place where he changes his clothes and puts on the disguise that ensures his success as a beggar. A proper Victorian father, St. Clair is so afraid that his children will find out that he has made his bundle by begging that he allows himself to be arrested as Hugh Boone, the well-known beggar with the twisted lip, who, quite suddenly is a suspect in the disappearance and possibly the murder of Neville St. Clair. At this point Mrs. St. Clair employs Sherlock Holmes to find out what happened to her husband.

Like all Conan Doyle stories about the great detective, this one works on the premise that if one observes carefully and thinks logically no mystery is insoluble. In this case Holmes formulates his first hypothesis—Neville St. Clair is dead—with one piece of information missing; therefore, it is the wrong hypothesis. The new piece of evidence in the case is a letter that St. Clair sends to his wife to quiet her fears about his disappearance. It proves that St. Clair is not dead and that Holmes is wrong; his working hypothesis doesn't work. The letter itself is of course an attempt on St. Clair's part to ensure domestic tranquility, another trait of a thoughtful, if errant, Victorian husband and father. It is clue enough to convince Holmes that Neville St. Claire is the unwashed Hugh Boone who is sitting in Bow Street jail. He would rather be there than have his wife and children know what he does after his commuter runs up to the city each working day. The sponge that Holmes packs in his kit bag to wash away Boon's disguised face solves the insoluble problem. No man who gets himself up with a twisted lip and changes his clothes in an opium den is any match for a detective who disguises himself as an opium addict and shoots a little cocaine.

If St. Clair is ashamed of his disguise, Holmes is ashamed of his addiction too. Holmes is a master of deduction, true; but he is that because he also flirts with criminality. He no more wants Watson to be embarrassed by his cocaine habit than St. Clair wants his wife to be embarrassed by his begging. Holmes is clearly good at deduction because he is so good at induction too. He knows how to get to his first premise because he frequently knows how his antagonists feel. Knowing this, he is able to establish how they think.

This is standard in a Sherlock Holmes story. This is perhaps best illustrated in "The Speckled Band" (1892). Helen Stoner comes to Baker Street all in a flutter and says to Holmes, "I have heard, Mr. Holmes, that you can see deeply into the manifold wickedness of the Human heart" (*Adventures* 174). This is true because Holmes knows something of his own heart. Notice how he and Dr. Grimesby Roylott, Helen Stoner's murderous uncle, are equally matched antagonists.

"I know you, you scoundrel! . . . You are Holmes, the meddler."

My friend smiled.

"Holmes, the busybody!"

His smile broadened.

"Holmes, the Scotland Yard jack-in-office!"

Holmes chuckled heartily. . . .

"I am a dangerous man to fall foul of! See here." He stepped swiftly forward, seized the poker, and bent it into a curve with his huge brown hands.

> "See that you keep yourself out of my grip," he snarled, and hurling the twisted poker into the fireplace he strode out of the room.
>
> "He seems a very amiable person," said Holmes, laughing. "I am not quite so bulky, but if he had remained I might have shown him that my grip was not much more feeble than his own." As he spoke he picked up the steel poker and, with a sudden effort straightened it out again. (183)

Roylott proves that he is violent, and his ingenious plan to kill his nieces proves that he is cunning as well. Just as in the "Twisted Lip," it takes Holmes two tries to get to the right hypothesis: the speckled band is not a gipsy band but a snake: "a swamp adder . . . the deadliest snake in India" (195). Holmes finally proves how cunning he is, just as he finally proves how violent he is. He strikes the serpent and forces it back on its master whom it kills. The story concludes with Holmes saying, "I am no doubt indirectly responsible for Dr. Grimesby Roylott's death, and I cannot say that it is likely to weigh very heavily upon my conscience" (197).

Disguise for disguise, fire poker for fire poker, snake for snake, stroke for stroke, Sherlock Holmes is no one to fall foul of. That is something that "The Man with the Twisted Lip" and "The Speckled Band" tell us, but there are other things we learn as well. Helen Stoner is on the verge of marriage. A domestic life much quieter and more secure than her uncle, Roylott, has allowed her or wants her to have. All he wants is her money that her marriage will give her and take from him.

"The Man with the Twisted Lip" begins with a happy domestic scene. Dr. Watson, after a hard day of rounds, is at home seated happily before his fire with his wife Mary, and he is just beginning to feel a bit sleepy when Mrs. Isa Whitney bursts into the room and reports that her husband has been missing for forty-eight hours; indeed, that he is in an opium den called the "Bar of Gold." The happy domestic scene at the Watsons' house is the norm, the standard. This is the way that a husband and wife should live together. It is the very thing that Helen Stoner wants for herself. The contrast to this is the opium den where Whitney lies in misery. That same opium den seems to have taken Neville St. Clair away from a domestic bliss similar to that of the Watsons. St. Clair manifestly fears destroying that. Holmes, playing crypto-marriage counselor, tells him he would have been a better husband if he had confided in his wife. The detective, who can reproduce in himself the traits of his cagey antagonists, nevertheless has a reverence for domesticity. Indeed, he who prefers deduction to affection carries domestic sensibility about as far as a bachelor with desultory habits[5] can, when, at the story's end, he says, "I think, Watson, that if we drive to Baker Street we shall just be in time for breakfast."

Breakfast reminds us that the story has gone from dark to light. It begins in the night just about bedtime and it ends in the morning just about breakfast time. Watson is dragged out of domestic bliss into an opium den where he succeeds in finding Isa Whitney and sending him home. That is the very place where he finds Holmes disguised as an opium addict looking for Neville St. Clair. The story opens in a challenging manner with a success for Watson and a failure for Holmes, who has yet no clue to St. Clair's whereabouts. Is Watson really better at preserving domestic tranquility than Holmes? For the moment, yes; in the end, no. While Watson sleeps at the St. Clairs' house in Lee, Kent, Holmes meditates. The solution to his problem comes at just about daybreak, at 4:25 a.m. In addition, the solution is arrived at in "a dense tobacco haze" that contrasts with the "vile, stupefying fumes of the drug" in the opium den. Holmes had disguised himself as an addict to gain information about St. Clair. Sherlock Holmes is a master of disguise, but in this story he is taken in, briefly, by another master of disguise. St. Clair's disguise is a mirror of the confusion of Holmes's mind in the opium den—a confusion that is dissipated in the tobacco smoke of St. Clair's house. As opium fumes turn into a tobacco haze, the night becomes day, the dark becomes light, the detective—sometime cocaine addict and sometime master of disguise—sees into the working of the illusive St. Clair's mind.

Holmes comes to his salutary conclusion of Boone as St. Clair because of the letter that Mrs. St. Clair shows him. She is the one who holds the clue to the mystery. He is the one who makes proper use of it. What this is then is a modern displacement of an old myth—that of Theseus and Ariadne. Ariadne held a clew of thread that guided Theseus into the labyrinth where he found the cannibal Minotaur, slew him, and followed the thread out of the labyrinth. One sees this sort of thing again and again in detective stories. Instead of a cannibal monster, half-man/half-beast, standing at the center of a labyrinth devouring virgin sacrifices, the detective story frequently gives us a killer who murders innocent victims. Dr. Grimesby Roylott murders his one niece with a deadly snake bite and tries to murder a second. The dead sister delivers a clue into Helen Stoner's hands before she dies when she mentions a "speckled band." Helen hands the clue on to Holmes who takes her place as a victim by his vigil in her bedroom. Then he slays the slayer. In the original myth, Theseus abandons Ariadne, who helped him, and returns home to Athens alone. There is a benign reflection of such disregard in Holmes too: if he returns home with anyone, it is Watson. He is fonder of the clue a woman gives him than he is of the woman who gives him the clue. Like Theseus and his modern-day counterparts who enter one kind of labyrinth or another, Sherlock Holmes cannot have emotional attachments that will prevent his using the clues of other Ariadnes and entering other labyrinths to slay other modern monsters.

> All emotions [Watson tells us as "A Scandal in Bohemia" begins] and that one [of love] particularly, were abhorrent to his cold, precise, but admirably balanced mind. He was, I take it, the most perfect reasoning and observing machine that the world has seen, but as a lover he would have placed himself in a false position. . . . for the trained reasoner to admit such intrusions into his own delicate and finely adjusted temperament was to introduce a distracting factor which might throw a doubt upon all his mental results. (*Adventures* 5)

Yet we know that one woman did make an impression on Holmes's life. He always referred to as "*the* woman." Her name is Irene Adler, and she appears in the first story of Holmes's *Adventures*, "A Scandal in Bohemia."

"A Scandal in Bohemia" is remarkable in many ways—not the least of which is that it takes us back to "The Man with the Twisted Lip" in presenting us with a Holmes who meets an antagonist who disguises herself better than he does, with a Holmes who resorts to the mean and criminal expedient of smoke-bombing of her house, and with a Holmes who once again becomes an actor in a story that clearly has a plot with mythic underpinnings.

The main theme of "A Scandal in Bohemia" is the split in most men between passion and reason. Watson has already shown us how dramatic a split that is in Sherlock Holmes: "Grit in a sensitive instrument, or a crack in one of his own high-power lenses, would not be more disturbing than a strong emotion in a nature such as his" (5). The story presents us with the King of Bohemia, once a lover of Irene Adler but now engaged to be married to another woman. When he was in love with Irene, he was, he tells Holmes, "mad—insane" (13). It presents us with a Dr. Watson who is married and who since his marriage has seen little of Holmes and therefore who is out of practice with criminal investigations. And finally it presents us with Sherlock Holmes, a "reasoning . . . machine." Holmes as the least involved with passion and love is the most capable of dealing with the problem facing the king, which is that Irene Adler threatens to make public a picture of the king and herself on the day his betrothal to Clotilde Lothman von Saxe-Meningen is publicly announced. This, of course, is a throwback to one of the most famous tales of passion in classical mythology: that of Jason, Medea, and Creüsa. When Medea is abandoned by Jason for Creon's daughter, she sends her a present on her wedding day. It is a poisoned cloak that kills her. Holmes not only becomes involved with circumventing domestic tragedy but with saving the king from disgrace in his own land. His problem is not an easy one because Irene Adler's mind matches her beauty. If she is "a lovely woman, with a face that a man might die for" (18), as Holmes says, she is nonetheless not simply a creature of emotions. She is also a fitting intellectual antagonist for Sherlock Holmes. "She has the face of the most beautiful of women, and the mind of the most resolute of men" (14).

Moreover, she holds together within herself the two elements that Holmes cannot: passion *and* reason.

Holmes disguises himself as a Nonconformist clergyman, gains entrance to Irene Adler's house by a ruse, has Watson toss a smoke bomb in the room in which he hopes to discover the hiding place of the picture of the king and herself. His intention, of course, is to steal it. But two can play such games, and Irene realizes that she has been set up by Holmes. Later the same evening, passing down Baker Street, she wishes him good night while disguised as a young lad. When Holmes arrives at her house the next morning to get the photograph, he finds that Irene has not only left with the man she has just married, Godfrey Norton, but also has left Holmes a note which pays tribute to his methods. It also reflects on her own methods of dealing with a clever man like Holmes and further indicates that she will not use the photograph against the king; however, she will hold on to it for self-protection.

One other thing that she leaves is a photograph of herself for the king as a remembrance of things past. Holmes exacts this as his only further payment from the king for his services (he had already received a £1,000 as a retainer!). He refuses to shake hands with the king because the king has led him to act shabbily and below himself in this case. Because Irene Adler has beat Sherlock Holmes at his own game, he praises her by referring to her as "*the* woman" (29). And this tribute nicely rounds out the adventure and reminds us that, as in the case of Medea, a woman has proved herself superior to the power, the reasoning, and the wealth of her male antagonists.

Holmes is not always scrupulous about breaking the law, as we have seen in some of the cases discussed. And in "Charles Augustus Milverton" (*Return* 157–75), he and Watson witness the murder of this eponymous blackmailer. Then Holmes rifles his safe, burns his papers, and refuses to help Inspector Lestrade investigate the murder, saying of Milverton, "I considered him one of the most dangerous men in London, and . . . I think there are certain crimes which the law cannot touch, and which therefore, to some extent, justify private revenge. . . . My sympathies are with the criminals rather than the victim, and I will not handle this case" (174). In "The Priory School" (*Return* 100-133), Holmes nonetheless scolds the Duke of Holderness for doing exactly what he does in "Charles Augustus Milverton": "You have condoned a felony, and you have aided the escape of a murderer" (131). The significant difference is that Holmes's idea of justice is perverted by Holderness who has endangered the life of his legitimate son, Lord Saltire, by aiding the escape of his illegitimate son, Wilder, whose kidnapping of Saltire has led to a murder. Milverton , however, as one of "the most dangerous men in London," makes society a better place for others by his violent death. He shares the same fate as Professor Moriarty and Colonel Moran, who were also described by Holmes as the most dangerous men in London in their time. So illegal doings in Conan Doyle's stories must be judged by justice being done or not being done. Whereas Holmes does not in every case square his criminal actions with justice, as his remorse in "A Scandal in Bohemia" suggests, he often does. And because this is so, Watson, thinking him dead in "The Final Problem," eulogies him as "the best and wisest man whom I have ever known" (*Memoirs* 268). Watson's words are almost identical to those that Plato used at the end of the *Phadeo* to praise Socrates, who gave his life for an ideal: "Such was the end . . . of our friend, who was, as we may say, of all those of his time whom we have ever known, the best and most righteous man."[6] The classical antecedent this time is not for wrong-doers who cross his path, but for Sherlock Holmes himself.

Like most men of his day—indeed, of ours too—Holmes has problems with love, to say nothing of passion and sex. He sublimates them by acting like a reasoning machine and satisfies them to an extent, I suspect, in subversive, androgynous actions like changing places with women and destroying those who would destroy them. For Holmes the creative principle that woman represents must be protected and saved. The criminal in the detective also reminds us that one of the lasting appeals of Conan Doyle's stories is that, subliminally, they evoke within us responses like their classical antecedents. They deal with basic strengths and frailties in human nature, they stir our sense of wonder and, if they do not appeal overtly to the darker side of human nature, they do suggest its presence while also showing, overtly, how the brighter and braver intellectual side of men and women can win the day. In a world like ours where it seems so hard to make intelligence telling, Conan Doyle tells the kind of stories in which, despite every sort of difficulty, intelligence wins the day; indeed, wins the day from night and the light from darkness. That is one myth, surely, that it would be a pleasure to recover for contemporary life—even for contemporary fiction—in any way we can.

NOTES

1. Holmes quoted by Green in the introduction to his edition of *The Return of Sherlock Holmes*, p. xi.

2. Hocking quoted by Roden in a note to his edition of *The Memoirs of Sherlock Holmes*, p. 320.

3. Conan Doyle quoted in Kestner, p. 29.

4. *Memoirs*, p. xxix.

5. At the beginning of "The Musgrave Ritual" Watson points out in detail that the orderliness of Holmes's mind has no counterpart in his housekeeping: "When I find a man who keeps his cigars in the coal-scuttle, his tobacco in the toe end of a Persian slipper, and his unanswered correspondence transfixed by a jack-knife into the very center of his wooden mantelpiece, then I begin to give myself virtuous airs. I have always held, too, that pistol practice should distinctly be an open-air pastime; and when Holmes in one of his queer humours would sit in an arm-chair with his hair-trigger and a hundred Boxer cartridges, and proceed to adorn the opposite wall with a

patriotic V.R. done in bullet-pocks, I felt strongly that neither the atmosphere nor the appearance of our room was improved by it" (*Memoirs* 113). The "V.R." stands for *Victoria Regina.* And Roden suggests that the "implication would seem to be that this was a celebration of the Golden Jubilee of her accession to the throne, i.e. that the shooting took place on or around 21 June 1887" (*Memoirs,* p. 295).

    6. Quoted by Roden, *Memoirs,* p. 321.

WORKS CITED

Conan Doyle, Arthur. *The Adventures of Sherlock Holmes.* Edited by Richard Lancelyn Green, *The Oxford Sherlock Holmes,* Oxford University Press, 1993.

———. *His Last Bow.* Edited by Owen Dudley Edwards, *The Oxford Sherlock Holmes,* Oxford University Press, 1993.

———. *The Memoirs of Sherlock Holmes.* Edited by Christopher Roden, *The Oxford Sherlock Holmes,* Oxford University Press, 1993.

———. *The Return of Sherlock Holmes.* Edited by Richard Lancelyn Green, *The Oxford Sherlock Holmes,* Oxford University Press, 1993.

Kestner, Joseph A. *Sherlock's Men: Masculinity, Conan Doyle, and Cultural History.* Ashgate, 1997.

Index

About the Editors and Contributors

Kenneth Womack is Dean of the Wayne D. McMurray School of Humanities and Social Sciences at Monmouth University, where he also serves as Professor of English. He is the author or editor of numerous books, including *Long and Winding Roads: The Evolving Artistry of the Beatles* (2007), the *Cambridge Companion to the Beatles* (2009), and *The Beatles Encyclopedia: Everything Fab Four* (2014). Womack is also the author of three award-winning novels, including *John Doe No. 2 and the Dreamland Motel* (2010), *The Restaurant at the End of the World* (2012), and *Playing the Angel* (2013). He serves as Editor of *Interdisciplinary Literary Studies: A Journal of Criticism and Theory*, published by Penn State University Press, and as Co-Editor of the English Association's *Year's Work in English Studies*, published by Oxford University Press.

James M. Decker is Professor of English, Humanities, and Language Studies at Illinois Central College. He is the author of *Ideology* (2003), *Henry Miller and Narrative Form: Constructing the Self, Rejecting Modernity* (2005), and *Henry Miller: New Perspectives* (2015), with Indrek Manniste.

Troy Bassett is Associate Professor of English at Indiana University Purdue University Fort Wayne. He has published numerous articles on Victorian authorship and publishing and is the creator of *At the Circulating Library: A Database of Victorian Fiction, 1837–1901*.

Martin Bidney is Professor Emeritus of English and Comparative Literature at Binghamton University. He has published twenty essays of epiphanological analysis of poetry, novels, and short stories based on the method used in his *Patterns of Epiphany: From Wordsworth to Tolstoy, Pater, and Barrett Browning*. He has also published ten volumes of original and form-faithful translated verse. His latest book is *A Unifying Light: Lyrical Responses to the Qur'an*, and his soon forthcoming book is *Shakespair: Sonnet Replies to the 154 Sonnets of William Shakespeare*.

Nancy Henry is Professor of English and Distinguished Professor in the Humanities at the University of Tennessee. She is the author of *George Eliot and the British Empire* (2001), *The Cambridge Introduction to George Eliot* (2008), and *The Life of George Eliot* (2012). She is also the co-editor of *Victorian Investments: New Perspectives on Finance and Culture* (2009).

Joseph Lennon is the Director of Irish Studies and associate professor of English at Villanova University. His book, *Irish Orientalism: A Literary and Intellectual History* won the Donald Murphy Prize from the American Conference for Irish Studies. Salmon Poetry published his first volume of poetry, *Fell Hunger*, in 2011. He has published in edited collections and in periodicals such as the *Times Literary Supplement, New Hibernia Review,* and *Poetry Ireland.*

Ira Nadel is Professor of English at the University of British Columbia. He is the author of biographies of Leonard Cohen, Tom Stoppard, David Mamet, and Leon Uris. He has also published *Joyce and the Jews, Biography: Fiction & Fact and Form,* and *Modernism's Second Act.* His study *Cathay: Ezra Pound's Orient* appeared in 2015.

Ruth Robbins is Professor of English Literature and Head of the School of Cultural Studies and Humanities at Leeds Beckett University. She is the author of several works about literary theory and about the late-nineteenth century including *Literary Feminisms* (2000); *Pater to Forster* (2003); *Subjectivity* (2005); *The British Short Story* with Emmal Liggins and Andrew Maunder (2010); *Oscar Wilde* (2011). She has also edited a five-volume edition of *Medical Advice for Women, 1830–1915* (2009).

Jeanette Shumaker is Professor of English at San Diego State University–Imperial Valley. She publishes on Victorian fiction, modern Irish writers, and Anglo-Jewish writers.

Alexis Weedon is UNESCO chair of new media forms of the book at the University of Bedfordshire. A specialist in publishing economics, quantification, and cross-media production, she is co-editor of the journal *Convergence* and author of *Victorian Publishing* (2003) and co-author of *Elinor Glyn: Novelist, Movie-Maker, Glamour Icon and Business Woman* (2014). She has recently published chapters in *The Book a Global History* (2013) and *Women, Celebrity and Cultures and Aging* (2015).

Joseph Wiesenfarth is Professor Emeritus of English at the University of Wisconsin–Madison. His books include *Ford Madox Ford and the Regiment of Women* (2005) and *Gothic Manners and the Classic English Novel* (1998). In addition to books on Jane Austen, George Eliot, and Henry James, he has published numerous articles on British fiction and edited two collections of essays on Ford Madox Ford. His revised editions of Jane Austen's "Jack and Alice" (2001) and "Three Sisters" (2004) were published by Juvenilia Press. He edited the authoritative critical edition of *No More Parades* from a typescript corrected by Ford for the second volume of Ford's tetralogy, *Parade's End,* which was published in 2011.

www.ingramcontent.com/pod-product-compliance
Lightning Source LLC
Chambersburg PA
CBHW032028120726
47901CB00002BA/568